The Charter School Solution

Challenging the popular perception that the free market can objectively ameliorate inequality and markedly improve student academic achievement, this book examines the overly positivistic rhetoric surrounding charter schools. Taking a multifocal approach, this book examines how charter schools reproduce inequality in public education. By linking charter schools to broader social issues and political economic factors, such as neoliberalism, race, and class, *The Charter School Solution* presents a more complete and nuanced assessment of charter schools in the context of the American public education system.

Tara L. Affolter is an Assistant Professor of Education Studies at Middlebury College, USA.

Jamel K. Donnor is an Associate Professor of Education at the College of William and Mary, USA.

Routledge Research in Education

For a full list of titles in this series, please visit www.routledge.com

162 **Reconceptualising Agency and Childhood**
New Perspectives in Childhood Studies
Edited by Florian Esser, Meike Baader, Tanja Betz, and Beatrice Hungerland

163 **Technology-Enhanced Language Learning for Specialized Domains**
Practical applications and mobility
Edited by Elena Martín Monje, Izaskun Elorza and Blanca García Riaza

164 **American Indian Workforce Education**
Trends and Issues
Edited by Carsten Schmidtke

165 **African American English and the Achievement Gap**
The Role of Dialectal Code-switching
Holly K. Craig

166 **Intersections of Formal and Informal Science**
Edited by Lucy Avraamidou & Wolff-Michael Roth

167 **Women Education Scholars and their Children's Schooling**
Edited by Kimberly A. Scott and Allison Henward

168 **The Improvised Curriculum**
Negotiating Risky Literacies in Cautious Schools
Michael Corbett, Ann Vibert, Mary Green with Jennifer Rowe

169 **Empowering Black Youth of Promise**
Education and Socialization in the Village-minded Black Church
Sandra L. Barnes and Anne Streaty Wimberly

170 **The Charter School Solution**
Distinguishing Fact from Rhetoric
Edited by Tara L. Affolter and Jamel K. Donnor

The Charter School Solution
Distinguishing Fact from Rhetoric

Edited by Tara L. Affolter
and Jamel K. Donnor

NEW YORK AND LONDON

First published 2016
by Routledge
711 Third Avenue, New York, NY 10017

and by Routledge
2 Park Square, Milton Park, Abingdon, Oxon, OX14 4RN

First issued in paperback 2018

Routledge is an imprint of the Taylor & Francis Group, an informa business

© 2016 Taylor & Francis

The right of Jamel K. Donnor and Tara L. Affolter to be identified as editors of this work has been asserted by them in accordance with sections 77 and 78 of the Copyright, Designs and Patents Act 1988.

All rights reserved. No part of this book may be reprinted or reproduced or utilised in any form or by any electronic, mechanical, or other means, now known or hereafter invented, including photocopying and recording, or in any information storage or retrieval system, without permission in writing from the publishers.

Trademark notice: Product or corporate names may be trademarks or registered trademarks, and are used only for identification and explanation without intent to infringe.

Library of Congress Cataloguing-in-Publication Data
Names: Affolter, Tara L., editor of compilation. | Donnor, Jamel K., editor of compilation.
Title: The charter school solution : distinguishing fact from rhetoric / by Tara L. Affolter and Jamel K. Donnor.
Description: New York : Routledge, 2016. | Includes bibliographical references.
Identifiers: LCCN 2016003286 | ISBN 9781138959569
Subjects: LCSH: Charter schools.
Classification: LCC LB2806.36 .A44 2016 | DDC 371.05—dc23
LC record available at http://lccn.loc.gov/2016003286

ISBN 13: 978-1-138-60025-6 (pbk)
ISBN 13: 978-1-138-95956-9 (hbk)

Typeset in Sabon
by Apex CoVantage, LLC

Contents

*Introduction: The Charter School Solution:
Distinguishing Fact from Rhetoric*   vii
JAMEL K. DONNOR AND TARA L. AFFOLTER

1   Chartering Charade in Washington State: The Anti-Democratic Politics of the Charter School Movement and the Removal of the Public from Public Education   1
WAYNE AU

2   Democracy, Charter Schools, and the Politics of Choice   19
ELENI SCHIRMER AND MICHAEL W. APPLE

3   Turning Over Teachers: Charter School Employment Practices, Teacher Pipelines, and Social Justice   41
SARAH M. STITZLEIN AND BARRETT A. SMITH

4   Charter School Teachers and the Consequences of Unionization   61
ELIZABETH MONTAÑO

5   Discursive Violence and Economic Retrenchment: Chartering the Sacrifice of Black Educators in Post-Katrina New Orleans   80
KEVIN LAWRENCE HENRY, JR.

6   Struggling for Community and Equity in New Orleans Public Schools: Lessons from a First-Year Charter School   99
JOSEPH L. BOSELOVIC

7   Segregated by Choice? Urban Charter Schools and Education Choices for Black Students and Disadvantaged Families in the United States   117
ERLING E. BOE, SHAUN R. HARPER, AND KATHERINE M. BARGHAUS

*Afterword: Schools of Education as Stakeholders in
the Charter School Debate* 139
VIRGINIA L. McLAUGHLIN

About the Editors 149
About the Contributors 150
Index 153

Introduction
The Charter School Solution: Distinguishing Fact from Rhetoric

Jamel K. Donnor and Tara L. Affolter

While publicly elected officials, education entrepreneurs, and business leaders assert that charter schools are best equipped to address the persistent underachievement of students of color and other traditionally underserved populations, this book argues to the contrary, that many of the purported attributes assigned to charter schools are unsubstantiated. Indeed, a paradox of charter schools is the policy assumption that competition and the free market can ameliorate inequality and boost student achievement. Schirmer and Apple (this volume) assert that charter schools have "become embedded within the ideological matrix of neoliberalism," whereby the "one best" (Tyack, 1974) model for schooling is no longer sufficient. Instead, the privatization of public goods, such as education, will improve instruction, efficiency, and learning outcomes.

This book challenges neoliberal policy assumptions by explaining how charter schools, under the auspices of choice, innovation, and efficiency, do not improve the overall educational well-being and advancement of students. In fact, charter schools as a whole do not outperform their traditional counterparts. As Chapman and Donnor (2015) point out:

> only 25% of U.S. charter schools exceeded their TPS counterparts in reading, and only 29% of the charter schools surpassed their TPS counterparts in math (CREDO, 2013). Moreover, 56% of charter schools have no difference in students' reading growth, and 40% of charter schools have no difference in students' math growth (CREDO, 2013). Disappointedly, 19% of charter schools perform worse than their TPS partners in reading, and 31% perform worse in math.
> (CREDO, 2013, p. 138)

Further, as the authors in this volume demonstrate, charter schools and their subsequent "way(s) of doing business" erode school-community ties (Montano), limit pedagogical innovation while dehumanizing both students and teachers (Steilzen and Smith), exclude the most vulnerable students (i.e., students with disabilities and English language learners), displace and marginalize teachers of color (Lawrence), increase racial segregation

(Harper et al.), divide families and neighborhoods (Boselvic), and generally threaten the democratic precepts underwriting the American public education system (Au; Schirmer and Apple).

Despite all of this, in September of 2015, the outgoing Education Secretary, Arne Duncan, pledged $157 million dollars to create and expand charters schools. Charter school expansion was also the cornerstone of Duncan's signature grant program, "Race to the Top," in which federal grant dollars were primarily awarded on the basis of lifting caps on the number of charter schools allowed under state law. Laws and policies surrounding charter schools seem to switch and morph to accommodate their continued proliferation. As Wayne Au asserts in this volume:

> Charter school reform in Washington State has been like a zombie: It is never quite dead, and just when you think you have killed it, charter school law somehow continues to move forward.

Indeed, as charter school expansion continues to lurch forward and consume the public's imagination regarding the purpose of education in the United States, the contributors to this volume expose some of the overlooked consequences resulting from the continued promotion of the "charter school solution."

Charter school advocates vigorously assert that the educational fortunes of students will improve because teachers and principals are free from the "monopolistic political control" of the state and teacher unions, respectively. In particular, proponents of charter schools argue that student from traditionally underserved populations will benefit directly and indirectly, because charter schools have the autonomy to create a learning atmosphere in which low-performing students can achieve. Lastly, charter school supporters posit that such environments are more conducive and responsive to student and familial preferences, interests, and values.

This book decouples the positivistic rhetoric surrounding charter schools by examining the broader political, economic, and social contexts of the American public education system by linking it to broader issues and exogenous factors, such as globalization, race, class, gender, and dis/ability. This includes highlighting how society's existing political economic and social institutions continue to marginalize low-income students and students of color by discussing how America's founding narratives (e.g., freedom, choice, and equality of opportunity) reproduce inequality according to race and class. Further, by debunking how the free market perpetuates a specific set of assumptions about human nature, including the idea of a "rational" actor, this book illustrates the complexity and enduring power of inequality.

In Chapter 1, "Chartering Charade in Washington State: The Anti-Democratic Politics of the Charter School Movement and the Removal of the Public from Public Education," Wayne Au interrogates the notion that charter schools are more democratic for families and communities. This chapter draws on a wide range of policy analysis and research, including the role of philanthropies like the Gates Foundation in policy development, the influence of conservative organizations like the American Legislative Exchange Council in shaping state-level policy development, the selective student enrollment exhibited by charters, the role of charter schools in subverting the power of teachers' unions, and the rise of charters in the midst of large-scale public school closings. Using this evidence, this chapter analyzes the multiple ways that the charter school movement expresses these fundamentally antidemocratic impulses.

Similarly in Chapter 2, "Democracy, Charter Schools, and the Politics of Choice," Eleni Schirmer and Michael W. Apple link charter schools to the increasing influence of neoliberal agendas and corporate interests. The authors use Kenosha, Wisconsin—where large amounts of funding and electoral pressure from national rightist organizations enabled the Right to take control of a local school system that has had a history of strong teachers unions and strong support of public education—to explore these tensions.

Sarah M. Stitzelein and Barrett A. Smith take a theoretical approach to exploring the dissonance between the key approaches of major education reform organizations and the employment practices that they endorse or embody, particularly within their affiliated charter schools, in Chapter 3, "Turning Over Teachers: Charter School Employment Practices, Teacher Pipelines, and Social Justice." The authors employ philosophical and interpretive methodologies and use the work of Karl Marx and the critical theorists who followed him.

Chapter 4, "Charter School Teachers and the Consequences of Unionization," by Elizabeth Montaño, reveals the tensions of unionization in a charter school founded by local community leaders, teachers, and funders. The charter school was deemed a success, yet the success they reached came at a great cost to the teachers, who expressed difficult working conditions and high turnover year to year. These conditions eventually led teachers to seek unionization. The chapter explores the consequences of such unionization on the teachers.

In Chapter 5, "Discursive Violence and Economic Retrenchment: Chartering the Sacrifice of Black Educators in New Orleans Post-Katrina," Kevin Lawrence Henry, Jr. examines the cost of the production and proliferation of charter schools in New Orleans on Black educators. This proliferation of charters coincides with the discursive marginalization of Black educators and the retrenchment of Black labor rights via White profit accumulation and power solidification. This chapter highlights how seemingly neutral, apolitical charter reform initiatives in New Orleans are shaped by White dominance that intersects with and is multiplied by other forms of oppression.

Joseph L. Boselovic also raises questions of community and various stakeholders in New Orleans in Chapter 6, "Struggling for Community and Equity in New Orleans Public Schools: Lessons from a First-Year Charter

School." He explores the transformation of school governance and operations in New Orleans from the vantage point of a charter school founded upon a community-based model. This analysis presents the limits to achieving progressive educational goals through the neoliberal framework of charter schooling.

Finally, authors Erling E. Boe, Shaun R. Harper, and Katherine M. Barghaus reflect on the (perhaps) unintended consequences of choice in Chapter 7, "Segregated by Choice? Urban Charter Schools and Education Choices for Black Students and Disadvantaged Families in the U.S." Using national data from the U.S. Department of Education's *School and Staffing Survey*, the authors found that urban charter schools, compared with urban regular schools, enrolled a much higher percentage of Black students, a lower percentage of Hispanic students, and equivalent percentages of White students.

When we, the editors, conceived of this book, we jokingly proposed the title, *The Charter School Hustle*. Our mentors dissuaded us from pursuing this title, suggesting that both contributors and future readers might be put off by the bias the title broadcasted. The essays in this collected volume suggest that our original impulse of calling out the hustle of charter school "reform" was on target. The empirical, theoretical, and case studies presented here should give politicians, "reformers," parents, educators, and community members pause and consider the damaging impact of charter school expansion in this country.

1 Chartering Charade in Washington State

The Anti-Democratic Politics of the Charter School Movement and the Removal of the Public from Public Education

Wayne Au

Introduction

The state of Washington has a unique and illustrative story when it comes to charter schools. The Washington State charter school story is unique because, unlike the majority of other states, we have resisted the legalization of charter schools for two decades (Au & Ferrare, 2014). Further, the Washington State story is illustrative because it highlights the particularly anti-democratic impulses behind charter school reform, specifically relative to the political-economic agenda of those seeking to redefine public education in terms more favorable to privatization projects. This chapter takes up the struggle over charter schools in Washington State, using that struggle as a case study (Stake, 2000) to illustrate the power relations within, and ideologies behind, charter school reform in the state. Here, I begin with a history of the legalization of charter schools in Washington State, including an in-depth analysis of which organizations and individuals played key roles in the most recent campaign to legalize charter schools there. I then move on to discuss the free market ideological investment in charter schools as articulated by Washington State's charter school law itself, and as an expression of the broader neoliberal project of the American Legislative Exchange Council. I then explain the version of school accountability and governance embedded in the charter school model, and use Washington State's first charter school, First Place Scholars, as an example of why that model of accountability and governance is not only insufficient, but is damaging to the population of students they serve. I conclude this chapter with a discussion of the September 4, 2015 ruling on the unconstitutionality of charter schools in Washington State, the fallout from that ruling, and some of the implications of charter schools for democratic governance of public schools and public monies.

Zombie Charter School Reform in Washington State

Charter school reform in Washington State has been like a zombie: It is never quite dead, and just when you think you have killed it, charter school law somehow continues to move forward. Like many other states, Washington has a system where, with enough signatures, initiatives can be filed with the state and become law with a majority vote by the public. Initiatives to legalize charter schools in Washington State have come to the voters four times, in 1996, 2000, 2004, and 2012. The first three times, Washington voters affirmed their opposition to charter schools by varying margins—a 54% majority in 1996, a 51.8% majority in 2000, and a 58.3% majority in 2004 (Au & Ferrare, 2014; Corcoran & Stoddard, 2011). However, in the 2012 general election, Washington State voters approved charter schools with a 50.69% majority yes vote on Initiative 1240 (Reed, 2012), making charter schools legal in the state.

I was personally involved in the public discussions leading up to the 2012 vote on Washington State's charter school Initiative 1240 (I-1240, hereafter), taking an active stance against charter schools in speaking events (Au, 2012b), blog posts (Au, 2012c), and in local newspaper editorials (Au, 2012a). I highlight this work to illustrate that I have been personally invested in the fight against charter schools and their role in a broader agenda associated with the remaking of schools vis-à-vis neoliberal markets (Au & Ferrare, 2015a; Fabricant & Fine, 2012; Lipman, 2011). As such, after watching the machinations of the campaign to get I-1240 passed by popular vote, I became interested in the policy actors and forces involved in the Yes on 1240 campaign itself. My research, which I completed and co-authored with my colleague Joseph J. Ferrare (see, Au & Ferrare, 2014), was revealing about the anti-democratic nature of charter school policy adoption in Washington State.

Who Was Behind I-1240 and the Yes on 1240 Campaign?

The legal origins of I-1240 can be traced to two companion bills that were introduced into the Washington State legislature in January of 2012 (Rosenthal, 2012). These bills outlined several typical aspects of potential charter school laws, like setting the number of charter schools to be opened over the course of five years, establishing charter school authorizers, and asserting a parent-teacher "trigger" provision that would allow a school to become a charter if a majority of teachers or parents signed a petition (Westbrook, 2012). These charter school bills eventually died in committee. Charter school advocates then drafted I-1240, which was officially filed with the State of Washington by then-League of Education Voters (LEV) staffer, Tania de Sa Campos (de Sa Campos, 2012; League of Education Voters, 2012). I-1240 contained several provisions for charter schools that were similar to the previous legislative bills: forty charter schools in five years, a state-level charter school commission, charter authorizers (either the state commission or local school districts), appointed charter school boards for oversight, and a parent-teacher conversion trigger, amongst others (de Sa Campos, 2012). Using $2.26 million donated mainly by Microsoft's Bill Gates, Jr., the Bezos family (of Amazon.com), Nick Hanauer (venture capitalist and board member of LEV), and Microsoft co-founder Paul Allen, paid gatherers collected enough signatures to get I-1240 onto the Washington State ballot (Callaghan, 2012).

Charter school advocates then formed the Washington Coalition for Public Charter Schools, which consisted of four organizations: Stand for Children, LEV, Partnership for Learning, and Democrats for Education Reform (Washington Coalition for Public Charter Schools, 2012). As evidenced by their "in kind" donations (Washington State Public Disclosure Commission, 2012c), these organizations coordinated the Yes on 1240 campaign, managing financial activities, handling media, and organizing volunteers (Washington State Public Disclosure Commission, 2012b). When election day arrived on November 6, 2012, the Yes on 1240 campaign had collected $10.9 million in donations, which at the time made it the third largest amount of money amassed for an initiative campaign in Washington State history (Washington State Public Disclosure Commission, 2012d). These millions were used for direct mailing, phone banking, field organizing, and signs, with $5 million of the total devoted to web, radio, and television advertising alone (Washington State Public Disclosure Commission, 2012b). Additionally, shortly before election day, Partnership for Learning (2012), in conjunction with researchers from the Center on Reinventing Public Education (CRPE), published a report that makes explicit reference to I-1240 as a good charter school law (Lake, Gross, & Maas, 2012), and CRPE founder and charter school advocate, Paul Hill, was featured prominently in a Yes on 1240 television advertisement advocating for the passage of I-1240 (Yes on 1240, 2012). After a large campaign to legalize charter schools, in November of 2012, the citizens of Washington State voted to approve I-1240 by a 50.69% majority, or 41,682 votes out of just over 3,020,000 total cast (Reed, 2012).

If we look at the relationships between the donors to the Yes on 1240 campaign and the core organizations of the Washington Coalition for Public Charter Schools who ran the campaign itself, we can see very clearly that a very small, elite group of wealthy individuals leveraged significant and disproportionate power in making charter schools legal in Washington State (Au & Ferrare, 2014, 2015b). In terms of individual donors, $10.65 million, or almost 98% of the $10.9 million total raised for the Yes on 1240 campaign, was donated by 21 individuals and organizations, each giving $50,000 or more (Washington State Public Disclosure Commission, 2012a, 2012c). Notably, at $3 million, Bill Gates, Jr. is the largest donor to the campaign, followed by the $1.7 million donated by Walmart heiress Alice Walton, and the $1.6 million donated by Paul Allen's Vulcan Inc. (I have to note here that originally, this donation was officially given by Paul Allen, but later the public record was changed to indicate that Paul Allen's company, Vulcan Inc., was the donor). At $1 million, Venture capitalist Nick Hanauer had the next largest donation to Yes on 1240, followed by Mike and Jackie Bezos (parents of Amazon.com's Jeff Bezos), who each gave $500,000 individually to the campaign. Connie Ballmer, wife of Microsoft CEO Steve Ballmer, also donated $500,000. Several other notable individuals came in at smaller amounts, including New York real estate mogul Eli Broad ($200,000) and Netflix's Reed Hastings ($100,000). Clearly, a select set of wealthy individuals, some of whom with no immediate connection to Washington State (e.g., Eli Broad and Alice Walton) demonstrated a vested interest in charter school policy in the state (see Au & Ferrare, 2014, for a more detailed list and discussion).

Relative to the current discussion, particularly to the activity of Democrats for Education Reform (DFER) as an organizing partner in the Yes on 1240 campaign, it is important to highlight the $50,000 donation from Education Reform Now! Advocacy, because this donation illustrates the interconnectedness of organizations and funding within education policy reform. New York State tax records from 2006 indicate that Education Reform Now! Inc., Education Reform Now! Advocacy, and DFER all share officers, personnel, office space, and paymasters (Libby, 2012b). Tax records from 2007 further indicate that Education Reform Now! Inc. and Education Reform Now! Advocacy share these same resources (New York State Office of the Attorney General, 2013). Thus, DFER, Education Reform Now! Inc., and Education Reform Now! Advocacy essentially operate as a financially intertwined cluster of three organizations with overlapping staff and resources. Consequently, even though we cannot fully understand the exact relationship, the $50,000 donation to the Yes on 1240 campaign from Education Reform Now! Advocacy is functionally also a donation from Education Reform Now! Inc. and DFER. On the surface it appears that, on the one hand, we have the four organizations constituting the Washington Coalition for Public Charter Schools and the CRPE coordinating the campaign, and on the other hand, it appears that there are seemingly disconnected donors to the Yes on 1240 campaign itself. However, if we look closer, we can see that these individuals and organizations are almost all connected by philanthropic foundations.

The Philanthropic Hook Up

The fact that Bill Gates, Jr., Eli Broad, and Alice Walton gave significant contributions to the Yes on 1240 campaign should not be surprising. Their respective foundations, the Bill and Melinda Gates Foundation (the Gates Foundation), the Eli and Edythe Broad Foundation (the Broad Foundation), and the Walton Family Foundation (the Walton Foundation) are well known for their consistent ideological and financial commitments to charter schools (Barkan, 2011; Ravitch, 2010; Reckhow, 2013; Reckhow & Snyder, 2014; Saltman, 2011). Research into the philanthropic foundations connected to wealthy Yes on 1240 donors reveals strong connections to prominent campaign organizers:

1) As of 2013, Education Reform Now! (functionally DFER) received over $6.5 million total funding from foundations associated with Yes on 1240 donors, mostly from the Walton Foundation and the Broad Foundation, with smaller funding from foundations associated with the Bezos family and other Yes on 1240 donors, Doris Fisher, Anne Dinning, and Michael Wolf.
2) As of 2013, the League of Education Voters had received over $5.2 million in funding from foundations associated with Yes on 1240 donors, mostly from the Gates Foundation ($4.79 million), with smaller awards from the Bezos Family Foundation and two other foundations.
3) As of 2013, Partnership for Learning had received $4.7 million from the Gates Foundation.
4) As of 2013, Stand For Children had received over $12.4 million from foundations associated with donors to the Yes on 1240 campaign, with $9 million coming from the Gates Foundation and over $2.8 million coming from the Walton Foundation.
5) As of 2013, the Center on Reinventing Public Education had received over $9.2 million in funding from foundations associated with donors to the Yes on 1240 campaign, including over $8.5 million from the Gates Foundation and small amounts from both the Walton and Broad Foundations.

(Bill & Melinda Gates Foundation, 2013; Foundation Center, 2013; Libby, 2012a, 2012b; New York State Office of the Attorney General, 2013; Stand for Children, 2013; University of Washington Bothell Office of Research, 2013; University of Washington Bothell Office of Sponsored Programs, 2013)

The web connecting major Yes on 1240 campaign donors, their affiliated philanthropies, and the Yes on 1240 coordinating and advocacy organizations is even more interconnected than what I have outlined here (see Au & Ferrare, 2014, for a more detailed analysis). However, even this relatively brief highlighting of the connectivity amongst charter school proponents and the Yes on 1240 campaign illustrates one layer of anti-democracy within charter school reform in Washington State. In the rawest sense, charter school policy was advanced in Washington State by a group of 21 wealthy individuals and organizations that donated significant sums of money to the Yes on 1240 campaign. Further, the philanthropic foundations associated with most of the individual major donors to the Yes on 1240 campaign have a history of funding the nonprofit and advocacy organizations that coordinated and operationalized the campaign itself. As such, these wealthy individuals wielded vastly disproportionate power over charter school policy reform relative to the average voter in Washington State. Further still, given the race and class demographics of these wealthy individual donors, and given that prominent ones, like Bill Gates, Jr., send their own children to elite private schools, these elites are essentially advocating and establishing policy not for their own children, but for everyone else's—an act that in its hubris looks to be one of patronizing neo-colonialism (Au & Ferrare, 2015b).

School Governance and the Free Market Ideology Lurking Within Washington's Charter Law

Given the wealthy elites who championed the Yes on 1240 campaign, it makes sense that I-1240, like many charter school laws, carries ideological baggage associated with deregulated, neoliberal, free market policy structures and assumptions associated with what many refer to broadly as corporate education reform (Au & Ferrare, 2015a; Fabricant & Fine, 2013; Lipman, 2011). While there are multiple facets to this education reform movement, here I will be focusing on two critical aspects related to the struggle over charter school law in Washington State: namely, the reconstruction of access to public education in the form of free market competition (i.e., charter schools and private school voucher programs), and the reliance on unaccountable and unelected NGOs, philanthropies, for-profit and nonprofit organizations, and corporations for guidance on, and implementation of, public education policy (Au & Ferrare, 2015a).

When looking at Washington State's charter school law, we can see a combination of the above aspects of neoliberal, corporate education reform—undemocratic governance and free market competition—clearly at play. Essentially, Washington State's charter school law establishes two appointed boards to govern charter schools at the state and local levels. At the state level (what became the Washington State Charter School Commission), these appointments are political appointments decided in the halls of the Washington State Legislature. At the local level, the charter school management organizations themselves appoint their governing boards (Au, 2012c; de Sa Campos, 2012). As Lipman (2011) notes, this is typical of the neoliberal shift from *government* to *governance*, where she states:

> The "triumph of market ideology" is coupled with an erosion of the idea that informed citizens should make decisions based on the general welfare. The shift from *government* by elected state bodies and a degree of democratic accountability to *governance* by experts and managers and decision making by judicial authority and executive order is central to neoliberal policy making . . . Public-private partnerships, appointed managers, and

publicly unaccountable bodies comprised of appointed state and corporate leaders make decisions about urban development, transportation, schools, and other public infrastructure using business rationales.

(p. 13, original emphasis)

I-1240's governance structure for charter schools establishes a foundationally important logic for the neoliberal education reform agenda: It means that charter schools can legally operate on the principle that public tax dollars for public education can follow the child into a charter school that is governed by an appointed, non-democratically elected board. This logic is critical for trying to reconstruct public schools as a system of market competition in a couple of ways. First, it establishes a climate of deregulation, where there are not publicly accountable, publicly elected institutions keeping track of both how public dollars are being spent and if the schools are behaving in a lawful manner. Second, within the deregulated market, "good" schools will attract a larger market share of students, and thus have enough fiscal resources to operate, because the money follows the child. Likewise, within these logics, "bad" schools will close since they will not attract enough market shares and will not have enough students to stay open. In this sense, charter schools are basically built upon a small business model, with startups popping up in various places, and once free market competition works its magic, only the "good" schools/businesses will be left standing. Indeed, one of the critical points to make in the current struggles over charter schools in Washington State has been to point out that the entire charter school model depends on closing schools (Au, 2015b).

It is important to recognize that there is a cluster of neoliberal policy characteristics at play here: charter schools with undemocratically elected boards, deregulation of charter schools, public money following children into deregulated charter schools that have undemocratically elected boards, and free market competition that is predicated on closing schools after market share is lost. It is a clear chain of logic, and the reason why it is so critical to the neoliberal, corporate education reform agenda is that it functionally is no different from private school voucher programs—where public monies are given to families in the form of vouchers, and those vouchers can be spent at any school, public, private, religious, or non-religious. As Ravitch (2010) observes, this is one of the reasons voucher supporters put their collective efforts behind the charter school movement in the late 1990s. They saw that charter schools provided a foothold for their own privatization agenda.

The fact that Washington's charter school law sought to redefine the "public" in "public school" as public money following the child into a deregulated market is a sure sign that other policy actors and agents were involved in the construction of I-1240 well beyond Tania de Sa Campos (who officially filed the initiative) and her employer, the League of Education Voters, discussed above. Indeed, a closer look at Washington State's charter school law finds that the American Legislative Exchange Council (ALEC) directly influenced the law there. ALEC is perhaps more widely known for promoting a broad privatization agenda, "stand your ground" gun laws, and anti-democratic voter registration laws, amongst others (Center for Media and Democracy, 2014). ALEC also has a privatization agenda for public education, including the promotion of charter schools generally, promotion of corporate charters and virtual schools specifically, private school vouchers, anti-union measures, "parent trigger" laws to flip public schools into privately managed charter schools, increasing testing, reducing (or eliminating when possible) the power of democratically elected local school boards, and limiting the power of public school districts (Underwood & Mead, 2012).

ALEC's presence within Washington State's charter school law is clear and most immediate in the inclusion of a "trigger" provision within Washington's law, allowing a small majority of teachers or parents to sign a petition and flip a regular public school into a charter school (Au, 2012c; de Sa Campos, 2012). ALEC has long been known to provide model legislation promoting similar trigger provisions for charter school laws (American Legislative Exchange Council, 2011b). There is evidence that portions of Washington State's charter school governance structure were plagiarized directly from ALEC model legislation. For instance, regarding the state-level commission governing charters in Washington State, I-1240, Section 208, Subsection 2 reads:

> The commission shall consist of *nine members, no more than five of whom shall be members of the same political party. Three members shall be appointed by the governor; three members shall be appointed by the president of the senate; and three members shall be appointed by the speaker of the house of representatives.* The appointing authorities shall assure *diversity among commission members*, including representation from various *geographic* areas of the state and shall assure that at least one member is a parent of a Washington public school student.
> (de Sa Campos, 2012, p. 11, emphasis added)

By way of comparison, here is the language from ALEC's "Charter School Growth with Quality Act" (American Legislative Exchange Council, 2011a) model legislation Section 3, Subsection C, Number 1 regarding state-level charter commissions:

> *Nine members, no more than five of whom shall be members of the same political party. Three members shall be appointed by the Governor; three members shall be appointed by the President of the Senate; and three members shall be appointed by the Speaker of the House of Representatives.* In making the appointments, the Governor, the President of the Senate, and the Speaker of the House of Representatives shall ensure statewide *geographic diversity among Commission members.*
> (n.p., emphasis added)

As another example, the language in I-1240, Section 208, Subsection 3, also regarding the governing board for the state-level charter school commission, reads:

> *Members appointed to the commission shall collectively possess strong experience and expertise in public and nonprofit governance; management and finance; public school leadership, assessment, curriculum, and instruction; and public education law. All members shall have demonstrated an understanding of and commitment to charter schooling as a strategy for strengthening public education.*
>
> (p. 11, emphasis added)

Again, by way of comparison, here is the language from ALEC's "Charter School Growth with Quality Act" model legislation Section 3, Subsection C, Number 2:

> *Members appointed to the Commission shall collectively possess strong experience and expertise in public and nonprofit governance, management and finance, public school leadership, assessment, and curriculum and instruction, and public education law. All members* of the Commission *shall have demonstrated understanding of and commitment to charter schooling as a strategy for strengthening public education.*
>
> (n.p., emphasis added)

The overlapping language between I-1240 and the ALEC model legislation has been highlighted here in italics, and it seems clear that whoever originally authored Washington State's charter school law plagiarized this language on charter school governance from ALEC's model legislation. Given ALEC's commitment to school vouchers and free markets, and given ALEC's influence in state politics around the country, the presence of their model charter school legislation in Washington State's charter school law should perhaps come as no surprise.

Common Schools, Closings, and the Risk of the Free Market

I see the forces of neoliberal privatization and the politics of anti-democracy lurking within the charter school movement, and as such see the defense of public schools as a critical piece of supporting the democratic ideal in the United States. Public schools are part of the commons: They are one of the last institutions in our country where nearly everyone is present and interacting with each other. Public schools are therefore also critical for diversity, critical thinking, and developing critical consciousness about how our world functions. It is for these reasons that I have been deeply involved in the struggle against charter schools in Washington State generally, and against

I-1240 specifically (Au, 2015a). Part of my involvement was agreeing to be a named appellant in a lawsuit challenging the constitutionality of I-1240, and after 10 months of deliberation, on September 4, 2015, the Washington Supreme Court handed down a ruling that I-1240 was indeed unconstitutional and should therefore be invalidated entirely (Madsen, 2015). Specifically, the Washington State Supreme court ruled that, "because charter schools under I-1240 are run by an appointed board or nonprofit organization and thus are not subject to local voter control, they cannot qualify as 'common schools' . . . ." (p. 11) under Washington's Constitution. Thus, because of the neoliberal governance structure that lacks direct public oversight, charter schools are not "common schools" in Washington State, and therefore are ineligible to receive public monies designated for public school funding. As such, without other funding sources, the nine charter schools operating in Washington State at the time of the state Supreme Court ruling would have to close their doors and stop serving the roughly 1,300 enrolled students (Rees & Franta, 2015).

Conservative and free market education reformers were furious about the Washington State Supreme Court decision. The Washington Policy Center (2015), whose tagline is, "Improving Lives Through Market Solutions," the CEOs of both the National Alliance for Public Charter Schools and the Washington State Charter Schools Association (Rees & Franta, 2015), right wing think-tank policy advocates (Whitmire & Rotherham, 2015), and several local politicians have called on the Washington State Legislature to "correct" the law by changing the funding structure so charter schools would receive tax dollars through a specific fund not associated with public schools (Cafazzo & Santos, 2015). Admittedly, the timing of the Washington State Supreme Court ruling was terrible for the nine existing charter schools in the state, some of which were already open and operating and faced potential closure. In turn, the looming closures were seized upon by free market advocates, like the Washington Policy Center (Finne, 2015), to assert that the ruling was bad because it closed schools—an assertion that, as discussed above, conveniently ignored that school closures are built into the charter school model they advocated for from the beginning (Au, 2015b). Further, in protesting the school closures, the free market, education reform advocates seemingly also ignore how their market models actually function.

To be clear, I am sympathetic to the plight of the students and parents who had signed up for charter schools in Washington, and thus faced the threat of their schools closing. I would guess that, at best, charter operators were inconsistent in communicating to the students and parents about the potential risks involved in enrolling in their charter schools given the then-pending Washington State Supreme Court ruling. It is even possible that some of the charter management organizations themselves may not have fully grasped the risks involved. However, this is the game one plays within the model of charter schools as small, independently operating businesses. Presumably, charter schools are supposed to offer "choice" and "competition" in the educational marketplace (Fabricant & Fine, 2012). Within this model, if you choose to invest in a risky product under risky market conditions, then you and the charter operators are assuming that risk. Those charter school operators opened their small businesses and the parents chose to enroll their children in an environment where there was very real risk that the constitutionality ruling could go against them and withdraw their state funding entirely. If your small business (charter) gets shut down because someone did not fully understand state regulations or fully comprehend the potential risk of opening a business (charter) in a hostile marketplace, so be it. That is how the free market model is supposed to function, and in this model, small businesses that make poor decisions about market conditions are supposed to close. Further, part of the risk of framing charters, as small businesses not governed by the public, is that they can and do close often, sometimes without notice. Charter closures have happened all over the country, many times because of financial problems (The Center for Popular Democracy & Integrity in Education, 2014). Indeed, between 2001 and 201,3 almost 2,500 charter schools closed, impacting almost 290,000 students (Persson, 2015b), and in the 2011–2012 school year specifically, charter schools were two and a half times more likely to experience closures than regular public schools (Persson, 2015a). School closures are simply a part of the charter school plan, and the lack of public accountability points to the risks faced by charter school students and families.

First Place Scholars and the After-the-Fact Accountability of Markets

First Place Scholars was the very first charter school to open in Washington State, and in many ways, it was the perfect example of the charter school promise. First Place Scholars was a conversion from an existing school that had previously been funded by other sources, and it also laudably served a very important and vulnerable population: homeless children. However, in its first year of operation as a publicly funded charter school, First Place Scholars faced several problems, many of which have to do with the deregulation agenda associated with privatization. Before continuing with the example of First Place Scholars, I want to be clear on a few points. First and foremost, those homeless children need and deserve the highest-quality education possible. Second, and just as important, I am sure that the staff at First Place Scholars was well intentioned and wanted to provide for their students. Third, based on the reports, I would guess that the board and staff of First Place Scholars might not have fully grasped the intricacies of running a charter school, including the full details of children's legal educational rights. Regardless, First Place Scholars serves as an example of what can happen when schools are run as deregulated institutions that lack accountability mechanisms outside of their own non-elected governing boards.

As was reported back in late fall of 2014 (Todd, 2014), then again in March of 2015 in a letter from the Washington State Charter School Commission (2015), and in September of 2015 in an Accountability Audit Report by the Washington State Auditor's Office (Jutte, 2015), over the course of its first year, First Place Scholars charter school:

1) Started with five of eight teachers not certificated (by October 2014, it was two of eight);
2) Did not perform criminal background checks, as required by state law, on a number of staff members;
3) Did not have a certificated special education teacher and did not provide special education services for its students from September 2014 to March 2015, despite a full 20% of its children being placed in special education;
4) Was not meeting the educational needs of its English language learners;
5) Was not properly implementing or tracking assessment of student progress;
6) Faced constant financial shortfalls so severe that the school was under regular threat to close its facilities;
7) Was not meeting the school education design outlined in their original charter contract;
8) Did not properly maintain documentation of staff certification;
9) Had out-of-date safety plans;
10) Did not adequately monitor and report student enrollment;
11) Lacked internal fiscal controls and documentation for monitoring finances, putting the school in danger of fiscal collapse;
12) Improperly used public funds to support the operations of First Place, Inc., the nonprofit established to manage the school;
13) Did not comply with lawful requirements to hold board meetings open to the public;
14) Was overpaid by $200,000 (of state education funds that should have gone to public schools, mind you) because of improper reporting and not providing promised and required special education services.

Thus, despite the ongoing assurances that charters schools provide a high-quality education, and the assertions that Washington State's charter schools will serve our highest needs students in a responsible way, we can see that the students at First Place Scholars did not receive many of the services they were legally entitled to and would have gotten had they attended a regular public school.

Unfortunately, First Place Scholars illustrates almost every single major problem with charter schools and the deregulated, neoliberal, free market model they are founded upon. The fact that First Place Scholars did not provide any special education services for the 20% of its students that are designated as being in special education is distressing, to say the least. That First Place was also found lacking in providing services for its English language learners is equally problematic. Unfortunately, both are consistent with nationwide issues, where charter schools have been found to underserve both English language learners and students in special education (Miron, Urschel, Mathis, & Tornquist, 2010), oftentimes because they do not provide adequate services for these populations (Welner, 2013). Additionally, while I would not assert that First Place Scholars was purposefully fraudulent, the evidence indicates that they were at least negligent in their reporting duties regarding enrollment and special education services, and as such received over $200,000 of public tax monies that should have remained in the regular public school system. Unfortunately, this kind of negligence is consistent with the financial waste, fraud, and abuse happening with charter schools nationally (The Center for Popular Democracy & Integrity in Education, 2014).

These issues, and the others listed here, highlight a fundamental flaw with deregulation and free market forms of accountability. As the example of First Place Scholars highlights, free market accountability amounts to after-the-fact accountability. The issues at First Place were only first noticed when a representative of the Washington State Charter School Commission happened to be on site for a meeting (Todd, 2014). This initial signal that there were problems was happenstance, not systematic. No one was actively keeping track of First Place Scholars. The state accountability audit did not happen until after the school was open and not adequately serving many of their students for six months. This is what happens at the crossroads of deregulation and a lack of public accountability: The mistakes and problems are figured out *after* the fact, *after* the students in special education don't receive any special education services for six months of the year, *after* months of English language learners not getting the services they require and deserve, *after* $200,000 is incorrectly allocated to them, *after* we find out that proper criminal background checks had not been completed, *after* a school spends most of the year on the brink of financial collapse and regularly cuts services for kids. The deregulated charter school version of after-the-fact accountability is always done in retrospect, and it means figuring out the problems *after* the damage has already been done and *after* the kids have already been hurt. In the charter school, small business, free market model, the "bad" schools close after they lose market shares, making this after-the-fact accountability a fundamental feature of how charters operate (Au, 2015b).

Conclusion

In this chapter, I have used Washington State as a case to illustrate how charter schools are fundamentally and purposefully anti-democratic. To make that case, I have drawn on the history of charter school law in the state, including the multiple times charter schools have been rejected by Washington voters and the wealthy elites who bankrolled a major campaign to legalize charter schools in the state in 2012. I then highlighted the logics underlying the charter school model, explaining the implication and neoliberal origins of the idea of redefining "public schools" as any school where "the money follows the child," regardless of the governance structure for accountability and oversight. As I argue, this model is functionally a model for private school vouchers, which is a major goal for free market conservatives. I then provided evidence that the anti-democratic governance structure found within Washington State's charter school law came directly from the hyper conservative, anti-public American Legislative Exchange Council. From there, I discussed the Washington State Supreme Court ruling, its implications for school closings, and the ways that school closures are fundamental to the charter school model. Finally, I offered First Place Scholars, Washington's first charter school, as an example of what happens with deregulation and a lack of public accountability: children's education gets hurt.

The Washington State Supreme Court's ruling against charter schools is a major rebuke of the privatization agenda. Overturning I-1240 establishes that here in Washington, without public oversight, charter schools are not "common schools" and hence are not really "public schools" eligible for public funding. Just as supporters of publicly financed charter schools understand the profound implications of the Washington State Supreme Court ruling, public school supporters also need to pay close attention. As Washington State's Supreme Court has said: If a school is not controlled by a public body, then it should not have access to public funds. Indeed, this point is at the heart of my argument here. The anti-democratic, anti-public governance of charter schools is purposeful, not accidental. Free market reformers see this as an essential and explicit goal for the restructuring of public schools. If we value democracy and high-quality education for all children, then we would do well to take heed of just who is advocating for charters and what the real effects of charters are on some of our most vulnerable student populations.

References

American Legislative Exchange Council. (2011a). Charter School Growth with Quality Act. Retrieved September 5, 2015, from http://www.alec.org/model-legislation/charter-school-growth-with-quality-act/

American Legislative Exchange Council. (2011b). Parent Trigger Act. Retrieved September 5, 2015, from http://www.alec.org/model-legislation/parent-trigger-act/

Au, W. (2012a). The false promise of charter schools. *The Seattle Times*. Retrieved from http://seattletimes.com/html/opinion/2017379325_guest31au.html

Au, W. (2012b, February). *Learning to read: Charter schools, public education, and the politics of educational research*. Presented at the Washington State PTA Public Charter School Forum, Seattle, WA.

Au, W. (2012c, October 22). Policy memo on Washington State Initiative 1240. Retrieved from http://seattleducation2010.wordpress.com/2012/10/22/policy-memo-on-washington-state-initiative-1240/

Au, W. (2015a, September 10). A perfect education storm in Washington State. Retrieved from https://www.washingtonpost.com/blogs/answer-sheet/wp/2015/09/10/a-perfect-education-storm-in-washington-state/

Au, W. (2015b, September 27). Dear Liv: Yes, a loss for ALEC and the privatizers makes me happy. Retrieved from https://seattleducation2010.wordpress.com/2015/09/27/dear-liv-yes-a-loss-for-alec-and-the-privatizers-makes-me-happy/

Au, W., & Ferrare, J. J. (2014). Sponsors of policy: A network analysis of wealthy elites, their affiliated philanthropies, and charter school reform in Washington State. *Teachers College Record, 116*(8). Retrieved from http://www.tcrecord.org/content.asp?contentid=17387

Au, W., & Ferrare, J. J. (2015a). Introduction: Neoliberalism, social networks, and the new governance of education. In W. Au & J. J. Ferrare (Eds.), *Mapping corporate education reform: Power and policy networks in the neoliberal state* (pp. 1–22). New York: Routledge.

Au, W., & Ferrare, J. J. (2015b). Other people's policy: Wealthy elites and charter school reform in Washington State. In W. Au & J. J. Ferrare (Eds.), *Mapping corporate education reform: Power and policy networks in the neoliberal state* (pp. 147–164). New York: Routledge.

Barkan, J. (2011). Got dough? How billionaires rule our schools. *Dissent, 58*(1), 49–57. Retrieved from http://doi.org/10.1353/dss.2011.0023

Bill & Melinda Gates Foundation. (2013). How we work: Awarded grants. Retrieved from http://www.gatesfoundation.org/How-We-Work/Quick-Links/Grants-Database

Cafazzo, D., & Santos, M. (2015, September 12). Washington charter schools: Officials can't agree on how to save them. *Tacoma News Tribune*. Tacoma, WA. Retrieved from http://www.thenewstribune.com/news/local/politics-government/article35046459.html

Callaghan, P. (2012, July 3). Might be a record: Sponsors of charter schools initiative say they have enough signatures. Retrieved from http://blog.thenewstribune.com/politics/2012/07/03/might-be-a-record-sponsors-of-charter-schools-initiative-say-they-have-enough-signatures/

Center for Media and Democracy. (2014). What is ALEC? Retrieved October 1, 2015, from http://www.alecexposed.org/wiki/What_is_ALEC%3F

The Center for Popular Democracy & Integrity in Education. (2014). *Charter school vulnerabilities to waste, fraud, and abuse*. Washington, DC: The Center for Popular Democracy, Integrity in Education. Retrieved from https://www.scribd.com/doc/221993993/Charter-School-Vulnerabilities-to-Waste-Fraud-Abuse

Corcoran, S. P., & Stoddard, C. (2011). Local demand for a school choice policy: Evidence from the Washington charter school referenda. *Education Finance and Policy, 6*(3), 323–353.

de Sa Campos, T. (2012). *Initiative measure No. 1240 concerns creation of a public charter school system*. Olympia, Washington. Retrieved from http://sos.wa.gov/_assets/elections/initiatives/FinalText_274.pdf

Fabricant, M., & Fine, M. (2012). *Charter schools and the corporate makeover of public education*. New York: Teachers College Press.

Fabricant, M., & Fine, M. (2013). *The changing politics of education: Privatization and the dispossessed lives left behind*. Boulder, CO: Paradigm Publishers.

Finne, L. (2015, September 17). Charter school opponent expresses joy at school closures. Retrieved from https://www.washingtonpolicy.org/blog/post/charter-school-opponent-expresses-joy-school-closures

Foundation Center. (2013). 990 finder. Retrieved from http://foundationcenter.org/findfunders/990finder/

Jutte, J. M. (2015). *Accountability audit report: First Place Scholars Charter School* (No. 1015230). Olympia, Washington: Washington State Auditor's Office. Retrieved from http://www.sao.wa.gov/local/Documents/1stPlScholarsCharter_accountabilityaudit.pdf

Lake, R., Gross, B., & Maas, T. (2012). *Examining charters: How public charter schools can work in Washington State* (p. 23). Seattle, Washington: Partnership for Learning; Center for Reinventing Public Education. Retrieved from http://www.partnership4learning.org/files/ExaminingCharters.pdf

League of Education Voters. (2012). Staff. Retrieved from http://www.educationvoters.org/about-2/staff/

Libby, K. (2012a). Doris and Donald Fisher education giving, 2003–2011. Retrieved from http://nepc.colorado.edu/blog/doris-and-donald-fisher-education-giving-2003-2011

Libby, K. (2012b). Education reform now advocacy committee. Retrieved from http://dferwatch.wordpress.com/connections-2/education-reform-now-advocacy-inc/

Lipman, P. (2011). *The new political economy of urban education: Neoliberalism, race, and the right to the city.* New York: Routledge.

Madsen, C. J. (2015). League of Women Voters et. al v. State of Washington, No. 89714–0 (Washington State Supreme Court September 4, 2015). Retrieved from http://www.courts.wa.gov/opinions/pdf/897140.pdf

Miron, G., Urschel, J. L., Mathis, W. J., & Tornquist, E. (2010). *Schools without diversity: Education management organizations, charter schools, and the demographic stratification of the American school system.* Boulder, CO and Tempe, AZ: Education and the Public Interest Center and Education Policy Research Unit. Retrieved from http://nepc.colorado.edu/files/EMO-Seg.pdf

New York State Office of the Attorney General. (2013). Charities nys.com. Retrieved from http://www.charitiesnys.com/RegistrySearch/show_details.jsp?id={4D9E71F8-0188-4433-9D6C-4892837A401C}

Partnership for Learning. (2012, October 18). New report examines how charter schools can work in WA. Retrieved from http://www.partnership4learning.org/node/3843

Persson, J. (2015a, June 16). Charter program expansion looms despite probes into mismanagement and closed schools. Retrieved from http://www.prwatch.org/news/2015/06/12859/charter-program-expansion-looms-despite-ongoing-probes-mismanagement-and-closed

Persson, J. (2015b, September 22). CMD publishes full list of 2,500 closed charter schools (with interactive map). Retrieved from http://www.prwatch.org/news/2015/09/12936/cmd-publishes-full-list-2500-closed-charter-schools

Ravitch, D. (2010). *The death and life of the great American school system: How testing and choice are undermining education* (e-book). New York: Basic Books.

Reckhow, S. (2013). *Follow the money: How foundation dollars change public school politics.* New York: Oxford University Press.

Reckhow, S., & Snyder, J. W. (2014). The expanding role of philanthropy in education politics. *Educational Researcher, 43*(4), 186–195.

Reed, S. (2012, November 27). November 6, 2012 general election results: Initiative measure no. 1240 concerns creation of a public charter school system. Retrieved from http://vote.wa.gov/results/current/Initiative-Measure-No-1240-Concerns-creation-of-a-public-charter-school-system.html

Rees, N., & Franta, T. (2015, September 5). Save Washington State public charter schools. Retrieved from http://www.huffingtonpost.com/nina-rees/save-washington-state-pub_b_8094048.html

Rosenthal, B. M. (2012). Charter schools on legislative agenda: "Worth the fight": Many say we can't wait longer for solution; others worry. *The Olympian.*

Retrieved from http://www.theolympian.com/2012/01/13/1946994/charter-schools-on-legislative.html
Saltman, K. J. (2011). From Carnegie to Gates: The Bill and Melinda Gates Foundation and the venture philanthropy agenda for public education. In P. E. Kovacs (Ed.), *The Gates Foundation and the future of U.S. "public" schools* (pp. 1–20). New York: Routledge.
Stake, R. E. (2000). Case studies. In N. Denzin & Y. S. Lincoln (Eds.), *The handbook of qualitative research* (2nd ed., pp. 435–454). Thousand Oaks, CA: Sage Publications.
Stand for Children. (2013). Annual report and financial statement. Retrieved from http://stand.org/national/about/annual-report-financial-statement
Todd, L. (2014, December 10). State's first charter school in disarray. *The Seattle Times*. Seattle, WA. Retrieved from http://www.seattletimes.com/seattle-news/statersquos-first-charter-school-in-disarray/
Underwood, J., & Mead, J. F. (2012). A smart ALEC threatens public education. *Education Week*. Retrieved from http://www.edweek.org/ew/articles/2012/03/01/kappan_underwood.html
University of Washington Bothell Office of Research. (2013). Office of research: Current awards. Retrieved from www.uwb.edu/research/reports/current-awards
University of Washington Bothell Office of Sponsored Programs. (2013). Request for information. Retrieved from www.uwb.edu/research/reports/current-awards
Washington Coalition for Public Charter Schools. (2012). Yes on 1240. Retrieved from yeson1240.com
Washington Policy Center. (2015, September 4). WPC calls on legislature to protect the charter school education of 1,300 children from the unjust decision of the state Supreme Court. Retrieved September 6, 2015, from http://washingtonpolicy.org/press/press-releases/wpc-calls-legislature-protect-charter-school-education-1300-children-unjust-dec
Washington State Charter School Commission. (2015, March 31). Letter of concern. Retrieved from https://www.documentcloud.org/documents/1699904-first-place-letter-of-concern-4-1-15.html
Washington State Public Disclosure Commission. (2012a). Washington State Public Disclosure Commission: 40 years of shining light on Washington politics: Cash contributions for Yes On 1240 WA Coalition for Public Charter Schools. Retrieved from http://www.pdc.wa.gov/MvcQuerySystem/CommitteeData/contributions?param=WUVTIFdDIDUwNw====&year=2012&type=initiative
Washington State Public Disclosure Commission. (2012b). Washington State Public Disclosure Commission: 40 years of shining light on Washington politics: Expenditures for Yes On 1240 WA Coalition for Public Charter Schools. Retrieved from http://www.pdc.wa.gov/MvcQuerySystem/CommitteeData/contributions?param=WUVTIFdDIDUwNw====&year=2012&type=initiative
Washington State Public Disclosure Commission. (2012c). Washington State Public Disclosure Commission: 40 years of shining light on Washington politics: Inkind contributions for Yes On 1240 WA Coalition for Public Charter Schools. Retrieved from http://www.pdc.wa.gov/MvcQuerySystem/CommitteeData/contributions?param=WUVTIFdDIDUwNw====&year=2012&type=initiative
Washington State Public Disclosure Commission. (2012d). *Washington State Public Disclosure Commission's "most money" journal*. Olympia, Washington: Washington State Public Disclosure Commission. Retrieved from http://www.pdc.wa.gov/archive/home/historical/pdf/MostMoneyJournal.pdf
Welner, K. G. (2013). The dirty dozen: How charter schools influence student enrollment. *Teachers College Record*. Retrieved from http://www.tcrecord.org/Content.asp?ContentID=17104

Westbrook, M. (2012). Why the Washington State charter bills are flawed. Retrieved from http://saveseattleschools.blogspot.com/2012/02/why-washington-state-charter-bills-are.html

Whitmire, R., & Rotherham, A. J. (2015, September 16). Why Washington's "common school" court decision runs counter to common good of students. Retrieved from https://www.the74million.org/article/opinion-why-washingtons-common-school-court-decision-runs-counter-to-the-common-good-of-students-and-communities

Yes on 1240. (2012). Yes On 1240: Prof. Hill. Retrieved from https://www.youtube.com/watch?v=tGLNzlImRNY

2 Democracy, Charter Schools, and the Politics of Choice

Eleni Schirmer and Michael W. Apple

Introduction

A longing for choice and "freedom" animates the charter schools movement in the United States. Charter schools began as a public alternative to traditional public schools, allowing parents and students to select educational environments seemingly better suited to their students' needs, interests, or goals. Supporters of charter schools maintain that enabling families to choose the best educational environment for their child maximizes the child's individual potential and aspirations. For this reason, charters commonly possess a tailored focus: for example, special subjects, such as the arts or computer engineering, or a specialized curriculum, such as English as a second language. In many instances, charter schools have been motivated by a desire for more democratic, responsive, engaging, and socially just education (for example, see Apple & Beane, 2007). Similarly, charter school and school choice programs aim to function as an equalizing mechanism for unequal markets, enabling low-income and under-resourced families to participate in the marketplace of school choice in which upper-class families regularly engage (Pedroni, 2007). Such developments reveal the fundamentally democratic sentiment embedded within part of the originating theory of charter schools, that of achieving the human longings of choice and freedom.

However, the drive towards choice and freedom presented by charter schools has become embedded within the ideological matrix of neoliberalism. The ideal of choice has become redefined in economic terms as a consumer's choice to select goods in a competitive marketplace. This understanding characterizes the current economic and political era not only in education, but also in all things social. Generally stated, neoliberalism is the dominant ideology in which material exchanges on a marketplace best fulfill human aspirations. Markets are the preferred means to coordinating the requirements of human flourishing, rather than states and politics, which are seen as inefficient at their best and obstructive to freedom at worst (Crouch, 2011). For charter schools, this means the human longing for choice operates through private markets rather than publicly managed institutions.

Although charter schools originated within public school districts, they have since proliferated as privately managed organizations (Kretchmar, Sondel, & Ferrare, 2013; Scott, 2009). A new marketplace has formed around these charter options, governed by the logic of consumer choice. Students and families are the "customers," and schools are the product. In this system of logic, the act of choosing alone constitutes a stance of empowerment and freedom. As one school choice organization emblematically claims, "[We] strive to empower families by advocating for quality educational options for families regardless of their zip code or income. We believe it is a parent's right to choose the best educational environment for their child" ("Choose Your School Wisconsin," 2015). As this formulation reveals, empowerment rests primarily in an individual's capacity to choose, not necessarily the possibilities and constraints embedded within the chosen option (see, e.g., Peterson, 2006).

Yet, what exactly is "choice"? How does a set of choices get defined? And how significant is the chosen object relative to the act of choosing? To further examine these questions, we turn our attention to a case study of political and economic changes within a paradigm case both of how this process of the neoliberalization of choice proceeds and of the conflicts it entails in the real, not idealized, world. We focus on Kenosha, Wisconsin's public education system as a key instance of the redefinition of choice. We trace the ideological shift towards a neoliberal definition of choice, and how it interacts with other significant elements of rightist educational and social politics, such as labor rights and the role of local governments.

However, before examining the case of Kenosha, it is important to note that this chapter by and large brackets a number of important critiques of charter schools that have already been correctly raised by many others. For example, despite the growth of choice rhetoric, meager attention is given to what gets chosen: the actual charter schools and the degree of social empowerment they may or may not offer to students and families (Sondel, 2015; Wells, Slayton, & Scott, 2002). Research on charter efficacy relative to traditional public schools reveals consistently mixed results; charters, it seems, can be claimed as neither inherently better nor worse than public schools (e.g., Miron, Mathis, & Welner, 2015). Furthermore, critical issues about the exclusionary character of charters abound. For example, a growing body of evidence suggests that charter schools tend to have inadequate services for students with special education needs. Frequently, such students get counseled out of charter schools, despite the fact that families of students with special education needs often choose charter schools because traditional public schools offered insufficient services for their students. (Fabricant & Fine, 2012; Wells, 2002; Welner, 2013).

This is a crucial point. Unlike public schools, private charter schools do not have an obligation to serve all students. Rather than a charge from the state to provide a certain standard of education, market forces structure charter schools. The viability of charter schools largely corresponds to their marketability, or their ability to outperform on a marketplace.

As such, charter schools increasingly rely on performance indicators, such as high-stakes test scores, to distinguish themselves from other "products" on the market. This gives charters an implicit incentive to remove low-performing students so as to enhance their perceived competitiveness. Schools must work to attract the highest-performing students from well-resourced families to ensure that the school's performance metrics are top notch. This means middle class and wealthy families get to choose schools for their children, with much less trouble. And it means that schools, in turn, get to choose which students they accept. As a result, school choice typically enhances racial segregation (Fabricant & Fine, 2012; Frankenberg, Siegel-Hawley, & Wang, 2010).

Finally, the lottery systems that characterize typical charter school enrollment policies are a subject of debate in themselves. Rather than an equal access entry mechanism, many scholars argue that the lotteries themselves constitute a subtle form of exclusion. As Brighouse and Schouten (2014) explain, "Just enrolling in a lottery requires effort and social capital that may effectively exclude many of the most disadvantaged parents—for example, parents without the time or resources to attend required recruitment events or to gather the necessary forms and documents for applications" (Brighouse & Schouten, 2014, p. 348). For all the reasons mentioned above, mounting evidence supports the claim that charters function as a basic level of educational privatization. And of course, the mechanisms of each of these dynamics would benefit greatly from further study. But these are not the only things that deserve further critical examination. The very meaning of democracy, the choices taken and left behind, the connections between (imposed) choice and the rights of teachers and other public employees, and who decides each of these issues—all of these are equally crucial. It is for these very reasons that we focus on Kenosha, Wisconsin, since it provides an object lesson in how all of this is in flux—and how all of it is moving in neoliberal directions.

The Basic Questions: Democracy, Choice, and Rightist Mobilizations

Between 2011 through the present, various educational policy changes have taken place in Kenosha: the hyper-financialization of the school district, a turn towards neoliberal strategies to manage drastically reduced public funding, a state-imposed voucher and charter expansion, changes to the legal rights of teachers' unions, a lawsuit against the teachers' union brought forward by a teacher in the school district, and a school board election that attracted national attention. As we shall see in the following pages, what remained consistent through this tumultuous series of events was how the rhetoric of choice was continually put forward as an educational goal. Yet, many in Kenosha were unwilling to accept the consequences of the proposed choice plans. This case study reveals a more nuanced understanding of choice, beyond its rhetorical summoning so frequently flashed in political discourse. Indeed, what comes to light in Kenosha is the understanding of choice as a mature calculus of not only the preferred outcomes, but also the preferred losses. In other words, choice becomes not simply the selection of what one wants, but also what one is *willing (or even forced) to abdicate*. In the case of Kenosha, in the face of growing pressure from neoliberal agendas that pushed for "choice," many people—including a majority on the school board—were unwilling to "unchoose" the basic democratic pillars of their public school system: public funding for public schools, a locally elected governance body, more efficient state-regulated systems, and protections of teachers' rights. By rejecting the proposed school choice policies, the Kenosha school board and their electorate chose educational policies they considered more democratic.

Unsurprisingly, these choices were not universally endorsed. Within the Kenosha school district, some preferred privatized notions of school choice; certainly, many outside of Kenosha supported and pushed forward these policies. In response to the Kenosha school board's repeated rejection of neoliberal notions of choice, groups outside of Kenosha mobilized—including the Koch brothers-backed Americans for Prosperity—took an active interest in the school board elections, providing financial backing and support to the candidates who supported conservative school choice programs. What this case suggests, therefore, is the ways in which dominant conservative forces suture together not only competing and contradictory notions of "choice" in schools, but in crucial instances when such programs were consistently contested by the local school board, well-funded conservative national and regional movements and organizations will proceed to take over the mechanism that made the choices themselves—in this case, the school board itself. Thus, this case study of school choice in the Kenosha Unified School District extends well beyond charters, shedding light into the complex texture of democracy itself and the complex ways choice gets defined and operationalized in neoliberal school districts. It provides a more complex analysis of the power relations and networks, and of the connections to the other parts of the conservative agenda that often stand behind the push for marketized choice in the real world of actually existing schools.

What comes to focus as the salient dynamic in our chapter, then, are not only the tensions represented by charters, but those that extend well beyond them: How do democratic spaces remain viable within in an increasingly aggressive neoliberal context? What role does "choice" play towards restricting or expanding democracy, especially in a time of fiscal crisis of the state? The chapter pays particular attention to the slippery way "choice" functions as an ideologically loaded rhetorical device, ambiguously and problematically changing meaning over time. Let us now turn to the specifics of Kenosha to show how these questions get answered in real life.

Kenosha, Wisconsin: Where Capitalism and Democracy Face Off

The downtown of Kenosha, Wisconsin buttresses against Lake Michigan, and sweeping views of the stretching blue-green horizon interrupt the rows of concrete buildings. Since 1902, the town has hosted automobile manufacturing plants, including those of the American Motors Corporation and later, the Chrysler Corporation. When the Chrysler Corporation shut down its Kenosha facilities in 1988, the factory was the oldest operating automobile manufacturing facility in North America. The local economy had long been dependent on the manufacturing industry and its unionized jobs for its economic vitality. Kenosha had a bustling downtown with a renowned symphony orchestra and public museums nestled between the union hall, pubs, and automobile factory. For years, Kenosha offered a blue-collar haven, where workers had unionized jobs, low costs of living, and access to high-quality public education and family-friendly neighborhoods.

By the early 1980s, Kenosha's economic dependence on automobile manufacturing thrust the town into unstable employment and income for residents, thanks to the cyclical and relatively weak nature of the American automobile industry. Workers decried the loss of jobs, particularly well-paying jobs with access to benefits. The racial effects of these job losses were also pronounced. A year after the factory closed, only one-third of Kenosha's Black and Latino residents had found new work, compared to 42% of white workers. Simultaneously, pro-business groups argued that Chrysler's unionized wages set a prohibitively high wage floor, creating disincentives for economic development. These groups celebrated Chrysler's closing in 1988 as an opportunity for increased commercial and industrial expansion.

The closing of the Chrysler plant triggered competing narratives for Kenosha's development prospects—one in which economic growth comes from relaxing regulations for capital, thereby maximizing profit growth for investors, and one in which economic growth comes from more equitable distributions of wealth, such as raising and stabilizing workers' wages and increasing employment (Moore & Squires, 1991, p. 169). In effect, both narratives hold some truth. Kenosha *had* witnessed a rise in pro-growth business groups. And wages *had* declined for workers, with particularly disproportionate wage loss for people of color. The rise in economic growth for top wage earners combined with a loss of unionized jobs accelerated economic inequality in Kenosha. In this regard, Kenosha, Wisconsin illustrates the all-too-common story of failed trickle-down economics.

Yet, more than simply competing, these dueling narratives clarified each other. The mirage of economic growth in Kenosha sharpened awareness of its uneven realities, crystallizing critiques of the social costs of corporate growth agendas, and mobilized action in the small town. The grim reality of lost jobs galvanized the unionized former Chrysler employees to organize for restitution from the multi-billion dollar corporation. Through their union, autoworkers at the plant fought for and won a settlement against Chrysler's use of federal funds to relocate its Kenosha operations to Detroit. Although the loss of well-paying jobs for working-class people exposed the grim social impacts of globalized capitalism and rising corporate strength, it also generated a spirit of activism in Kenosha. The autoworkers struggle against Chrysler reinvigorated a public sector committed to socially just policies, such as increased employment, especially for people of color. In the wake of Chrysler's closure, the ideology of privatization faced a growing challenge from activists, workers, and public officials in Kenosha (Moore & Squires, 1991). Yet the tension between the private-sector and public-sector governance in Kenosha was far from over.

Almost exactly twenty years after the Chrysler plant closed its Kenosha plant, global political-economic changes again erupted in Kenosha after the 2008 financial collapse. These economic changes provided rich ground for the subsequent political changes, ushering in a neoliberal regime to compete with Kenosha's municipal democracy. In particular, three key events heightened tensions between the reign of market governance and democratic principles in Kenosha: the financialization of the school district, the leadership's turn toward "managerial" reforms, and the mounting external pressures from the neoliberal state. Each of these events exposed the deep friction between the needs of capital growth and the Kenosha school district. More specifically, perhaps, they reveal the deep friction between the requirements of private markets and the requirements of a school districted committed to a public good.

The Financialization of Kenosha Unified School District

Like many school districts in the early 2000s, the Kenosha Unified School District faced rising health care costs and declining state aid and eagerly sought solutions for its budget shortfalls caused by reduced state funding. When the district's trusted financial advisor, David Noack, presented "collateral debt obligations" (CDOs) as the "best investment" possible to the school board in June 2006, members listened eagerly. As Noack explained, this investment would require the district to borrow large amounts of money from an overseas bank and then purchase corporate bonds, what Noack described as a "collection of bonds from 105 of the most reputable companies that would pay the school board a small return every quarter." These would be sold to the school district by the Royal Bank of Canada, which had a relationship with Noack's company (Duhigg & Dougherty, 2008). The three hundred-plus pages of documents presented to the school board members on this complicated financial mechanism seemed impenetrable. But board members became quickly convinced to accept the plan, given both the financial success such mechanisms had yielded for New York investment bankers and the assurance presented by Noack to the school board that it would take "15 Enrons" for this investment to fail (Flores, 2011c). As a Kenosha school board member Mark Hujik told the *New York Times*, "Everyone knew New York guys were making tons of money on these kinds of deals. It wasn't implausible that we could make money, too."

What could go wrong? Unfortunately, all too much. Mr. Noack's description of CDOs failed to encompass an accurate portrayal of the risks at hand, nor did it account for the growing instabilities of global capitalism. If only a mere 6% of the bonds defaulted, the school district would lose all its money. What's more, Noack and his employing investment company, Stifel, Nicolaus and Company, failed to communicate how risky the school district's actual investments were. The investments performed poorly from the outset; within the first 36 days of closing the account, 10% of the investments were placed on negative watch. None of this information, however, was communicated to the Kenosha school board or the four other Wisconsin school districts that had collectively invested $200 million dollars in Noack's plan. As one financial advisor and Kenosha school board member told the press, "I've never read the prospectus. We had all our questions answered satisfactorily by Dave Noack, so I wasn't worried" (Duhigg & Dougherty, 2008). This statement makes evident the expert knowledge bestowed to financial elites, obviating local and democratically elected decision-makers of their own deliberations, a hallmark feature of managerial regimes (Apple, 2006; Clarke & Newman, 1997). More significantly, the school board's pursuit of high-risk, speculative investments to finance the school district's operating budget revealed the larger trend of neoliberalism: state divestment from public institutions. Declining state aid to public education, coupled with rising health care costs, ushered school districts like Kenosha into unstable financial markets of private investment.

After several months, the Kenosha school district administrators and the other districts began receiving notices that their investments had suffered a series of downgrades and were on the verge of failure. By 2010, the remaining investments lost all value, and the lender seized the trust's assets. The financial management firm was charged with fraud, the first time a private securities firm had been charged for fraudulent dealings with a government entity. The U.S. Securities and Exchange Commission alleged that David Noack in particular had "misrepresented the risk of the CDOs and failed to disclose "material facts" to the districts" (Flores, 2011c). The school districts had lost not only all of the $200 million they had invested—including the $163 million they had borrowed—they also suffered severe credit rating downgrades. This loss of funds, in addition to the massive shortfalls in state aid of 2011, painted a financially bleak picture for the Kenosha Unified School District. When the state's public aid to schools began dwindling, the school district took it upon itself to engage in high-risk speculative loans—the currency de jure of mainstream economics—to increase the district's financial assets. When these investments came crashing down, the district fell into even deeper financial straits, making it more susceptible to calls to increase the economic efficiency of the school district at the expense of educational quality, educational equity and democratic working conditions. Like a municipal shock doctrine, the financial crisis also provided extremely fertile ground for more conservative policy changes in the district.

Economic Crisis Meets Education Reformer

When Michele Hancock, the new superintendent, arrived to Kenosha in 2010, she faced a bleak situation. In addition to the district's collapsed investments, Governor Scott Walker's 2011–2013 budget issued the biggest funding cuts the state had seen until that point (Shaw & Kelley, 2012). Yet, the financial swings of an institution hardly fazed Hancock. A former "human capital officer" from the Rochester, New York School district, Hancock was immersed in the corporate management of education. Rochester Superintendent Jean-Claude Brizard, for example, was trained by the Broad Foundation, a corporate foundation known for its role in promoting top-down, corporate-management styles in public education (Ravitch, 2013). In Rochester, community members and teachers became increasingly frustrated with the administration's top-down, aggressive leadership in 2010. Through a series of public forums, members of the Rochester community asserted that the administration's leadership had caused schools to become more racially segregated, teachers' work less supported, and students' academic and college preparation downgraded. When the Rochester Teachers Association officially issued a no-confidence vote in the administration in 2011, Hancock and the superintendent and other top-ranking administrators sought employment elsewhere. Brizard joined the administration of the Chicago Public School district, a district known for its corporate-style management; Hancock came to Kenosha as superintendent (Friedman, 2011a; Friedman, 2011b; Lipman, 2004, 2011; Saltman, 2009).

Within a few months of her tenure as superintendent in Kenosha, Hancock issued "The Transformation Plan" to the Kenosha Unified School District. In a pitch eerily consistent with the policies of Rochester School district and the Broad Foundation, this several-hundred-page document offered an analysis and roadmap for Hancock's education vision, largely centered around education reform buzzwords like building "life and career skills," deploying "relevant global knowledge," and increasing the use of technology in the classroom.

Yet the gap between Hancock's rhetoric and the actual practices in schools felt jolting to many teachers and community members. Although the school district was still struggling from the subprime financial investments, the Transformation Plan proposed investing in increased technology for the school district, such as laptops, iPads, and online textbooks (Hallow, 2011). Meanwhile, the district's financial hardship, coupled with state budget cuts, laid the groundwork for massive staff layoffs. Near the end of the 2011 school year, Hancock issued layoff notices to over three hundred teachers in the district (Flores, 2011b). In addition to providing devastating job losses to the town's largest employer and unionized work force, the drastic reduction in staff changed the education provided across the district. For example, class sizes in the district jumped; some kindergarten classes packed more than 30 students into a classroom. Foreign language teachers were replaced by the online instruction program Rosetta Stone. In a school district with a very quickly growing Spanish-speaking population, the decision to eliminate foreign language instructors and replace them with computer programs signaled a sharp divestment from some of the community's key resources. The loss of jobs combined with increased class sizes and changes to curriculum priorities frustrated parents and teachers alike. Meanwhile, the district administrators spent hundreds of thousands of dollars on hotels, restaurants, and other travel expenses (Gunn, 2013). As one teacher stated bluntly, "I can also paint my home with a toothbrush. Please, trust your teachers when they say this plan is not right for children. Thirty students will not get the attention they need in the classroom . . . many will get lost . . . Don't let my students get lost in the transformation" (Flores, 2011a).

Besides significantly depleting district morale, Hancock's Transformation Plan had few positive effects on educational outcomes. An independent curriculum audit conducted in 2013 revealed very little progress in the actual adoption of technology by students or in pursuit of the district's educational goals. More seriously, the curriculum audit suggested that the Transformation Plan did very little to address the significant race and class inequalities in the school district. As the audit states, "The strategies listed in the Transformation Plan are worded in very broad and generic terms and do not invoke a clear sense of how the Kenosha Unified School District is going to significantly change its professional practices in order to address identified system needs—particularly reducing the predictive factor of a student's race and family income on academic achievement. While each of the strategies contained within the transformation plan may have some merit as part of an overall improvement process, alone they do little to build the capacity of staff to achieve different results" (Clegg et al., 2013).

As the audit suggests, the Transformation's Plan's myopic failure to address race and class inequities had an impact on educational outcomes. The plan presented no systemic response to the poverty or racial segregation in the city, and the school district's policies exacerbated these social inequalities. Teachers and administrators disproportionately suspended African American and Latino students, while under-enrolling them in special curricular offerings or advanced programs. Programs specifically designed for English language learners (ELL)—largely Latino students—were grossly under-resourced. As one site administrator reported in the curriculum audit, "We have equity issues in our building. The ELL kids don't have any computers or even tables to put them on" (Clegg et al., 2013, p. 210). Although more than 25% of Kenosha's school district is Latino, only 4% of the district educators are.

Furthermore, students of color and low-income students were also less represented in the district's school choice program. The Kenosha Unified School District had developed a well-respected district-sponsored school choice program, offering several public charter schools, an open-enrollment policy, and an in-district transfer policy (Flores, 2013a). However, as is often the case in many school districts, the school choice programs were not equally accessible to all Kenosha families. Many of the schools were not accessible by bus, thereby restricting access. Selection into choice programs was determined by lottery, imposing a language and education barrier to those under-represented families who did not have the background information necessary to participate (Clegg et al., 2013, p. 211).

Superintendent Hancock's prioritization of technology over staff—of efficiency over equity—in Kenosha embodies a characteristically neoliberal and managerial regime. As the global economic crises and risky financial speculation seeped into the school district's own ledgers, the administration adopted an austerity regime of laying off staff while simultaneously increasing investments in technology and administration. As Pauline Lipman and others have eloquently described, the increased financialization and other high-risk debt management techniques often provide justification for the rollback of public services. Rather than defined as vital social institutions, such as public education, these services are calculated in terms of return on investment and profit margins (Lipman, 2011). In Kenosha, both the district's bleak financial condition that welcomed Hancock and her subsequent call for district reorganization embody these effects of neoliberalism, and the managerial regime to which it gave its way.

Between 2010 and 2013, the Kenosha school district followed the classic neoliberal roadmap: The financial collapse provided justification to reorganize elements of the state, altering both the content of the social services and their organization. This reorganization placed new premiums on efficiency, market nimbleness, and choice as the central mechanisms of social provision. Meanwhile, racial and class inequalities in the school district got no better or even worsened. While Hancock and her administration did not independently cause any of the economic preconditions for this reorganization—in either the economic collapse or the district's financial response—they responded with the inflection of what one of us has called the "new managerial" class (Apple, 2006). As Apple states, "As experts in efficiency, management, testing and accountability, [new managerial class] provide the technical expertise to put in place the policies of conservative modernization. Their own mobility *depends* on the expansion of both such expertise and the professional ideologies of control, measurement and efficiency that accompany it" (p. 48). Hancock's vision characterized the former mode of coordination as rule-bound, ossified, and interfering systems; the new proposal, on the other hand, was "innovative," "externally-oriented," and "strategic" (Clarke & Newman, 1997). Although these labels signaled educational effectiveness to Hancock and her cadre of new managerial reformers, many in Kenosha found the actual educational impacts detrimental to the community.

In the face of budget shortfalls, Hancock invested in technological enhancements, rather than adequate staffing and equal resources. She issued significant layoffs and reorganized the priorities of the school district to emphasize technological investments, such as the Rosetta Stone language instruction programs and iPads noted above, while schools scrambled to cover classes with less staff. Many parents and community members in Kenosha felt Hancock's optimism and "can-do" attitude in the face of austerity actually exacerbated the budget realities, rather than mitigating them (McDarison, 2013). Kenosha teachers and parents wished Hancock's vision had not cost so many teachers their jobs, a decision that made the district's class sizes swell.

Furthermore, many would have preferred that Hancock invest more resources in improving access for what were seen as the district's promising educational initiatives, such as public alternative charters. The charters contain a number of innovative programs, such as a special program for teenage parents, a medical sciences preparation program, and a graphic design academy. Most of the charter schools operate well beyond their capacity and have large waitlists. However, the student demographics in the charters are racially segregated; African American and Latino students are highly underrepresented, while white students and economically advantaged students are over-enrolled. As one charter administrator reported, "Charter school enrollment doesn't represent the district. Those in the know make the choice. We use a lottery system but they [families] have to sign up" (Clegg et al., 2013). The audit of the Transformation Plan revealed many teachers' and administrators' dissatisfaction with the existing model, commenting that there was significant work to be done to make the school district more equitable for all students. "[There is] nothing systematic in place to address high concentration of poverty," claimed one site administrator. Despite widespread concern about these problems, Hancock and her managerial framework did not prioritize addressing these issues with the district's scarce resources.

The State of Wisconsin: The External Neoliberal Agenda

Notably, the arguments for neoliberal and managerial reforms emerged both within the state, in the case of Hancock's administration, and outside the state, through an influx of conservative advocacy organizations, as we will soon see. Yet an important dynamic in the case of Kenosha was the ways in which different layers of the state interacted.

Although Hancock's Transformation Plan crystallized a neoliberal agenda within the Kenosha school district, significant external forces influenced the school district's political and economic realities. In 2011, one year after Hancock's arrival to Kenosha, Governor Scott Walker issued the largest budget cuts in the state's history to public education. These cuts were especially hard-hitting in districts such as Kenosha, which contain high proportions of low-income students, for one critical reason: The reductions in state revenue were more than twice as large in high poverty school districts as in low poverty school districts (Shaw & Kelley, 2012). Walker's budget cuts, initiated during his first term in office in 2011, continued to grow over the 2013 and 2015 years. His educational agenda cut support services for educational staff, expanded the state's voucher program, and relaxed charter authorizations. Each of these three proposals—voucher expansion, charter expansion, and curtailed collective bargaining rights—came to a head in Kenosha, Wisconsin. As we shall see, the increased calls for choice embodied by each of these policy reforms revealed deep contradictions in the requirements of publicly accountable institutions and privately managed ones.

First, the Walker administration identified Kenosha as one of nine districts targeted for a voucher program expansion. Under this program, districts that had received failing marks in the state's report card accountability system and had more than 4,000 students would have a portion of their state aid converted to support vouchers. Yet, the Kenosha school board and district principals unanimously opposed this move, arguing that not only would it reduce state aid to the schools, but that it was unnecessary in Kenosha, given their robust public charter schools. As Superintendent Hancock claimed, "We do not need choice schools here in Kenosha. We already offer so many choices to our students via our charter schools, our in-district transfers and our open enrollment" (Flores, 2013b). The school board passed a resolution opposing the voucher expansion. In the resolution, the board asserted that every district should decide for itself whether voucher plans were best for them. One board member expressed frustration with the lack of autonomy given to local school districts: "We don't have any control what the state does. If the governor wants to do it . . . we will do what we can to convince him that this not right for us in Unified" (Flores, 2013a). The school board's resolution directed the superintendent to actively reach out to state legislators, parents, and other community members to speak out against the voucher system. In this way, the school board articulated what they were and were not willing to choose.

Second, Walker continued to expand his school choice program, this time taking aim at *publicly* operated charters. In the 2013–2015 budget, Walker proposed legislation that loosened regulations on charter authorization, increasing the number of agencies around the state that would be legally able to approve charters. What's more, the proposed legislation required the elimination of publicly operated charter schools, threatening the future of the five renowned programs in Kenosha. Known as instrumentality charter schools, publicly operated charters, such as Kenosha's charters, have broad autonomy over their curriculum and educational focus, but follow district personnel requirements and receive district support services.

The proposal to eliminate the publicly funded charter schools, unsurprisingly, alarmed Kenosha's principals, who again felt they had been offered no choice in the matter. As Angela Andersson, the principal of one of Kenosha's technical education charters, stated, "We never wanted to be an instrumentality school, my board and I" (Smith, 2014a). In addition to feeling a loss of autonomy and choice, many principals objected to the changes, preferring to be part of the public school operation because of the resources and expertise it offers. Andersson elaborated, "The district can do things like payroll and benefits and technology support in a way that would be very difficult for a single school to do. I would not want to operate without a special education department or a finance department or a technology department or any of those things. We really benefit from having those experts" (Smith, 2014b).

Finally, Walker's 2011 legislative changes to the collective bargaining rights of public-sector employees—basically removing the right to collectively bargain—of which teachers comprised the largest majority, struck a chord with many in Kenosha. Already vulnerable from Hancock's layoffs, the Transformation Plan, and budget cuts, already mobilized pro-labor and public education supporters took action themselves in the Kenosha school board in 2011. Alarmed by the direction of both Walker and Hancock, the Kenosha school board adopted an active posture to protect the rights of teachers. Led by former teacher and long-time school board member JoAnne Taube, the Kenosha school board wanted to be sure to protect workers against more state-initiated austerity regimes, but also against the district and local extension of programs such as those enacted by Hancock. In Taube's campaign for school board, she made it clear that she opposed cuts to funding and supported workers' rights to collective bargaining (Taube, 2014).

Yet, the mobilization against Walker's agenda was far from one-sided in Kenosha; it also galvanized conservative forces in Kenosha. One of the chief ways this occurred was through the organized efforts to recall Kenosha's Democratic state senator, Bob Wirch, a lifelong Kenosha resident who had served as a public official in the district for the past twenty years. When it became clear that Walker and his administration were unwilling to negotiate the extreme budget cuts and legal changes to public employees' rights, Wirch and 12 other Democratic state senators left the state for nearly two weeks, thereby preventing the quorum required to pass the bill, in an attempt to force Republicans to modify their proposal. Unsurprisingly, this tactic enraged conservatives around the state. In Kenosha, in response to this, a group of conservative citizens, dubbed "Taxpayers to Recall Robert Wirch" began a campaign. As one Wirch recall supporter said at a campaign kick-off rally, "[Wirch] should be out because he didn't do his job" (Steinkraus, 2011). The campaign to recall Wirch drew the first out-of-state groups to begin investing money in Kenosha politics. More than half of the campaign donations came from non-local groups; the largest donation the campaign received was from The Madison Project, a Washington, D.C.-based group committed to electing conservative politicians (Olson, 2011). Although Wirch survived his attempted recall election, the campaign itself made conservatives even more active in the area, and stimulated national interest in Kenosha politics.

Meanwhile, members of the Kenosha school board took careful note of the unfolding state-level political drama. After the attempt to recall the governor failed, as well as the failed attempt to recall enough Republican senators for Democrats to gain control of the state legislature, the recourse strategy shifted to an attempt to legally overturn Act 10 itself, the law that prohibited collective bargaining. Responding to a suit brought forward by the Madison teachers union challenging the constitutionality of Act 10, municipal judge Juan Colas ruled in September 2012 that certain portions of Act 10 were indeed unconstitutional. This meant that municipal state employers, like school boards, were no longer legally prohibited from bargaining with teachers' unions, as Act 10 mandated. This fact is crucial to understanding the reasons behind the focus on Kenosha by conservative national groups.

Members of the Kenosha school board seized this opportunity to restore bargaining with the district teachers' union. In October 2012, they approved employment contracts with the district's teachers, rather than mandating the employee handbooks that had become the common replacement. Whereas handbooks unilaterally dictated teachers' employment conditions, the contracts were produced through mutual negotiations between teachers and school boards. Overruling Act 10 meant that teachers' unions not only restored collective bargaining, but also restored a number of important institutional mechanisms of unions, such as automatic dues deduction—allowing for automatic withdrawal of union dues from employees' paychecks, regardless of whether or not they have elected to become a member of the union. The philosophy behind this policy is based on fair-share dues: Worker benefits won through union negotiations—such as higher wages, safer working conditions, and equitable treatment—are administered to all employees, not simply those who have elected to join the union. In addition to mandating an equitable investment mechanism for workers, dues withdrawal strengthened the union, as it guaranteed its financial sustenance. In a climate of increasing conservative legal hostility to public education and labor unions, the Kenosha school board's willingness to bargain contracts with the teachers' union went against the political current and challenged the "new common-sense" of conservative modernizers, which opposed strong forms of collective and democratic organization, such as unions.

At first glance, the Kenosha school board's protection of teacher's rights to collective bargaining seems entirely disconnected from their stance against vouchers. Similarly, Walker's policies restricting public workers' collective bargaining appeared to be disconnected from his support of school choice and voucher programs. Yet, school choice programs and attacks on teachers' unions are intricately linked. Both policies stem from a conservative critique of the welfare state and a desire to be free from its bureaucratic binds, in favor of proclaimed "free" market operations. The seeming disjointedness between the two issues—restricting collective bargaining rights for public-sector workers and expanding school choice programs—illustrates the contradictions required to fashion new ideologies and common-sense (see Apple, 2006). This is a crucial point. Neoliberal agendas in education—and in all thing social—require the fundamental restructuring of common sense and of the meanings of the concepts we use to evaluate our institutions, such as democracy, justice, and fairness, and the government's role in guaranteeing the conditions supporting these things (Apple, 2006, 2013).

The policies link to each other in their mutual foundation in a fundamental critique of the state. The Right's arguments against the welfare state center around three dominant critiques: 1) The *costs* of the welfare state—public services are too expensive; 2) The *effects* of the welfare state—welfare enables irresponsible behavior by "bad" and "lazy" people; and 3) The *problem of the welfare state itself*—as a system itself, it is poorly organized, with too much red tape and too little impact, not structured enough for consumer choice and obtusely immune from the "real world" pressures of competition and forced innovation (Clarke & Newman, 1997, p. 14).

Yet, the Right also extends this critique specifically to education, attacking public school institutions themselves as unduly bureaucratic and unreceptive to students' needs. This critique has fueled a movement centered around school choice, in which families act as consumers and education becomes a product on the market, and also around teachers' unions (Chubb & Moe, 1990). School choice programs build on people's understanding of themselves as rational actors, capable of making savvy and personal choices to best fulfill their needs, in ways that the bureaucratic and professionalized arrangements of the welfare state could not. Here, teachers' unions are seen as further ossifying the legal and bureaucratic structures that make public schools "failures" (Apple & Pedroni, 2005).

Therefore, the Kenosha school board's willingness to defend teachers' union rights, and to vocally oppose voucher expansion and the neoliberal positions underpinning the changes in charter school regulations displayed a willingness to resist the Right's agenda. It also represented an important redefinition of "choice"—the democratically elected school board and its supporters did not select Walker's neoliberal changes to education.

Ideological Mobilizations and the Clash in School Board Elections

Naturally, the Kenosha school board's opposition did not go unnoticed by conservative groups in Wisconsin. Both school choice policies and anti-collective bargaining forces attracted the Koch brothers-funded organization, Americans for Prosperity, to Kenosha. Americans for Prosperity began political organizing work in Wisconsin during the 2011 gubernatorial elections, with an avowed commitment to reducing collective bargaining rights for public sector workers. Although their previous activity in Wisconsin had largely been around the 2011 recall elections, now the group turned their attention to shifting an understanding of public schools. In the winter of 2013, Americans for Prosperity held a special panel about school choice specifically in Kenosha. David Fladeboe, Americans for Prosperity's deputy state director, explained the group's interest in turning to places like Kenosha to expand voucher programs. As he stated, "We're just talking about it in general terms, and we want to hear from the communities. We want to talk to people in each community and hear what they think about it, and hopefully educate them on why it's a good idea"("Board opposed to private school voucher proposal," 2013). In this way, Americans for Prosperity turned to Kenosha to form new "common-sense" links between school choice politics and reduced union rights for public sector employees. Yet, this common-sense formation occurred through more than just conducting educational meetings. The Right also pursued legal sanctions against the resistant school board.

Within a few months of the school board's approval of teachers' collective bargaining agreements, they came under fire once more. The school district's legal standing for bargaining with the teachers' union was shaken. In September 2013, the state Supreme Court overturned Judge Colas's ruling against the constitutionality of Act 10. Immediately, two anti-union teachers in the district sued the school board and the Kenosha teachers' union, KEA, for violating Act 10, once its constitutionality had been upheld by the state Supreme Court. The conservative, libertarian public interest law firm, Wisconsin Institute for Law and Liberty (WILL), funded by the conservative Bradley Foundation, backed the anti-union teachers' lawsuit (Murphy, 2011). The teachers, one of whom had recently left her job teaching in the school district, sued the school board and the union for collecting union dues through automatic dues withdrawal, basically because it was "not democratic" and thus abridged personal choice. As one of the plaintiff teachers, Kristi LaCroix, wrote in an op-ed to the *Milwaukee Journal Sentinel*, "Teachers are not blue-collar laborers; they are academic professionals like lawyers, scientists and engineers. Industrial-style union representation does not advance the respect that educators deserve in Wisconsin or nationwide" (Lacroix, 2013). In addition to deeming the class associations of labor unions irrelevant, LaCroix disputed the political direction of the union, particularly its opposition to Act 10 and Governor Walker, while they were supporting liberal politicians ("Former teacher: I know my own worth," 2015).

In their case against the school district, these teachers claimed legal standing as "taxpayers." Interestingly, this legal standing positioned the plaintiffs as pseudo-employers of the district teachers, entitled to an audit of the salary funds. As "taxpayers," the teachers positioned themselves as entitled to public benefits. Simultaneously, by labeling themselves as "taxpayers," this authorized the teachers to dictate the financial decisions of the school board. Such claims characterize the common-sense alchemy of neoliberalism, which is rooted in notions of possessive individualism, in which an individual is the sole proprietor of his or her skills, and has the unfettered right to market these skills (see, e.g., Apple, 2014). The individual owes nothing to society, but rather is entitled to dictate the terms of one's social participation, based on responsibilities as a taxpayer. Furthermore, the possessive individual seeks freedom from state-enforced regulations.

The rhetoric of choice plays a key role in enabling these positions—the individual participates in society as he or she chooses. As LaCroix elaborated, "We need to empower teachers to not only have the tools they need to succeed but give them the facts to make the choice for themselves how to be represented. It is not only important for today's teachers but the future of a shrinking workforce" (Lacroix, 2013). According to LaCroix and others, teachers should feel free to choose whether or not they have union representation.

In this case, the plaintiff teachers sought freedom from fair-share dues payments enforced by collective bargaining agreements. The school board and KEA, however, defended their rights to bargain using the procedural grounds established by both the Judge Colas's circuit court in 2012, and also legal stays enforced by the Court of Appeals and the Wisconsin Supreme Court in March and November, respectively (*Defendant Kenosha Education Association's Brief in Opposition to Plaintiff's Motion for Temporary Injunction*, 2013). In spite of the plaintiff's extensive backing from outside conservative organizations, the courts initially denied WILL and LaCroix's attempt to void the union contract.

Having failed to legally overturn the school board's decision to continue to extend teachers' contracts, right-wing groups looked to insert their influence by occupying the school board itself. After a court-ordered injunction stalled WILL's lawsuit, LaCroix's father, Dan Wade, decided to run for a seat on the district's school board. In the February primary, the incumbent board president and union-supported candidate JoAnne Taube earned the most votes. Yet, Kenosha's landscape had shifted between the February primary and the April election. In those two months, national groups such as American Majority and the Koch-funded Americans for Prosperity (Smith, 2014c) poured resources into Dan Wade's campaign. In addition to providing direct campaigns to the candidates, these groups flooded the town with mailed flyers, radio ads mud-slinging at Taube and the other progressive candidate, and newspaper advertisements for Wade. Furthermore, they conducted their own organizing, bringing in outside staff to conduct door knocking and phone calling to Kenosha voters.

This involvement from major corporate groups in local elections upset many in Kenosha. As an ironworker stated at a rally to protest Americans for Prosperity's involvement in the elections, "I think that local people should be in control of who wins their elections, and outside money needs to stay out." Further, this same ironworker made a nuanced distinction between corporate influence in education and union influence in education. He stated bluntly, "The difference between unions and the Koch brothers is that when unions spend money, they have elected representatives that are making decisions. The union members are the ones voting. The Koch brothers are two guys who are spending money to buy politicians" (Giles, 2014).

Money and the work of powerful organized interests, however, *do* make a difference. Despite the dissent among some Kenosha voters, Wade and Kucinich defeated Taube and the other union-supporting candidate, Mike Falkofske, in the March 2014 elections. The extensive increase in advertising, phone banking, and outside field organizers changed the nature of the district's elections, from a neighbors-voting-for-neighbors brand of politics to one in which major corporate and philanthropic money continually transformed the politics. This affected not simply the 2014 school board race, but also was a major element in constructing a much more conservative common sense. With the new conservative majority in the school board, the board ruled to void the union contracts, and settle the lawsuit with plaintiffs Kristi LaCroix and WILL (Smith, 2014d).

The school board's willingness to take a politically oppositional stance threatened conservative organizations, triggering their interest and persistence in the district's political affairs. What started out as a local issue became a national testing ground for conservative mobilizations (see Apple, 1996 for other examples).

Conclusion

In our examination of Kenosha, it is clear that the *larger context counts* and that it counts in crucial ways. As we documented, charter schools—and how they are used and by whom—need to be seen as part of a larger ideological agenda. A key here is to understand the larger conflicts over the meaning of democracy, of who defines what it is, and who controls that meaning over time. And all of this is deeply connected to political economy, to local, regional, and national mobilizations, many of which are decidedly *not* progressive.

In Kenosha, Wisconsin, it wasn't the economic scale of the school board elections that drew groups like Americans for Prosperity into the race. It was the fact that the existing school board and institutions used their authority to defend and deepen the democratic nature of public institutions that had been weakened by high-risk finance, corporate-influenced school reformers, and out-of-state corporate advocacy groups like Americans for Prosperity. What was at stake in the Kenosha election was the struggle for the meaning of our common-sense ideas about democracy and fairness, not only in "choice" and schooling, but also how teachers and teaching should be seen.

The Kenosha school board became a site for the Right to closely connect school choice arguments with right-to-work arguments. Because of the school board's capacity to articulate policy priorities, it became attractive to both school choice proponents and those opposed to teachers' unions. These two policy programs found mutual ground in their diagnosis of the state as imposing undue "freedoms." Yet ironically, they turned to the state itself to administer their political program. In this way, Kenosha became a struggle over two competing narratives: one in which the state—through institutions like schools and labor laws—restricts individual freedom, and one in which the state's policies enables equality and collective well-being.

The triumph of conservative actors in Kenosha reveals three key lessons in the success of rightist movements, lessons that are crucial to our understanding of how the Right works and how to interrupt it. First, it highlights the Right's growing commitment to small political spaces, and the political persistence necessary to take control of them. By both waging lawsuits against the liberal school board and by running political candidates to take over the school board, the Right successfully occupied micro-political spaces. Second, conservative movements give people identities that provide attractive forms of agency. For example, as "taxpayers," individuals are able to position themselves as entitled to public benefits *and* authorized to dictate the terms of these benefits. Finally, the Right combined ideological elements to form a more unified conservative movement, connecting momentum from anti-collective bargaining mobilizing with pro-vouchers programs.

The story of Kenosha has many lessons to teach those of us who are committed to a critically democratic education for all of our children. Those of us who believe in the value of democratic institutions must have an acute awareness of the vulnerability of things that we too often take for granted. But we must do more than simply defend these spaces. We need to continue the long and never-ending struggle to build an education that does not divide us by class and race and that is respectful of diversity (see Apple, 2013)—and that is equally respectful of the teachers who now labor so hard in uncertain conditions in our public schools. We must continue to define—richly and collectively—the education system we are willing to choose.

References

Apple, M. W. (2006). *Educating the "right" way: Markets, standards, God and inequality* (2nd ed.). New York: Routledge.

Apple, M. W. (2013). *Can education change society?* New York: Routledge.

Apple, M. W. (2014). *Official knowledge: Democratic education in a conservative age* (3rd ed.). New York: Routledge.

Apple, M. W., & Beane, J. A. (Eds.). (2007). *Democratic schools: Lessons in powerful education* (2nd ed.). Portsmouth, NH: Heinemann.

Apple, M. W., & Pedroni, T. C. (2005). Conservative alliance building and African American support of vouchers: The end of Brown's promise or a new beginning? *The Teachers College Record, 107*(9), 2068–2105. doi:10.1111/j.1467-9620.2005.00585.x

Board opposed to private school voucher proposal. (2013, February 22). Channel 3000. Madison. Retrieved from http://www.channel3000.com/news/Board-opposed-to-private-school-voucher-proposal/-/1648/19046792/-/100trmd/-/index.html
Brighouse, H., & Schouten, G. (2014). To charter or not to charter: What questions should we ask, and what will the answers tell us? *Harvard Educational Review*, 84(3), 341–365. Retrieved from http://her.hepg.org/index/6346P42623827838.pdf
Choose Your School Wisconsin. (2015). Retrieved from http://www.chooseyourschoolwi.org/take-action.html
Chubb, J. E., & Moe, T. M. (1990). *Politics, markets, and America's schools*. Washington, DC: Brookings Institution Press.
Clarke, J., & Newman, J. (1997). *The managerial state*. London: Sage Publications.
Clegg, R., Kulas, O. M. A., Proffitt, E., Nisbett, K., Shidaker, S., Tuneberg, J., & Van Hoozer, S. (2013). *A curriculum audit of Kenosha Unified School District*. Bloomington, IN: International Curriculum Management Audit Center, Phi Delta Kappa International.
Crouch, C. (2011). *The strange non-death of neoliberalism* (pp. vi–70). Malden, MA: Polity Press. Retrieved from http://www.tandfonline.com/doi/full/10.1080/14782804.2012.711164
Defendant Kenosha Education Association's brief in opposition to plaintiff's motion for temporary injunction, LaCroix v. Kenosha Unified School District Board of Education, No. 2013CV001899 (Wis. Cir. Ct. Branch 1, Kenosha Cnty., December 16, 2013).
Duhigg, C., & Dougherty, C. (2008, November 2). From Midwest to M.T.A., pain from global gamble. *The New York Times*, p. A1. New York. Retrieved from http://www.nytimes.com/2008/11/02/business/02global.html?pagewanted=all&_r=0
Fabricant, M., & Fine, M. (2012). *Charter schools and the corporate makeover of public education: What's at stake?* New York: Teachers College Press.
Flores, T. (2011a, March 3). Unified OKs transformation plan. *Kenosha News*. Retrieved from http://kenoshanews.com/news/unifi ed_oks_transformation_plan_335146617.html
Flores, T. (2011b, April 28). Unified layoffs affect nearly every school. *Kenosha News*. Retrieved from http://www.kenoshanews.com/home/unified_layoffs_affect_nearly_every_school_136429303.html
Flores, T. (2011c, August 10). SEC charges Stifel with fraud. *Kenosha News*. Retrieved from http://www.kenoshanews.com/home/sec_charges_stifel_with_fraud_207348082.html
Flores, T. (2013a, February 18). Proposed expansion of school vouchers to Kenosha disappoints Unified officials. *Kenosha News*. Retrieved from http://www.kenoshanews.com/news/at_unified_choice_schools_waiting_lists_abound_473875489.html
Flores, T. (2013b, February 18). Voucher plans upset Unified. *Kenosha News*. Retrieved from http://kenoshanews.com news/proposed_expansion_of_school_vouchers_to_kenosha_disappoints_unifi ed_offi cials_470179962.html
Former teacher: I know my own worth. (2015). Wispolitics.com. Retrieved from http://quorumcall.wispolitics.com/2015/02/former-teacher-i-know-my-own-worth.html
Frankenberg, E., Siegel-Hawley, G., & Wang, J. (2010). *Choice without equity: Charter school segregation and the need for civil rights standards*. Los Angeles, CA: The Civil Rights Project/Proyecto Derechos Civiles at UCLA; www.civilrightsproject.ucla.edu.

Friedman, M. (2011a). 94.6% No Confidence and the Following Storm. Retrieved from https://failingschools.wordpress.com/2011/02/20/94-6-no-confidence-and-the-following-storm/
Friedman, M. (2011b). Challenges ahead: Brizard's departure to Chicago. Retrieved from https://failingschools.wordpress.com/2011/04/24/challenges-ahead-brizards-departure-to-chicago/
Giles, D. (2014, March 29). Demonstration draws 60 to ESC. *Kenosha News.* Retrieved from http://www.kenoshanews.com/news/demonstration_draws_60_to_esc_476321192.html
Gunn, S. (2013, May 3). Kenosha, Wisconsin schools ran up huge tabs for hotels, rental cars, restaurants and airlines in 2011–12. *EAGnews.* Kenosha. Retrieved from http://eagnews.org/kenosha-schools-ran-up-huge-tabs-for-hotels-rental-cars-restaurants-and-airlines-in-2011-12/
Hallow, L. (2011, September 1). "We need to be optimistic" Unified superintendent encourages parents, teachers to stay positive. *Kenosha News.* Retrieved from http://www.kenoshanews.com/home/we_need_to_be_optimistic_221238606.html
Kretchmar, K., Sondel, B., & Ferrare, J. J. (2013). Mapping the terrain: Teach for America, charter school reform, and corporate sponsorship. *Journal of Education Policy, 29,* 742–759.
LaCroix, K. (2013, September 2). Association offers fresh start for Wisconsin teachers. *Milwaukee Journal Sentinel.* Retrieved from http://www.jsonline.com/news/opinion/association-offers-fresh-start-for-wisconsin-teachers-b9985309z1-221866951.html
Lipman, P. (2004). *High stakes education: Inequality, globalization, and urban school reform.* New York: Routledge.
Lipman, P. (2011). *New political economy of urban education: Neoliberalism, race and the right to the city.* New York: Routledge.
McDarison, K. (2013). Sign of the times: Parents, teachers, students picket outside Kenosha Unified School District offices. Retrieved from http://wisconsinhappyfarm.com/sign-of-the-times-parents-teachers-students-picket-outside-kenosha-unified-school-district-offices/
Miron, G., Mathis, W., & Welner, K. (2015). Review of "Separating Fact & Fiction: What You Need to Know About Charter Schools." Boulder, CO: National Education Policy Center. Retrieved from http://nepc.colorado.edu/thinktank/review-separating-fact-and-fiction.
Moore, T. S., & Squires, G. D. (1991). Two tales of a city: Economic restructuring and uneven economic development in a former company town. *Journal of Urban Affairs, 13*(2), 159–173.
Murphy, K. (2011, July 12). Kenosha teacher backs governor in fight over collective bargaining. *Kenosha News.* Retrieved from http://www.kenoshanews.com/home/kenosha_teacher_backs_governor_in_fight_over_collective_bargaining_178420122.html
Olson, M. (2011, March 30). Wirch recall group has received nearly $11,000. *Kenosha News.* Retrieved from http://www.kenoshanews.com/home/wirch_recall_group_has_received_nearly_11000_118415117.html
Pedroni, T. (2007). *Market movements: African American involvement in school voucher reform.* New York: Routledge.
Peterson, P. E. (Ed.). (2006). *Choice and competition in American education.* Lanham: Rowman and Littlefield.
Ravitch, D. (2013). Meet the Broad Superintendents. Retrieved from http://dianeravitch.net/2013/08/15/meet-the-broad-superintendents/
Saltman, K. (2009). The rise of venture philanthropy and the ongoing neoliberal assault on public education: The Eli and Edythe Broad foundation Kenneth.

Workplace: A Journal for Academic Labor, 53–72. Retrieved from http://prophet.library.ubc.ca/ojs/index.php/workplace/article/view/182244

Scott, J. (2009). The politics of venture philanthropy in charter school policy and advocacy. *Educational Policy*, 23(1), 106–136. Retrieved from http://epx.sagepub.com/content/23/1/106.short

Shaw, J. J., & Kelley, C. (2012). Making matters worse : School funding, achievement gaps and poverty under Wisconsin Act 32, 1–31.

Smith, D. (2014a, January 10). Proposed charter bill worries Kenosha Unified principals. *Kenosha News*, 36.

Smith, D. (2014b, January 10). Proposed charter bill worries Kenosha Unified principals. *Kenosha News*.

Smith, D. (2014c, March 24). Americans for prosperity throws its weight into Kenosha Unified School Board race. *Kenosha News*. Retrieved from http://www.kenoshanews.com/news/americans_for_prosperity_throws_its_weight_into_kenosha_unified_school_board_race_476239373.html

Smith, D. (2014d, June 6). Kenosha School Board voids union contract in legal settlement. *Kenosha News*. Kenosha. Retrieved from http://www.kenoshanews.com/news/kenosha_school_board_voids_union_contract_in_legal_settlement_477375131.html

Sondel, B. (2015). Raising citizens or raising test scores? *Theory and Research in Social Education*, 43(3), 289–313. doi:10.1080/00933104.2015.1064505

Steinkraus, D. (2011, February 26). Angry volunteers rally at Wirch recall drive. *The Journal Times*. Retrieved from http://journaltimes.com/news/local/angry-volunteers-rally-at-wirch-recall-drive/article_6d6a3a8e-4231-11e0-a7df-001cc4c03286.html

Taube, J. A. (2014). I lost my seat to the Koch brothers. *The Progressive*, 78, 51–52.

Wells, A. S. (Ed.). (2002). *Where charter school policy fails: The problem of equity and accountability*. New York: Teachers College Press.

Wells, A. S., Slayton, J., & Scott, J. (2002). Defining democracy in the neoliberal age: Charter school reform and educational consumption. *American Educational Research Journal*, 39(2), 337–361. doi:10.3102/00028312039002337

Welner, K. G. (2013). The dirty dozen: How charter schools influence student enrollment. *Teachers College Record*, (April), 1–7. Retrieved from http://nepc.colorado.edu/files/welner-charter-enrollment-teachers-college-record.pdf http://www.tcrecord.org

3 Turning Over Teachers

Charter School Employment Practices, Teacher Pipelines, and Social Justice

Sarah M. Stitzlein and Barrett A. Smith

"We cannot enter the struggle as objects in order later to become subjects."

—Paulo Freire[1]

Secretary of Education Arne Duncan has repeatedly proclaimed quality and equitable education as "the civil rights issue of our generation" (U.S. Department of Education, 2010). This sentiment has been expressed by educational reformers both before and after Duncan, from Wendy Kopp's sense of civil rights injustice that urged her to develop Teach for America as a corps to overcome inequities related to teacher shortages she witnessed in schools in the 1980s (Kluger, 2008), to Michelle Rhee more recently asserting that the civil rights issue underlying the continued poor performance of some of our schools requires drastic measures of school takeover or turnover as part of StudentsFirst (Rhee, 2012). These leading figures in the reform movement rightly highlight the importance of education for creating a more socially just society. And insofar as rights claims often serve as political trump cards (Sandel, 1996, p. 41), urging people to act on their behalf, using this rhetoric has goaded a flurry of major new approaches to preparing, hiring, leading, and firing new teachers. This is especially the case in the charter school movement, which, in many instances, has chosen to bear the flag of civil rights when it comes to education reform.

In this chapter, we aim to reveal a troubling dissonance between the key approaches of education reform at some charter schools and the employment practices that they endorse or embody. We argue that while their ends may be ensuring greater civil rights through more socially just and equitable education via charter schools, the means they use to do so may not only undermine that end, but may actually work to further injustice in some cases. Employing a philosophical and interpretive methodology derived from the works of Karl Marx and the critical theorists who followed him, we will analyze the labor practices of major educational reform organizations and related charter schools, including examining how they define educational success and its influence on how teachers are conceptualized and employed, especially as members of the precariat. To do so, we investigate some practices endorsed by these reformers and their charter schools, including instituting short teaching commitments, facilitating high teacher turnover, and requiring rigid disciplinary procedures of teachers. Finally, we consider how the new charter-inspired pipelines to teaching established by these reformers actually circumvent treating teachers as professionals altogether.

Throughout the analysis, we seek to better align the means and ends of achieving quality education for all as a civil rights feat. By pointing out the disconnect between the practices and goals of some leading charter schools, we hope to give them and those who support them pause. We mean to redirect the understandably hurried rush to improve schools toward more just employment practices that are better aligned with the goals of civil rights and quality education. Importantly, we intend to draw attention to more internally consistent and socially just practices that may improve the lives of teachers, communities, and children, aligning the means and ends of reforming education.

Philosophical Foundations

> If we may take an example from outside the sphere of material production, a school-master is a productive worker when, in addition to belabouring the heads of his pupils, he works himself into the ground to enrich the owner of the school. That the latter has laid out his capital in a teaching factory instead of a sausage factory, makes no difference to the relation.
>
> (Marx, 1990, p. 644)

Marxist conceptions of productive activity, labor, and alienation can be powerful tools in examining the philosophical foundations and limitations of many charter schools within the education reform movement. The metrics by which both student and teacher success are measured in these schools ultimately narrow the role of teachers and alienate both teachers and students from their productive activity. Despite employing social justice and civil rights rhetoric, the divisive, capitalist, and colonizing philosophies and practices of many reform organizations limit their efficacy in achieving positive change while simultaneously upholding some of the most problematic aspects of the current social order.

Nearly all education reform programs recently—especially national efforts from federal policies like No Child Left Behind and Race to the Top, but also organizations like Knowledge is Power Program (KIPP) and Teach for America (TFA)—formulate their missions around the achievement gap. The stated goal is to bring about educational equity by closing that gap, often by any means necessary. This goal situates their work squarely within larger efforts at racial and social justice, although, as we will show, their position is grounded more in rhetoric than practice or effect. At the center of these efforts is indeed "a potentially revolutionary premise—the explicit, direct commitment to eliminating the achievement gaps that have long existed between the academic success of White and middle- and upper-income children and those of children of color and children from low-income homes" (Skrla, Scheurich, García, & Nolly, 2010, p. 259). However, this premise is not a revolutionary certainty, because an "equally strong potential exists for both positive and negative effects of such policy on educational equity" (p. 260).

Metrics gathered from standardized testing can be useful when they provide an empirical basis for naming the (re)production of inequity and when they indicate progress in narrowing that inequity. The situation becomes problematic, however, as the metrics for determining success shift the understanding of the purposes of education. Reform organizations represent the achievement gap not as merely symptomatic of inequity, but as inequity incarnate. If the achievement gap can be closed, then equality in schooling will have been achieved. This says nothing of broader unequal social conditions—the issue of inequity in education can be solved wholly within the (right) classroom. The data-driven approaches to measuring and constantly re-measuring the achievement gap shift the focus of public education from qualitative ends, ranging from developing good citizens to igniting lifelong learning, to narrowly quantitative ends of numeric performance and equity between groups. The indicator ultimately becomes the ends as teacher and student labor becomes more and more beholden to a quantitative metric.

An insightful glimpse into the ideological work of affirming this metric itself can be found in Michelle Rhee's (2013) *Seattle Times* op-ed "MAP Boycott Is About Keeping Test Scores Out of Teacher Evaluations." In her editorial, Rhee responds to the Garfield High School teachers who unanimously voted to boycott the MAP test. In a public letter, these teachers enumerate their "objection to the MAP test specifically and particularly to its negative impact on our students" (Straus, 2013). The objections include the fact that for high school students, "the margin of error is greater than the expected gain," (which analytically renders the test utterly useless); the lack of "alignment between the Common Core and MAP"; the amount of missed instructional time in administering the test; a related concern that the test "may violate the rights of groups of students for whom schooling already constitutes an uphill battle"; and the MAP test's introduction under a superintendent who was also at the time on the board of the company that sells the test (Straus, 2013). On the whole, the concerns seem to center around the educational value of the test, while also taking into account the legitimacy of the test itself and even rights claims of students. The boycott is indicative of a complex democratic act of the teachers: organizing to speak and act in a unified and, even more impressive, a unanimous way.

Rhee's op-ed, however, works to demand the legitimacy of the test, to misconstrue the nature of teacher and community concerns, and to position the teachers as disinterested in providing their students with a quality education. Belying the reform movement's deep-seated aversion to the democratic process, she begins her op-ed with a refusal to acknowledge the unanimity and solidarity of the Garfield High School teachers: "Some local teachers union members have decided to reject Washington state's student assessment program, and that's unfortunate because every great teacher knows that student assessments can be a great tool" (Rhee, 2013). The standardized tests themselves are conflated with assessment—an incredibly broad category of evaluating student learning—and called "a great tool." Rhee automatically gives the MAP test legitimacy because it is *an* assessment of student learning. Rhee is most upset that by boycotting the test, teachers are not "engaging in a constructive discussion." Instead, the teachers should administer the test and "take the assessments seriously." Not once in her argument does Rhee acknowledge the limitations of the test or even the rights claims evoked by the teachers. Rhee ends her editorial with a broad indictment of the Garfield teachers for not working to better the education of their students, claiming that "the debate over the nuts and bolts of the MAP robs the public of a much more meaningful dialogue about how to ensure a high-quality education for every American student." Accepting and implementing (even flawed) standardized assessments are Rhee's means of "ensuring a high-quality education" for all students. In her editorial, Rhee demonstrates how the ideological stance of many education reform organizations demands the legitimacy of quantifying student learning. In this case, for Rhee, notions of efficacy, community, and even rights claims were not worth acknowledging.

The focus on the production of a quantitative product (not to mention the strict allegiance to the legitimacy of its means of extraction) has deep implications for the curriculum, pedagogies, daily activity, and, therefore, for teacher and student labor. Marx's concepts of productive activity and alienation offer useful insight here. From this perspective, teachers can be said to perform their productive activity upon students, and students can therefore be seen as the products of the education process. According to Ollman (1971), the creation of an objective product is a necessary consequence of many productive activities: "Man's productive activity, however, is objectified in his products in all societies" (p. 142). The objectification of teacher labor in his or her students holds across the spectrum of philosophical approaches to education, from more traditional approaches that critical theorist Paulo Freire calls "banking models" (2007) to more critical, feminist, and postmodern approaches.

In a more traditional banking model, this claim is not controversial and is widely accepted: The student is transformed by receiving information in ways that can be easily measured and quantified. In this model, the students themselves are quantifiable, objectified, and commoditized products.

Proponents of a critical approach here would likely reject the idea of a teacher acting *upon* a student and situating the student as a product of the teacher. Throughout critical discourses, the language of working *with* is strongly preferred and emphasized. Even in this more critical approach, however, students stand as products because the end goal is conceived of as a transformation (or liberation) of the student (alongside the teacher and broader community). The student stands in the position of a product, but as a complex and human product that is neither objectified nor commodified. The critical question for those developing a curriculum or educating teachers is therefore: What type of products should the teacher work to produce? Should productive activity be focused on developing communities, critical consciousness, democratic citizens, or quantifiable learning gains?

In either case, a teacher's labor is objectified in students; however, the products are radically different. If the goal is citizenship, the products are human and the metrics are widely varied, communal, and performed: the ability to create knowledge across difference, critical questioning, concern for others, public speaking. Teachers' labor is objectified in students, but there is no alienation—that is, the product is not externalized, not "an alien object that has power over [the worker]" (McLellan, 2001, p. 89). Both teachers and students emerge in a position from which they maintain control over their products and may "engage in further productive activity" (Ollman, 1971, p. 143). Teachers' labor in this model is not just objectified in students, but also necessarily in the teachers themselves and the community. However, if the goal is derived from purely quantitative metrics, those confined to a realm of number two pencils and scantrons, student and teacher productive activity is necessarily limited in scope.

Worse, purely quantitative metrics narrow the view of students: "[B]y reducing students to numbers, standardized testing creates the capacity to view students as things, as quantities apart from their human qualities" (Au, 2011, p. 37). The teacher's labor is still objectified in the students, but the students are separated from their social contexts, quantified, and then commodified to influence funding and to evaluate their teachers. These products are those that "exist outside [the producer], independently, as something alien to him" (Ollman, 1971, p. 142) and stand opposed to their producers in a way that does not allow for further engagement in productive activity. This quantification, individualization, and alienation "allow[s] for the efficient categorizing and sorting of human populations; in the process they commodify human beings, thus allowing learners to be viewed and treated as products" (Au, 2009, p. 20). The categorization and sorting (particularly disaggregating data by race and income level) can be an excellent tool for identifying and measuring inequity. When teaching and learning are reformulated as commodities, however, the resulting alienation opens up educational labor to be understood and managed in ways that broadly reproduce capitalist social relations both inside and outside the classroom.

The appropriation, or coerced disassociation, of a teacher's labor culminates on high-stakes standardized testing days, when the ability of both teachers and students to exercise power is radically limited. On ordinary days in the classroom, teachers make complex decisions about curriculum and instruction: from the generation, differentiation, and scaffolding of learning materials to analyses and implementations of methodology, all of which find expression during complex interpersonal interactions with students, colleagues, and administrators. Most drastically, on testing day itself, teachers' labor is appropriated and narrowed as professional educators are transformed into watchmen for the test—they are to stand guard, controlling students' bodies and monitoring behavior in an effort to ensure the "validity" of the test. The curricular, instructional, and interpersonal aspects of teachers' labor disappear, as they are asked to step back and enforce silence while punishing attempts at collaboration and cooperation (which constitute cheating on assessments designed to measure, compare, and sort students as individuals).

These teaching practices are bolstered by a disturbing and dehumanizing change to the understanding of students in a testing-focused environment. As Wayne Au explains, "By reducing students to numbers, standardized testing creates the capacity to view students as things, as quantities apart from their human qualities" (2011, p. 37). Au goes on to rightly conclude that high-stakes testing makes students into commodities that are objectified because they are presumed to have no differences coming into the classroom and are held to the same standards going out of the classroom. Students are reduced to products that can be objectively measured and compared to determine the efficiency and quality of the school or teacher that produced them. Moreover, under the pressure to produce measurable results of efficiency, teachers and students become alienated from one another because teachers have to stomp out student creativity and intellectual curiosity in order to keep them on task toward achieving the prescribed end (Au, 2011).

The effect is felt beyond just testing day: Leading up to the high-stakes test, a teacher's labor begins to be appropriated by preparations for the test. Curricular decisions are more and more taken over by those who write the test (not only by way of test content and form, but also practice materials). These increasingly nationalized, profit-driven efforts are often dissociated from the interests, needs, and values of local school communities in which they occur. Days and weeks of instructional time, often referred to as the classroom's "most precious commodity" by reformers, are unquestioningly sacrificed. The "opportunity cost" is enormous, especially for "our neediest students." The distortion of labor is evident, but the effect of testing regimes in alienating teachers from their labor and commodifying students is more pervasive and far-reaching than just test day.

Adopting more critical, feminist, and postmodern approaches would create opportunities for teachers to resist alienating practices. In contrast, a focus on objective, quantitative products of education facilitates the integration of the capitalist logic of production, where labor is depersonalized, increasingly deskilled, and alienated. The philosophical outlook that promotes objectification, the individualization of opportunity for both students and teachers, and the alienation of both has observable consequences in our schools.

Precarious Positions

Marx describes the proletariat as a class who does not own their means of production (Marx, 1990). Instead, in order to survive under capitalism, they are coerced into selling their labor power, typically for relatively low pay. Often, they are exploited by those with more power or wealth. While we do not see teachers as neatly fitting within this class, the depiction of teachers above, especially as constrained and usurped in charter schools and under accountability policies that alienate and objectify while depriving teachers of professional voice and practice, positions teachers and many elements of their work under this umbrella.

Recently, some sociologists and economists have begun to analyze classes anew within the shifting conditions of neoliberal capitalism, where a segment of the traditional proletariat now suffer greater precariousness, leading them instead to be called "the precariat" (Standing, 2011). This type of social class not only sells their labor to live and experiences relatively low pay, but also lacks power and status with employers, therefore facing increasing uncertainty and instability as job security wanes. Whereas the proletariat historically worked under well-established, known local employers in stable jobs with set hours and clear avenues for promotion, often with the protection of unions and collective bargaining, the precariat lacks these safeguards and the guarantees they provide. The proletariat did not originally enjoy such stability and protections, but rather fought hard to secure them over time, often through unionization. New forms of labor struggle may be necessary if the precariat are to earn similar safeguards today.

We recognize that there is ongoing debate amongst economists, sociologists, and Marxists regarding exactly whether the precariat is a social class and what its boundaries are. We do not wish to take a stand on that debate, but rather to engage the category rather loosely as a framework for analyzing changes in the teacher workforce and employment practices as a result of some charter schools and the neoliberal capitalism that guides them. Again, while not neatly captured by this term, teachers, especially those employed and prepared in some charter school settings, increasingly demonstrate key elements of the precariat, such as lack of unionization, long and unpredictable work hours under extreme pressure to ameliorate the achievement gap, raises that depend on student test scores, oversight by managers from afar rather than known local education leaders, high teacher turnover rates, massive teacher layoffs, shortened teaching stints, lack of commitment to and identity as a career educator, and feeling forced to employ pedagogies and disciplinary techniques that counter their own professional knowledge or personal beliefs. Here, we explore those elements of charter school teachers' lives and employ the contentious category of the precariat to raise awareness about the possible implications for teacher labor that may be unfolding in shifting employment and preparation practices that are couched within a larger market logic of neoliberal competition. In the midst of trying to bring about greater equality amongst student groups, many charter school practices effectively further fragment the teaching class, in some instances causing or reaffirming other forms of inequity and injustice.

The largest employers within the charter school sector are education management organizations (EMOs). Most are private, for-profit companies that manage public schools. For-profit EMOs are usually owned by investors looking to make money. Being profit-driven distinguishes most EMOs from other charter schools that are mission driven, although schools in both camps often employ similar social justice imagery and focus on the achievement gap. They educate about 44% of the more than two million students in U.S. charter schools (NEPC, 2013). Some of the largest EMOs include K12 Inc., National Heritage Academies, Charter Schools USA, Edison Learning, White Hat Management, and the Knowledge is Power Program (a nonprofit EMO) (NEPC, 2013). Most EMOs do not have teachers' unions, depriving teachers of the typical protections of working conditions (such as maximum numbers of pupils per class or manageable and defined work hours) and guarantees (such as a step salary scale). Indeed, it is common within these schools to require teachers to be present at the building or available by phone for extended hours and on weekends, and many have starting salaries lower than nearby traditional public schools. In return, these schools offer the moral and economic allure of overcoming the achievement gap and potential merit pay based on raising student test scores, which are unpredictable and, in some cases, incredibly difficult to achieve. Each of these conditions leads to a more precarious working state for teachers.

Whereas traditionally teachers are employed by local school districts, long-standing institutions in their communities, EMO charter schools are often run by corporations housed far from the community where the school actually operates, and principals and teachers may be imported into that community to staff the school. This distance can hamper teachers, parents, and local media from engaging these new managers and holding them accountable. Some of these schools have only been recently established as new ventures within the community or have been brought in to take over previously failing schools. The separation between community locale and corporate oversight suggests a new form of separation and distinction between both those who own the schools and those who work in them, as well as between the workers and the citizens of the community they serve. Furthermore, EMO teachers may be unfamiliar with or have backgrounds quite different from the communities where they are sent to teach. This becomes particularly problematic when, in an effort to address the achievement gap, the EMO school is located in a high-poverty, high-minority community—the demographics of most of our lowest-performing schools—while the EMO teachers may not themselves be from such a community or have knowledge of how to work in it successfully.

Unlike traditional public schools, where decision-making about employment and teaching practices is made open and transparent by elected school boards at public meetings, EMOs often have unelected and non-local corporate leaders who make decisions behind closed doors, further separating themselves from their employees and the communities they serve (Stitzlein, 2013). In their study of EMO governing boards, Wells and Scott (2001) found that "those who are handpicked to govern are not always those with the most vested interests—parents and educators. Instead, they are the ones with the most money, expertise, and connections" (p. 236). EMO governing boards are also kept closely in check by corporate overseers rather than by community members at meetings or local elections. These conditions create distances between teacher employees and their employers, making it more difficult for teachers to express their needs or professional judgment to their overseers. These distances also render it more difficult to ensure that EMO schools are truly meeting the needs and interests of the communities where they are located, rather than goals (typically test performance and narrowing of the achievement gap) or profit expectations set by corporate leaders elsewhere.

Charter schools, partially due to these circumstances of oversight, have experienced significantly higher teacher turnover rates, nearly twice those in traditional public schools (Stuit & Smith, 2010, 2012). Additionally, turnover rates have been the highest in the country's poorest schools (Di Carlo, 2015). Teachers with the least experience, strongest academic records, and least union protection were the most likely to leave their jobs. Most expressed dissatisfaction with their working conditions, in the case of EMOs in particular, because they found the workload to be too demanding and unmanageable or because they felt that their students were not being socialized well or disciplined fairly. At some online charter schools in particular, teachers struggle with class sizes that are nearly double or triple those of traditional public schools, further exacerbating the disconnect many of them feel from their students and leading them to conclude that they could not possibly deliver the personalized education their students need to ensure a quality education, or have the time to professionally connect with their teaching colleagues behind computer screens miles away (Molnar, 2014; Morgan, 2015). Back in the brick-and-mortar setting, the long hours, extreme conditions placed on teachers and students, and high teacher turnover rates at the famed Success Academy Charter Schools were recently publicly documented by the *New York Times* (Taylor, 2015).

Elsewhere, many EMO charter schoolteachers expressed feeling a lack of autonomy in their classrooms. They felt that they had no say in decisions that impacted their classrooms, reflecting the working conditions and de-professionalization we described earlier (Torres, 2014a, 2014b). Noted researcher Richard Ingersoll, who has estimated teacher turnover to cost schools upwards of $2.2 billion annually, explains that

> One of the main factors is the issue of voice, and having say, and being able to have input into the key decisions in the building that affect a teacher's job. This is something that is a hallmark of professions. It's something that teachers usually have very little of, but it does vary across schools and it's very highly correlated with the decision whether to stay or leave.
>
> (Phillips, 2015)

Given that charter schools tend to deprive many of their employees of sufficient voice, it is no surprise that turnover rates are even greater within their walls.

Outside of the charter network, the status of teachers' jobs across the country has become more tenuous in recent years. We have witnessed massive teacher layoffs in Philadelphia, Chicago, New Orleans, Los Angeles, New York City, and Washington, D.C. While many estimates are much higher, some of the most conservative data suggests that in 2012 alone, as many as 150,000 teaching jobs were cut across the country (Kessler, 2012). One leading education reform organization, The New Teacher Project (2011), documents that, due to layoffs traditionally being decided by seniority, the schools that are hardest hit by layoffs are those that have the most new teachers. Those schools tend to be located in some of the poorest communities and to have the lowest test scores and largest achievement gaps. In that regard, the increasing precariousness of teaching positions further exacerbates struggles in our lowest performing schools. Moreover, within some districts, such as Washington, D.C., under the direction of Michelle Rhee, new teachers have been hired en masse, only for other experienced teachers to be quickly laid off en masse a short while later, creating a cycle of unpredictability, turnover, shortened teaching stints, and decreased teacher experience (National Council on Teacher Quality, 2010).

All of this turnover, however, is not merely a troubling employment practice, but rather one that also runs in contradiction to the stated goals of many of the schools, especially the charters, who claim to be putting student achievement and narrowing of the achievement gap above all else. Eight years' worth of data on more than 850,000 New York City students confirms that students who encountered higher teacher turnover "score lower in both English language arts (ELA) and math and that these effects are particularly strong in schools with more low-performing and Black students" (Ronfeldt, Loeb, & Wyckoff, 2013). If these schools truly want to achieve those ends, then their means—including teacher retention—must be better aligned with the outcomes they desire. Additionally, they should ensure better professional conditions for the fair and equitable treatment of their employees.

Producing Pipelines

Teacher turnover produces instability within schools, communities, and teaching workforces. This is especially true of charter schools, which experience higher turnover rates than traditional public schools. For EMOs and schools that sustain high turnover year after year, a steady supply of new teachers becomes a necessity. Traditional teacher training, however, is a years-long endeavor. Accordingly, several organizations and pathways have opened by which teachers can be quickly and steadily supplied. These new pipelines are preferable, because teachers can be trained and put in front of a class much more quickly than in traditional education programs. The shorter training period also tends to supply teachers that lack understanding of different theoretical frameworks of teaching and who can therefore be more easily molded ideologically into more obedient workers within placement schools.

Perhaps the most prominent of these organizations, and one with many close ties to charters and charter networks, is TFA. In 1989, TFA was founded on the premise of recruiting "elite" college students to serve as teachers for two years in high-need areas where teacher supply could not meet teacher demand. The original premise is that an "elite" college student, trained for six weeks, will be better for students than a rotating cast of substitutes. First and foremost, TFA was an attempt to compensate for teacher shortages.

Since 2010, however, TFA has been rebranding itself as a supply line of effective teachers on the forefront of the struggle for social justice. Using the metric of standardized math and reading scores, one experimental study concluded that TFA corps members are as effective or more effective than other teachers (Clark et al., 2013; Decker, Mayer, & Glazerman, 2004). On the basis of Decker et al. (2004) and several other "quasi-experimental" studies, TFA applied for and received a $50 million Investing in Innovation (i3) grant to expand the size and regional scope of their teaching corps. According to the grant application, TFA hoped to rapidly grow the corps by 80% within a four-year span, while expanding TFA into 12 new regions (Teach for America, 2010). The stated goal was to "establish proven pipelines for recruiting, training, placing, and developing 'highly effective' teachers in 52–54 regions across the country . . . and accounting for approximately 20% of new hires in high-need schools across these regions" (p. 8). Simultaneously, to aid its recruiting efforts, TFA has more strongly promoted itself as an organization quickly and actively working to further social justice. The fact that it is such a quick pipeline into teaching has attracted many young people who are already somewhat skeptical of the organization because it is the quickest, easiest, but admittedly not the best path into a classroom. And, in the name of acting quickly on behalf of underserved children, poor-quality educational and professional employment practices are rationalized. TFA is no longer a stopgap for communities with a teacher shortage, but instead actively promotes itself as a supplier of "highly effective" teachers.

Accordingly, TFA has expanded into regions with no shortage of teachers and has persisted—and even expanded—concurrently with massive teacher layoffs. As part of its Investing in Innovation grant, TFA expanded into the state of Ohio. We have chosen to focus on Ohio specifically because it is one of TFA's newest regions, it is where we both live and teach, and it has a substantial number of charter schools. TFA is also being increasingly incorporated into the educational landscape, as the pending Ohio budget has just allocated $2 million to the organization for recruiting and training teachers. Previously, TFA had been barred from Ohio because of the Ohio Department of Education's strict requirements for teacher licensure. At the secondary level, candidates are required to have the equivalent of an undergraduate major of credit hours in the desired subject area. This content requirement demands that Ohio teachers have an extensive content background in their subject and effectively created a barrier to licensing many of Teach for America's corps members because most obtained degrees in areas other than the content they were assigned to teach by TFA and their partnering schools. In 2011, however, a law was passed modifying the state laws that dictate the requirements for teacher licensure (33 Ohio Rev. Code). This change created an alternative pathway to provide licenses specifically for TFA corps members. The law requires that the corps member holds a bachelor's degree, has maintained a 2.5 GPA, passes the appropriate state examination, completes the TFA-run summer institute, and will remain a corps member throughout the two-year commitment. The content requirement was waived entirely, so that a candidate not qualified for the traditional or even the state's own alternative pathway could gain a license in their Teach for America placement subject. Many corps members, therefore, not only lack the student teaching experience and education-related study, but many also lack content background in their subjects.

This Ohio law is written in a way that not only legally endorses TFA's selection and training practices, but also binds corps members to the organization. The corps members are tied to TFA because as licensure candidates, they cannot stand on the merit of their own coursework or experience. Instead, the law reads:

> [T]he state board shall revoke a resident educator license issued to a participant in the teach for America [sic] program who is assigned to teach in this state if the participant resigns or is dismissed from the program prior to completion of the two-year teach for America [sic] support program.
>
> (33 Ohio Rev. Code, para. E)

If a corps member changes his or her mind about the organization and decides to leave, his or her license is revoked by the state. In more traditional pathways, that candidate could take his or her course credits and experience to another institution or to another state. For corps members using TFA as a path into a secondary subject they would not otherwise be qualified for, continuing with TFA is their only option. The legal framework itself works to keep corps members within the organization, which in turn affects the scope of training they receive as teachers.

Beyond just training, corps members and their professional stature become reduced to their affiliation with TFA, thereby denying them full and equitable professional standing. It is worth noting that TFA sometimes provides access to traditional schools of education. The training that corps members receive through TFA, however, is often narrow in scope and comes from recent TFA corps members with limited experience. This breeds a sort of association with the organization whereby TFA's teachers identify primarily as "corps members" before "teachers" (Veltri, 2010). This is perhaps a factor in explaining TFA's high turnover. TFA actively recruits candidates with little interest in staying in education by offering a brief, just over two-year commitment to a struggle for social justice in schools. Consequently, TFA's teachers rapidly leave the profession. Heineke, Mazza, and Tichnor-Wagner (2014) have compiled and cited alarming statistics and are worth quoting at length:

> In New York City, TFA teachers left after the 2nd year of teaching at triple the rate of traditional teachers and double the rate of other alternately certified teachers; after 4 years, 15% of TFA teachers remained in the district (Boyd et al., 2008). In Houston, 85% of TFA teachers departed after 3 years (Darling-Hammond et al., 2005). Data from Louisiana similarly showed that few TFA teachers stayed beyond a 3rd year (Noell & Gansle, 2009). In Baltimore, many teachers remained for a 3rd year, but 60% left after 3 years and 80% after 5 years (MacIver & Vaughn, 2007). Synthesizing the regional literature, Heilig and Jez (2010) stated that four out of five TFA teachers left within 2 years after the 2-year requirement.
>
> (p. 753)

Even studies that push back against the narrative of corps members as "two-years-and-out" publish statistics that concede that less than one in two corps members stay in their placement school after just two years (Donald & Johnson, 2010 as cited by Heineke et al., 2014, p. 754). Although a higher percentage "stay in the profession," there remains an undeniable exodus from teaching after the two-year commitment. This turnover should stand in sharp contrast to TFA's rebranding and subsequent endorsements as an organization providing "highly effective" teachers. Is a teacher truly "highly effective" if he or she leaves within two years? 2010)

Charter School Teacher Training

In addition to TFA, another development in teacher pipelines has significantly impacted the charter school terrain: certifying teachers directly through schools of education located within charter networks. Major alternative certification and teacher preparation programs have opened in Chicago (Noble Charter Schools connected to the Relay Graduate School of Education), Boston (the Match Charter Public School connected to the Sposato Graduate School of Education), Atlanta (the Georgia Charter Schools Association connected to the Georgia Teacher Academy for Preparation and Pedagogy), San Diego (High Tech High connected to the High Tech High Graduate School of Education), and elsewhere. The connections between these teacher preparation programs and charter schools are strong. For example, the Relay Graduate School of Education is led by charter school network founders and was created by three education management organizations: the Knowledge is Power Program, Achievement First, and Uncommon Schools, who overtly set out to "develop a new pipeline of well-trained, well-aligned teachers for their growing networks of schools" (Relay Graduate School of Education, 2013). In a similar spirit, Match proclaims:

> Our program is 100% geared towards preparing teachers for a specific type of urban charter school that tends to offer a very different experience for teachers and students than the surrounding district schools. Because of that, we strongly believe that our graduates will be most effective in these types of charter schools. We also have great relationships with charter school leaders around the country, which we leverage to help our teachers get jobs.
>
> (Match Education, 2012)

Finally, in Atlanta:

> The goal of GCSA GaTAPP is to assist schools and teachers with compliance for highly qualified status and teacher certification via a non-traditional route to teacher preparation and certification geared specifically to teachers employed in the charter school sector, including independent and system charter teachers.
>
> (Georgia Charter Schools Association, 2014)

These teacher preparation programs, then, seek to place their graduates immediately into charter school jobs and many even get a head start on this by allowing or requiring not-yet-certified teachers to complete their degrees while already working in charter schools. Moreover, graduates of these programs receive special preference for open jobs in charter schools, which is particularly problematic when new charters are being commissioned even as large numbers of traditional public schools in cities like Chicago face closure (Ash, 2014). Like their counterparts elsewhere, the Noble charter/Match partnership proclaims, "This is one of the things we've always wanted charters to do—grooming our students to come back and work in our space and become advocates in our charter schools" (Ash, 2014). Education critic and historian Diane Ravitch rightly warns, "There is something incestuous about a 'graduate' program created by charter schools to give masters' degrees to their own teachers" (Ravitch, 2012, p. 4).

Ravitch's concern becomes even more alarming when you trace the likely implications of these relationships on the practices and beliefs of the teachers they prepare. The insular nature of these relationships may reduce where graduates can effectively teach to only those charter schools that share particular missions and serve specific sets of students. So even though these programs may be entitled to award state teacher certification, proclaiming their graduates fit to teach in any public school, they may not be adequately prepared to do so. Given that these schools of education are directly affiliated with and often even partially housed in charter schools, participants in the programs are likely to be enculturated to support charter schools. Such support is not a bad thing in and of itself, but one is left to wonder whether these schools of education provide sufficient space for critiquing charter school movements, the ethicality of their practices, the problems with their employment strategies, and their rigid adherence to achieving test scores with a no-excuses approach. We must be careful to avoid indoctrinating new teachers into specific definitions of education success that are narrowly quantitative and guided by benchmarks set by non-teacher education leaders and reformers who are spearheading the charter movement. Instead, teacher preparation programs should provide opportunities for future teachers to become professionals who intelligently debate and shape practice in their field.

De-professionalizing teachers occurs in multiple ways within these new charter teacher pipelines. Many of these programs, with the notable exception in certain regards of the High Tech High Graduate School of Education, avoid teaching educational theory, educational psychology, or the research basis for various teaching techniques. As a result, participants are taught one specific way to teach and are told it is the best way to do so to achieve efficiency without explanation for how the process works, what ethical implications it may raise, or whether better alternatives might be considered or constructed—the very types of conversations held by professionals. One of us, a former Match tutor, discovered that while Match leaders rarely engaged professional questions of *how* or *why*, they frequently offered "what-to-dos," which were inflexible and certain. Renowned teacher education expert Kenneth Zeichner is worth quoting at length on this issue:

> What is important to note about the alternatives being encouraged though is that they are often closely linked with a technicist view of

> the role of teachers and with efforts to erode teachers' autonomy and collegial authority. A number of scholars have carefully documented the transformation of the occupation of teaching in many parts of the world to what has sometimes been called "the new professionalism" that accepts the view that decisions about what and how to teach and assess are largely to be made beyond the classroom rather than by teachers themselves. The same ideas that have resulted in the new professionalism for teaching have now entered the world of teacher education to try and ensure that teachers are prepared to assume their limited roles as educational clerks who are not to exercise their judgment in the classroom.
>
> (Zeichner, 2010, p. 1545)

Research has shown that pre-service teachers who fail to engage in critical and self-reflective analysis of the contexts, theories, and purposes of teaching are not only poorer-quality professional teachers, but also are unable to participate effectively in education reform (Penny, Harley, & Jessop, 1996). So while charter school operators may turn to their schools of education to further their reform efforts, their approach to educating teachers does not emphasize the skills or knowledge needed for teachers to themselves engage in or lead reform.

Finally, when these teacher preparation programs fail to engage new teachers in overtly complex and professional conversations, those new teachers may become socialized into a narrow perspective of a teacher as technician, focused on efficiently delivering measurable test results without the ability or desire to critique that goal, thereby jeopardizing their professional stance. Another noted expert on teacher education, Marilyn Cochran-Smith, also criticizes the technician-like approach:

> Teaching has technical aspects to be sure, and teachers can be trained to perform these. But teaching is also and, more importantly, an intellectual, cultural, and contextual activity that requires skillful decisions about how to convey subject matter knowledge, apply pedagogical skills, develop human relationships, and both generate and utilize local knowledge.
>
> (Cochran-Smith, 2004, p. 298)

These new teacher preparation programs, then, might be better understood as teacher training than as teacher education, for, "[t]he uses of training are replicative and applicative. The uses of education are associative and interpretive" (Johnson, 1967, pp. 132–133). The name "teacher training" better reflects the focus on replicating applications geared heavily toward student test achievement, rather than developing a skill set that renders one professionally capable of interpreting and critiquing educational practices and the theories that underlie them.

In much the same spirit of neoliberal competition and deregulation that justifies the proliferation of charter schools, these alternative teacher pipelines challenge

> the "monopoly" of the universities. Within this logic, competition should make schools better, and regulation should be kept to a minimum—or at least, the appearance of governmental regulation, since not all regulation is unwanted. And therein lies the insidious logic of neoliberalism: regulation that reflects a social-welfare system is governmental "intrusion," whereas regulation that benefits those already privileged is governmental "support."
>
> (Kumashiro, 2010, p. 59)

These supports take many forms, from funding to influence. Cochran-Smith et al. (2015), in their recent review of more than 1,500 teacher preparation programs, found that

> the greater the alignment of research to the neoliberal program of education reform, the more centralized and funded the research was, and the more likely it is to inform state and/or federal policies and practices related to teacher preparation and certification... Although many of the studies, across programs of research, were about "equity" and "access," few raised questions about who does and does not have access in the first place, why and how systems of inequality are perpetuated, under what circumstances and for whom access makes a difference, and what the role of teachers (and teacher education) is in all of this.
>
> (p. 118)

Charter schoolteacher pipelines, as part of the neoliberal approach to education reform, then, are attracting the attention of funders and policy makers, and yet overlooking systemic issues that perpetuate the very inequalities they claim to seek to alleviate.

Conclusions

There appears to be a dissonance between education reform institutions and their employment practices. As endeavors aimed at greater equality and reducing the achievement gap, holistic practices that focus on employee retention and long-term investment would be more internally consistent. In order to maintain a true commitment to social justice, we must ensure that our founding philosophies and practices resist alienation, objectification, and commodification. A commitment to social justice is a commitment to our communities and individuals within those communities. We therefore must resist philosophies and practices that dehumanize students and deprofessionalize teachers, while fracturing and otherwise dismantling communities. We must better align the means and ends of achieving quality education.

Note

1 From bell hooks[0], *Teaching to Transgress*.

References

33 Ohio Rev. Code. § 3319.227 (2011). Retrieved from http://codes.ohio.gov/orc/3319.227

Ash, K. (2014, February 25). Charter network taps alumni to grow teacher pipeline. *Education Week*. Retrieved from http://www.edweek.org/ew/articles/2014/02/26/22noble.h33.html

Au, W. (2009). *Unequal by design: High-stakes testing and the standardization of inequality*. New York: Routledge.

Au, W. (2011). Teaching under the new Taylorism: High-stakes testing and the standardization of the 21st century curriculum. *Journal of Curriculum Studies, 43*(1), 25–45.

Clark, M. A., Chiang, H. S., Silva, T., McConnell, S., Sonnenfeld, K., Erbe, A., & Puma, M. (2013). *The effectiveness of secondary math teachers from Teach for America and the Teaching Fellows programs: Executive summary*. Washington, DC: National Center for Education Evaluation and Regional Assistance, Institute of Education Sciences, U.S. Department of Education. Retrieved from http://ies.ed.gov/ncee/pubs/20134015/pdf/20134016.pdf

Cochran-Smith, M. (2004). The problem of teacher education. *Journal of Teacher Education, 55*(4), 295–299. doi:10.1177/0022487104268057

Cochran-Smith, M., Villegas, A. M., Abrams, L., Chavez-Moreno, L., Mills, T., & Stern, R. (2015). Critiquing teacher preparation research: An overview of the field, part II. *Journal of Teacher Education, 66*(2), 109–121. doi:10.1177/0022487114558268

Decker, P. T., Mayer, D. P., & Glazerman, S. (2004, June 9). *The effects of Teach for America on students: Findings from a national evaluation*. Champaign, IL: Mathematica Policy Research, Inc. Retrieved from http://www.mathematica-mpr.com/~/media/publications/PDFs/teach.pdf

Di Carlo, M. (2015, January 22). *Update on teacher turnover in the U.S.* Washington, DC: Albert Shanker Institute. Retrieved from http://www.shankerinstitute.org/blog/update-teacher-turnover-us

Freire, P. (2007). Banking v. problem-solving models of education. In R. Curren (Ed.), *Philosophy of education: An anthology* (pp. 68–75). Oxford: Blackwell Publishing.

Georgia Charter Schools Association. (2014). CharterTeacher GaTAPP: Georgia Teacher Academy for Preparation and Pedagogy. Retrieved from http://www.gcsagatapp.org/#!charter-teacher-gatapp/cor2

hooks, b. (1994). *Teaching to Transgress: Education as the practice of freedom*. New York: Routledge.

Johnson, M. (1967). Definitions and models in curriculum theory. *Educational Theory, 17*(2), 127–140.

Kessler, G. (2012, June 12). Spinning the number of teacher layoffs. *The Washington Post*. Retrieved from http://www.washingtonpost.com/blogs/fact-checker/post/spinning-the-number-of-teacher-layoffs/2012/06/12/gJQAgAMdYV_blog.html

Kluger, J. (2008, May 12). Wendy Kopp. *Time.* Retrieved from http://content.time.com/time/specials/2007/article/0,28804,1733748_1733754_1736227,00.html
Marx, K. (1990). *Capital volume I.* New York: Penguin Putnam.
Match Education. (2012). Frequently asked questions. Retrieved from http://match-education.org/match-teacher-residency/faq
McLellan, D. (2001). Economic and Philosophical Manuscripts. In *Karl Marx selected writings* (2nd ed., pp. 83–120). New York: Oxford.
Molnar, A. (2014, March). Virtual schools in the U.S.: Politics, performance, policy, and research evidence. National Education Policy Center. Retrieved from http://digitalcommons.sacredheart.edu/cgi/viewcontent.cgi?article=1175&context=ced_fac
Morgan, H. (2015). Online instruction and virtual schools for middle and high school students. *The Clearing House: A journal of Educational Strategies, Issues and Ideas, 88*(2), 72–76. doi:10.1080/00098655.2015.1007909
National Council on Teacher Quality. (2010, February). Teacher layoffs: Rethinking "last-hired, first-fired" policies. Retrieved from http://www.nctq.org/p/docs/nctq_dc_layoffs.pdf
National Education Policy Center (NEPC). (2013, November 26). Private education management organizations running public schools expand. Retrieved from http://nepc.colorado.edu/newsletter/2013/11/EMO-profiles-11-12
The New Teacher Project. (2011, February). The case against quality-blind teacher layoffs: Why layoff policies that ignore teacher quality need to end *now*. Retrieved from http://tntp.org/assets/documents/TNTP_Case_Against_Quality_Blind_Layoffs_Feb2011.pdf
Ollman, B. (1971). *Alienation: Marx's conception of man in capitalist society.* London: Cambridge University Press.
Penny, A. J., Harley, K. L., & Jessop, T. S. (1996). Towards a language of possibility: Critical reflection and mentorship in initial teacher education. *Teachers and Teaching, 2*(1), 57–69. doi:10.1080/1354060960020105
Phillips, O. (2015, March 30). Revolving door of teachers costs schools billions every year. *NPR.* Retrieved from http://www.npr.org/sections/ed/2015/03/30/395322012/the-hidden-costs-of-teacher-turnover
Ravitch, D. (2012). A very bizarre graduate school of education [Web log post]. Retrieved from http://dianeravitch.net/2012/07/08/a-very-bizarre-graduate-school-of-education
Relay Graduate School of Education. (2013). Our history. Retrieved from http://www.relay.edu/history/
Rhee, M. (2012, October 25). Michelle Rhee: Communities need parent trigger laws. *U.S News & World Report.* Retrieved from http://www.usnews.com/debate-club/is-there-a-need-for-parent-trigger-laws/fixing-our-failing-schools-is-a-civil-rights-issue
Rhee, M. (2013, March 5). Op-ed: MAP boycott is about keeping test scores out of teacher evaluations. *The Seattle Times.* Retrieved from http://www.seattletimes.com/opinion/op-ed-map-boycott-is-about-keeping-test-scores-out-of-teacher-evaluations/
Ronfeldt, M., Loeb, S., & Wyckoff, J. (2013). How teacher turnover harms student achievement. *American Educational Research Journal, 50*(1), 4–36.
Sandel, M. (1996). *Democracy's discontent.* Cambridge: Harvard University Press.
Skrla, L., Scheurich, J. J., García, J., & Nolly, G. (2010). Equity audits: A practical leadership tool for developing equitable and excellent schools. In C. Marshall & M. Oliva (Eds.), *Leadership for social justice: Making revolutions in education* (2nd ed., pp. 259–283). Boston: Allyn & Bacon.
Standing, G. (2011). *The precariat: The new dangerous class.* London: Bloomsbury Academic.

Stitzlein, S. M. (2013). Citizenship education in for-profit charter schools? *Journal of Curriculum Studies, 45*(2), 251–276.

Straus, V. (2013, January 11). Teachers refuse to give standardized test at Seattle high schools—Update [Web log post]. *The Washington Post.* Retrieved from http://www.washingtonpost.com/blogs/answer-sheet/wp/2013/01/11/teachers-refuse-to-give-standardized-test-at-seattle-high-school/

Stuit, D. A., & Smith, T. M. (2010, June). Research brief: Teacher turnover in charter schools. National Center on School Choice/Vanderbilt Peabody College. Retrieved from http://www.vanderbilt.edu/schoolchoice/documents/briefs/brief_stuit_smith_ncspe.pdf

Stuit, D. A., & Smith, T. M. (2012). Explaining the gap in charter and traditional public school teacher turnover rates. *Economics of Education Review, 31*(2), 268–279.

Taylor, K. (2015, April 6). At success academy charter schools, high scores and polarizing tactics. *The New York Times.* Retrieved from http://www.nytimes.com/2015/04/07/nyregion/at-success-academy-charter-schools-polarizing-methods-and-superior-results.html?_r=1

Teach for America. (2010, May 11). Scaling Teach for America: Growing the talent force working to ensure all our nation's students have access to quality education. Investing in Innovation (i3) Fund Application. Retrieved from https://www2.ed.gov/programs/innovation/2010/narratives/u396a100015.pdf

Torres, A. C. (2014a). "Are we architects or construction workers?" Re-examining teacher autonomy and turnover in charter schools. *Education Policy Analysis Archives, 22*(124), 1–23. Retrieved from http://dx.doi.org/10.14507/epaa.v22.1614

Torres, A. C. (2014b). Is this work sustainable? Teacher turnover and perceptions of workload in charter management organizations. *Urban Education, 14,* 1–24. doi:10.1177/0042085914549367

U.S Department of Education. (2010, July 2). U.S. Education Secretary Duncan commemorates 46th anniversary of the Civil Rights Act. Retrieved from http://www.ed.gov/news/press-releases/us-education-secretary-duncan-commemorates-46th-anniversary-civil-rights-act

Veltri, B. T. (2010). *Learning on other peoples' kids: Becoming a Teach for America teacher.* Charlotte, NC: Information Age Publishing.

Wells, A. S., & Scott, J. (2001). Privatization and charter school reform: Economic, political, and social dimensions. In H. M. Levin (Ed.), *Privatizing education: Can the school marketplace deliver freedom of choice, efficiency, equity, and social cohesion?* (pp. 234–259). Boulder, CO: Westview Press.

Zeichner, K. (2010). Competition, economic rationalization, increased surveillance, and attacks on diversity: Neoliberalism and the transformation of teacher education in the U.S. *Teaching and Teacher Education, 26,* 1544–1552. doi:10.1016/j.tate.2010.06.004

4 Charter School Teachers and the Consequences of Unionization

Elizabeth Montaño

Introduction

The Charter Schools Act of 1992 established up to 100 charter schools, all eligible to bypass many of the regulations required of traditional public schools. California's Charter Law, only the second of its kind in the nation after Minnesota, became legislation as a concession to the voucher laws circulating the California assembly (Kerchner et al., 2008). Defenders of public schools, including teacher unions, criticized charter schools for inciting a movement to privatize education. Charter school supporters argued that they offered a choice for parents and students, particularly in low-income areas. In Los Angeles, there existed a unique convergence of interests between parents who sought an alternative to the large school district bureaucracy of the Los Angeles Unified School District, and the interests of school choice supporters.

Local community leaders, teachers, parents, and funders founded Hope Charter School (a pseudonym) in the year 2000. The school founders believed that a longer school year, longer school day, and a focus on literacy, critical thinking, and social justice would benefit the mostly Latina/o population of the area. Initially, there were two sites, which grew to three by 2001. By 2005, Hope Charter School (HCS) was a growing community of teachers, leaders, and parents who wanted the best educational opportunities for traditionally underserved students. The success they reached came at a great cost to the teaching force, which expressed challenging working conditions and faced high turnover year to year. That same year, teachers met and spoke about the possibilities of unionization. The teachers were divided. Some believed that a union would get in the way of the work that had been accomplished at HCS. Others were cautious about which type of union they could create that would meet their unique needs. Another group of teachers who had been there from the beginning warned their colleagues about the devastating effects that it could have on the school culture. They had tried to unionize back in 2001 and were unsuccessful after HCS opened an additional site and the union lost the numbers to move forward. Despite the warnings, teachers at all of the sites voted and authorized a teachers union through the California Teachers Association (CTA).

The teachers and school leaders were suddenly on different teams, and the governing board, appointed businessmen and women, questioned their ability to operate a charter school while having to negotiate with a "third party": the teachers' union. The experiences of teachers in this charter school are at the center of this chapter, which asks, "What consequences did teachers at Hope Charter School face when they decided to unionize?" Teachers spoke about broken relationships with the management of the school. Even though many relationships were broken, teachers gained a voice and presence in the organization. This chapter presents the experiences of teachers in a charter school and examines the consequences they faced when they decided to unionize.

Charter Schools and Unions: An Unlikely Beginning

In a series of speeches, starting in 1985, the late American Federation of Teachers President Al Shanker presented the concept of a charter school as a publicly funded school with high levels of teacher autonomy that would provide a choice for families (Kahlenberg, 2007). His vision was partly influenced by governmental pressures, specifically the publication of *A Nation at Risk* (National Commission on Excellence in Education, 1983), a report commissioned by President Reagan's National Commission on Excellence in Education. The report pointed to the failure of the public school system, particularly in maintaining accountability for schools and teachers (Gyurko, 2008). Shanker envisioned a charter school reform system centered on the role of the teachers' contract, which would "go beyond collective bargaining to the achievement of true teacher professionalism" (Gyurko, 2008, p. 6 as cited in Kahlenberg, 2007). He argued that when schools valued teachers' voices, they would achieve higher levels of success in the long run because if teachers felt valued, then the workforce would be more attractive to capable and innovative educators (Gyurko, 2008). Shanker was confident that his vision for charter schools would achieve teacher professionalism and ultimately would provide educational opportunities for the overwhelming majority of students underserved by the public school system.

In 1991, when Minnesota signed the first charter school law in the country, it did not fulfill Shanker's original vision (Gyurko, 2008). Instead of working within schools and with teachers, charter school operators created structural changes, such as exemptions from state education codes, public school regulations, and pre-existing collective bargaining agreements with teacher unions (Gyurko, 2008). By virtue of the Minnesota charter school legislation, teachers' rights were left out of the discussion in public school reform. In addition, the establishment of charter schools set out to fulfill the public's view that public schools should demonstrate high levels of autonomy and accountability (Ravitch, 2010). Accountability, measured by standardized test scores, would further blame teachers and their unions for the failure of public education, particularly in large urban centers, further prompting reform efforts in large cities (Ravitch, 2010). Fueled by the public's suspicion of public schools and of teacher unions, charter schools emerged and flourished without the unionization of its teaching force (Gyurko, 2008; Ravitch, 2010).

Teachers who have worked at charter schools have often not sought the protections that the teaching force has earned in the last 40 years of collective bargaining rights (Johnson & Landman, 2000). In 2015, the Los Angeles Unified School District (LAUSD) had 282 charter schools where fewer than 10% of teachers are unionized. Some conversion schools remained with the local district union, United Teachers Los Angeles (UTLA), while start-up charter schools typically organized independently through the California Teachers Association (CTA) or the California Federation of Teachers. Not only have charter school operators been opposed to unionization, teacher unions have traditionally been opposed to charter expansion until recently (Cohen, 2015). In 2015, teachers working for the Alliance College-Ready Public Schools in Los Angeles voted to unionize with UTLA and are facing a backlash from administration (Cohen, 2015). Charter school teachers across the country have faced similar backlash from management when they have voted to unionize (Blume, 2009; Cohen, 2015; Sawchuck, 2009). In order to examine the true impact of the charter school movement, it is imperative to look into the experiences of teachers who work in these deregulated spaces.

Teaching in Charter Schools: A Literature Review

Various studies have detailed the challenging working environments for teachers in charter schools. In 1998, the UCLA Charter School Study reported findings on the effects of the then-recent charter school movement in ten California school districts. The research team concluded that although charter school teachers enjoyed the freedom and empowerment of working within smaller schools, they faced the possibility of "burn-out" due to the added responsibilities, lack of time, and overall exhaustive workload (UCLA Charter School Study, 1998). Across all 17 schools in the study, most of the veteran teachers questioned the sustainability of the charter school workload (UCLA Charter School Study, 1998). The teachers in this study were all part of conversion charter schools that had retained their district union contracts and therefore were subjected to job protections that teachers in charter schools are not normally granted. Even though teachers were protected by their union contracts, they still did not feel that they could work in charter schools in the long run.

Most teachers in charter schools work in environments that are deregulated and free from union contracts. In fact, teachers oftentimes come to charter schools because they want the "freedom to make their own instructional and curricular decisions and an environment that fosters professional opportunities for collaboration with like-minded colleagues" (Malloy & Wohlstetter, 2003, p. 227). Several studies have found that freedoms associated with being a charter school teacher such as choosing their curriculum, creating their own assessments, negotiating their salary, and taking on administrative roles eventually become a burden for charter school teachers (Margolis, 2005). What they find when they arrive is that teacher autonomy does not translate to improving the "bread and butter" issues, such as workload, pay, and benefits, that would keep teachers committed to charter schools (Malloy & Wohlstetter, 2003). Charter school teachers have shared concerns about the scope and definition of their responsibilities, their role in the design and governance of the school, their right to raise complaints, and the guarantee of job security and fair pay (Johnson & Landman, 2000). Studies have concluded that charter schools are the least favorable to teachers and that the flexibility granted to charter school operators is not automatically extended to its teaching force (Johnson & Landman, 2000).

Ultimately, charter schools were designed as schools of choice. Margolis (2005) suggests that although "choice and competition may lure teachers to a charter school—these business-world facets of school life are not often enough to sustain teachers long term" (p.105). He further argues that the market-like environment of charter schools might not fit with a teaching force that naturally seeks community and collaboration to sustain itself. In addition, when teachers speak out about their working conditions, the charter school governance has questioned the teachers' loyalty to the organization (Johnson & Landman, 2000; Sawchuck, 2009). Because the power in charter schools goes to the governing board and to the administration, teachers have no guarantees about the nature of their workplace and whether it will be fair, responsive, and supportive.

Since the 1998 UCLA Charter School study, few studies have looked at the experiences of unionized charter school teachers and what they face to improve their working conditions. In 2007, the NewSchools Venture Fund released a case study documenting the working environment of Green Dot Public Schools (GDPS) teachers in Los Angeles. Teachers reported having a higher sense of security, control, representation, and respect due to their union representation (NewSchools Venture Fund, 2007). Yet, despite this, many teachers left each year, and most did not find the time to be active members in the union due to the heavy workload of working for GDPS (New Schools Venture Fund, 2007). In addition, teachers at GDPS did not fight for tenure in their collective bargaining agreement. According to the case study, despite being unionized, teachers continued to face high levels of turnover and low levels of participation in the union.

Other charter management organizations (CMOs) have not been so open to unionization, and many have opted out of the increased bureaucracy and the perceived antiquated labor practices brought on by teachers' unions (Malin & Kerchner, 2006). In 2008, charter school teachers at a Knowledge is Power Program (KIPP) school in New York City voted to unionize under the United Federation of Teachers. That same year, when the KIPP management discovered the teachers' organizing efforts, they placed pressure on the teachers' union to decertify (Sawchuck, 2009). In March 2015, charter school teachers with Alliance Public Schools in Los Angeles voted to unionize with UTLA and faced backlash from the community, other teachers, as well as the administration (Cohen, 2015). In June 2015, 17 charter school teachers, part of the Urban Prep Academy in Chicago, were allegedly fired for unionizing. Even after over 25 years of a charter movement, there exists a lack of understanding over the role of teachers' unions and the collective bargaining rights of teachers within charter schools.

Studies on teachers in charter schools have documented the benefits of autonomy when teachers can create their own curriculum, their own assessments, be leaders within the school, and work with like-minded colleagues (Malloy & Wohlstetter, 2003; Margolis, 2005; UCLA Charter School Study, 1998). Yet, these studies have also pointed to charter school environments as the least favorable for teachers, where teachers are overworked and do not get the same rights as teachers in traditional public schools (Johnson & Landman, 2000). Even teachers who worked in unionized charter schools felt too overworked to participate in the union (NewSchools Venture Fund, 2007). In addition, the unionization of some charter schools has led to harsh consequences for teachers who voted to unionize (Blume, 2009; Cohen, 2015; Sawchuck, 2009). The participants profiled in this chapter described their experiences working within a charter school and documenting the consequences they faced as a result of their unionization.

Methodology

To capture the experiences of teachers in a charter school, I utilized a qualitative case study methodology. The objective of this case study was to capture a phenomenon of a group of charter schools that decided to unionize. The case study design provided insights that could help structure future research in order to advance the field's knowledge base.

Site and Participants

Hope Charter School has been in existence since the year 2000, when it opened two school sites in a densely populated section of Los Angeles. By 2012, HCS was a CMO, educating over 2,500 students on five campuses. Ninety-eight percent of the student population in K–12 were Title 1 (economically disadvantaged), 98% were classified as Hispanic/Latino/a, and 48% of students were classified as English language learners. In 2012, all of the Hope Charter schools ranked 10 out of 10 on the Academic Performance Index (API measures are an outcome of California's Public Schools Accountability Act of 1999), placing them in the top 10% of all schools serving similar demographics. During the 2011–2012 school year, within a six-month period, I conducted interviews and focus groups with 17 former and current teachers of HCS. In addition, I observed leadership meetings of the Hope Charter School Teachers Association (HCSTA) and analyzed historical documents from the organization.

This case study employed a convenience and purposive sampling in order to ensure that teachers who knew the workings of the union were part of the sample. Seven union leaders, former HCS teachers who founded the union, were contacted individually and interviewed about the formation of the union. Four current teachers, who were leaders of HCSTA and who were also part of the founding of the union, participated in interviews regarding the current practices and beliefs of the teachers' union. The four current teachers were also invited to join one of two focus groups to provide historical context if issues regarding the founding of the union emerged. Three out of the four current teachers were available and participated in the focus groups. All union members were emailed and invited to participate in one-hour focus groups. The ones who responded and attended made up the focus groups. Nine teachers, all union members from mixed grade levels and from all five different HCS campuses, participated in the focus groups.

Data Collection

The data collection process consisted of interviews, focus groups, observations, and document analysis. Interviews with founding members were conducted with an interview protocol and outside of school hours, starting in July 2011 through February 2012. All of the interviews were audio recorded and transcribed. The observations of union leadership meetings occurred from October 2011 through February 2012. These observations were limited in scope, since there were few meetings, and I was also a participant in the meetings. I took handwritten notes and created researcher memos after the meetings. In order to triangulate with the themes that emerged in the interviews and focus groups, I examined a collection of historical documents kept by the union. All of the documents were publicly shared and addressed to the teaching force. The documents included the teachers' collective bargaining agreement, the governing board's meeting notes, letters from the union to teachers and from the management to teachers, and other forms of communication collected since the establishment of the teachers' union.

After interviewing ten individual teachers, I conducted focus groups with current members of the HCSTA. The focus groups served to bring in the voices of current HCS teachers and their views on the union today. In addition, because current HCS teachers who were part of the founding were also invited to the focus groups, they would serve to provide context about the founding of the union, therefore allowing me to focus on facilitating the discussion. The focus groups took place in January 2012 after all of the previous data had been coded and analyzed. Nine teachers attended two focus groups in my classroom. These were held at one of the school sites to allow access to the participants. The discussions lasted about one hour and were audio recorded.

Data Analysis

The data for this study consisted of transcribed audio-recorded interviews, transcribed audio-recorded focus groups, observation notes, and documents existing in the union's historical files. After conducting and transcribing the interviews, I utilized an inductive analysis to extract the themes that emerged (Hatch, 2002). The inductive analysis method allowed me to process large amounts of data while still assuring confidence that the themes emerging were representative of the overall data. Once I read and coded the interview transcripts, I used the emerging themes to create questions for the focus groups. After the focus groups, I transcribed the audio and read and coded the transcripts. I used the emerging themes to analyze historical documents and observation notes. I took quotes from the documents that corresponded to the themes presented by the teachers in the interviews and focus groups. In addition, I returned to the interview transcripts to find themes that resonated with the themes present in the documents and the focus groups. Throughout the data collection process, I returned to the inductive analysis to ensure that the themes were emerging from the data, rather than from the researcher.

This study chronicled the experiences of unionized teachers within one charter school organization. My positionality within this study included my role as member of the community, a former union leader, HCS teacher, and researcher. Because I was a part of the union's founding team, I ensured that the interviews reflected the teachers' experiences in their own words, as opposed to my own experiences. In this chapter, I included utterances of experiences that I did not experience or agree with. Although I was no longer in the union leadership throughout the duration of this study, the qualitative methodology allowed me to develop an insider perspective (Hatch, 2002). Guba and Lincoln (1981) discussed the benefits of qualitative research in that the researcher is close to the data, yet there exists a higher risk for researcher bias. They suggest the use of triangulation and an audit trail to decrease researchers' bias (Lincoln & Guba, 1986). In this study, I have ensured triangulation between data from various interviews, focus groups, document analysis, and observations, as well as within the data.

There are limitations inherent to the study due to the specific demographics and location of HCS. Because many charter schools in California are serving a large number of Latino/a students, and most of the charter schools in California are within the LAUSD, the limitations of this study were diminished. In addition to the limitations inherent in the study, there were limitations set by the researcher that impacted the generalizability of the study. The story is told from the perspectives of teachers in the union who were part of the unionization efforts and/or who were members and leaders in the union. It does not share the perspective of the management, governing board, or the teachers who were not part of the union or those teachers who resisted unionization.

HCS Teachers Unionize

The experiences of HCS teachers in seeking unionization are explored as part of a larger study (Montano, 2012). Teachers described a strong sense of community, one that they had not been able to encounter at other places, and one where initially they did not feel they needed a union (Montano, 2012). Yet HCS teachers also saw high turnover from teachers and administrators. They had a longer school day and a longer school year than the local district schools, yet they were paid the same. Sonia, a union member, reflected:

> Getting A-Z done is what makes us so successful, but getting A-Z done means working pretty outrageous hours. There's something to that. There's so much joy working here because there's so much positivity and productivity, so when you leave, you feel how great it was. But you leave because you can't have two kids and do all of this at the same time.

Teachers felt exhausted and they wanted to have a say in their working conditions. Valeria, a founding member, recalled:

> It came to a point where people really wanted to stay at Hope and felt really committed to the mission but the quality of life was deteriorating to the point where people said If I stay, I can only give another year, but I want to stay for the next few years, so what is it going to take?

The idea that many teachers wanted to continue working, but felt that they could not continue working at this pace was one of the main factors leading teachers towards unionization. In addition, they were led to believe that it was a teacher-led school, but they found that they had little control over their working conditions. They had a teacher representative and a parent representative on the governing board, but those two people had no voting rights. After unionization, the governing board removed the teacher and the parent representative, citing, "Collective bargaining represents a change in the way that we have done business in the past." In a letter to teachers dated September 20, 2006, the board president reminded teachers that, "Our intention was to create a small neighborhood school that was totally controlled by local decision-makers." Although the board claimed to be collaborative in its founding of HCS, having to answer to a group of teachers was not the collaboration they were seeking.

Teachers began to see that their school operated within a larger business model with a governing board made up of funders (Montano, 2015). Before unionization, many teachers saw themselves distanced from a governing board that most of them had never met. In the 2004–2005 school year, teachers from the different sites came together to discuss unionization. They also met with union representatives from UTLA and GDPS. Although their meetings were held in secret, some teachers discussed plans with the management of the school. It should not have been a surprise, since teachers had also formed a union in 2001, one that was de-certified when HCS opened a new site, and with the hiring of new teachers, the union vote was no longer a majority. Teachers discussed the pros and cons and whether a union was necessary. They wanted an organic union, one that represented them and their unique needs (Montano, 2012). They met for several months and spoke about the pros and cons of unionizing as an independent entity or with the local district union UTLA. They approached every teacher in the voting process, yet they found that some teachers were against unionization. Some teachers stayed away and were wary due to prior negative experiences with teacher unions, their ties to the administration, or their previous experience trying to unionize at HCS. In the spring of 2005, HCS reached a majority vote and established an independent union. The subsequent year, the teachers' union began an 18-month negotiation process that tested the unity of the HCS community.

Consequences from Unionization

The process of unionization and the ensuing contract negotiations divided a once-united HCS community. Following are the voices of teachers who shared their experiences in organizing a union and negotiating their first collective bargaining agreement.

Relationship with School Leaders

The first strain was a result of how the unionization occurred. Teachers felt that although administrators were fully aware of their concerns, teachers had to be secretive in their unionization efforts. Kelly, a founding member, recalled, "We had been advised that it needed to be secretive so that it wasn't squashed before it got too far. Judging by their reaction, I think it was a surprise to them." The secretive aspect of the unionization efforts was one of the factors that led to a strained relationship between teachers and their administrators. Valeria, a founding member, recalled, "I received emails from them, emails that said, 'I'm very hurt by this. I feel like it's dividing our school. I feel like you guys are being secretive.'" Luna, a current teacher who had been at HCS since unionization, recalled, "The principal at the time came into my room and she cried. She was really scared of what unionizing meant . . . I felt bad for her because I saw her as my friend and not my boss." Teachers, who had previously been friends with their principals, felt torn by their efforts to unionize. Kelly, a founding member, reiterated that unionization was not a personal attack on the leaders of the schools. She stated, "It wasn't against the management on a personal level. We didn't think, 'We don't like these people, we're going to go against them.'" HCS teachers and their school leaders had been accustomed to collaboration, yet the process of unionization created a strained relationship between both parties.

When teachers realized that site administrators could not respond to their working conditions, teachers decided to unionize. Union organizers stressed that the unionization effort was never against the school leaders. Rather, the union was in response to board policies and the lack of fair processes that existed. Karina, a union member who was at HCS during unionization, reflected:

> We were fighting for the recognition of the work we were doing, hours we were putting in, and equality, and that had nothing to do with administration. They're [principals] not the ones in charge of giving us the figures or deciding the calendar days. It was above them, so why were they taking it personal?

The process of unionization had to be secretive; therefore, some school leaders felt betrayed by the teachers. Other principals, who had worked in unionized environments before, felt strongly against the role of a union at HCS. At the high school, a new campus, the school leader felt very strongly about the impact of unionization on his school. Julie, a founding teacher, recalled:

> He [the principal] said, 'I believe in teacher unionizing. I was a representative of CTA. However, I don't think we need that here. Unions get in the way of real work and if we're doing such a great job, why do we have to get involved in that level of animosity?' I felt that him saying that was very discouraging and intimidating to my other colleagues that were less inclined to speak out.

The division between the teachers' union and HCS site leaders further deteriorated during negotiations, when teachers faced the high school principal at the bargaining table. George, a founding teacher, recalled,

> People didn't want it to be nasty, but they [management] weren't afraid to be nasty. When they pulled in [High School principal], they proved it. From everything that I heard of those meetings, he was just the perfect management person and he did his best to crush it [the union] at the beginning.

Teachers initially felt that the unionization would be against the governing board and the executive director, but when a principal joined the management's team at the bargaining table, it further deteriorated the relationships between teachers and their school leaders. Not only did teachers regret this as an unfortunate consequence of unionization, they reflected on how this strained relationship affected the culture at HCS. Kim, founding member, recalled, "It just felt uncomfortable and I felt that we had such an amazing relationship and we had such a nice community and it felt like we were all throwing each other under the bus." The contentious negotiations and the organizing efforts further tested the relationships between teachers and management. Kim described being "exhausted and kind of beaten down" from the unionization efforts. The conflicts between teachers and administration stemmed from the initial unionization but transferred to the negotiation table, where tensions grew between teachers and the management.

Relationship with the Governing Board

The act of unionization and the first collective bargaining process divided the school. The teachers became the "union" and the school leaders joined the governing board as the "management." Most teachers had not met the board members and described the governing board as "disconnected." Elisa, a current teacher who has been at HCS since unionization, recalled, "The board members, they didn't know us. A lot of them hadn't been into the schools to watch us teach. They didn't know the students." In a letter to teachers dated October 25, 2006, the union president at the time wrote:

> I was recently visited in my classroom by our HCS board president and I was amazed that as board president he had not ever visited a class. Yet, it does explain the dilemma faced by administrators having to work with a governing board that is disconnected from our school, our teachers, and our students. This I believe, more than any other factor, appears to be the stumbling block in finalizing a fair contract.

Teachers felt an added challenge during negotiations was bargaining a contract against a board that did not understand the issues leading teachers towards unionization. Luna, who had been at HCS since before unionization, recalled:

> It's difficult for the board members to walk in our shoes. They're not educators. It's whatever they see delivered on those Power Points presented by the CEO. Statistics, graphs, and pie graphs, and there's a human element of teaching and being with children, children who are at risk.

Michelle, a founding member, recalled, "The school board people are not elected and at the time there were a lot of sort of big business corporate people who didn't understand what we were trying to do because that's not their model." Teachers described working with a board of non-educators, businesspeople, who were not involved in running the day-to-day operations of the schools. When unionization occurred, the board responded in various ways. In a letter to teachers regarding unionization dated February 3, 2005, the board president stated:

> Therefore, I think that it is very important that our school administrators and board be included in dialogue and discussions that affect the school and its staff. Some of you might disagree with this premise, believing that certain matters must be decided unilaterally and presented by a union. I don't believe that this premise is consistent with the spirit of our school. When important decisions are made, I believe that all parties should be included and have a chance to personally air their fears and concerns, without the intervention of a 3rd party such as a union.

The governing board joined with the administration to place themselves as a party within the schools, while they placed teachers as a third party. Yet it was the board that was the third party in the eyes of teachers. Michelle, a founding member, stated, "At the end of the day, people who didn't work in our buildings were making all these decisions." After unionization, and during the negotiation process, the management team had a different vision for collaboration. Valeria, a founding member, recalled:

> I felt that there was a lot of bitterness about the fact that we had unionized, and there was not an acceptance of us as a true union. The people at the [negotiating] table did not want to hear what we had to say. They had already decided before we walked in that they weren't going to give us anything in the end.

Teachers felt that the management's perspective about maintaining flexibility became a symbol of their unwillingness to come to the table and bargain fairly. Kelly, a founding member, recalled, "They didn't come with anything. There was no movement, their answer was no to everything, they were just delaying and their proposals and their counters were the existing contract." Teachers came to a school where they believed in a charter founded upon a collaborative model, yet the culture of choice dictated an environment where management maintained a unilateral power over the employees.

Although teachers had unionized to create better working conditions, job security, and sustainability for the profession, they realized that the management did not share the same sentiment. Despite some teachers openly discussing unionization with the management, the management took the unionization hard. Valeria reflected, "I think it became an issue of pride obviously for the management and it would be for anyone if they feel like people are biting the hand that feeds them." Teachers believed that the management had various concerns about the unionization efforts at HCS. From the beginning, the governing board of HCS refused to view the union as a partner in governance.

Not only were board members against the unionization efforts, they used the fact that the board was a fundraising entity to further divide people at HCS about the union issue. George, a founding member, recalled hearing a response from the board president regarding unionization:

> I remember him [board president] saying, 'You can't make it public that we're a union school—we got people that are giving us money that are.' He didn't say people that are anti-union, but you can tell the way he was talking that he was worried about getting funding for the school because of what happened.

Teachers understood that the board never meant to share power with the union and that the real concern was about the union's threat to the board's fundraising interests. In a letter to teachers dated February 3, 2005, the board president stated:

> We have become known for quality instruction and teachers, exceptional administrators, stable fiscal management, and an inspiring vision for a community school. This success has made it easier for us to attract resources such as money and good teachers to the school. Obviously, this is a trend that depends upon a united school community.

In the eyes of board members, the teachers' union represented a threat to the governing board's fundraising efforts. In a letter to teachers dated November 3, 2006, another board member wrote, "The [HCS] board, which is responsible for managing the interests and meeting the expectations of multiple stakeholders, considers the expectations of our financial benefactors to be quite important." Teachers understood and valued the work of board members to govern and fundraise for the benefit of the charter schools. The board members claimed that the union was taking away the collaborative aspect of running their charter school.

Another concern was the public perception that unionization would have on the charter school community in Los Angeles. Valeria stated:

> Obviously, management was very unhappy that we were doing it because of the message that it would send to the outside world . . . despite having high test scores and high student achievement, we had unhappy teachers that wanted better working conditions.

Despite these concerns, teachers moved on with unionization efforts and organizing efforts that were often contentious. Teachers did not see unionization as a way to limit the flexibilities of the charter school; instead, they saw it as a way of protecting the vision that the school was founded upon. Michelle, a founding member stated, "We wanted to have the best school that we could have and we respected the management leaders. We respected those people, the community leaders and educators that founded that school." Even though there existed a respect for the work of the founders, funders, and managers, during negotiations, teachers found that the same respect was not reciprocated.

There was a sense of disappointment when teachers learned that different people in management and their lawyer repeatedly made comments at the bargaining table that demoralized teachers and questioned their intentions in unionizing. The management team repeatedly rejected proposals where they questioned the moral decisions of some teachers, even identifying them as "bad apples." The teachers interviewed spoke about being called "bad apples," which later became a slogan that they used on t-shirts and buttons to organize during negotiations. Marisol, a current teacher, recalled:

> I was very disappointed that I worked in an organization that allowed teachers to be called bad apples. Knowing that our leadership at that time was at the negotiating table to just sort of demonize what we were doing and demonize our desire to have fair rights and establish our working conditions which would then empower us to be better teachers for our students.

Teachers began to realize that although their intention in unionizing was to create a better school for the community, the management did not appear to share the same values as they did. The HCS mission was focused on building critical thinkers who were agents of change within a college-preparatory environment. Yet, teachers felt that the same progressive ideologies were not being extended to them, particularly when they were demanding a change in their working conditions. Marisol added:

> There seemed to be so much animosity and lack of understanding. We were at a school that was supposedly trying to promote agents of social change for our students, yet we were not given the same sort of rights to be socially just in our work conditions.

Teachers recognized the difficulty of working for an organization that did not extend them fair rights; yet teachers remained loyal to the school's mission, to the students, and to each other. Michelle, a founding member, stated, "For a progressive school, in terms of curriculum and what they believe to be true for kids, I think it's just sad that it happened that way." This type of backlash was one of the consequences of unionization that teachers did not expect, especially from a school founded collaboratively and within the community.

Consequences of Unionization 75

Unionization and the ensuing negotiations had become a personal attack between teachers and the management of HCS. Teachers called it an unintended and unfortunate consequence of unionization. Michelle, a founding member, reflected:

> [One regret was that] there was no bridge built . . . that teachers and management could have bargained this as collaboratively as we wanted [but] it continued to be confrontational. I know my principal at the time felt really damaged by it—for as hard as we worked as a teacher group to try to be inclusive, it's just too bad that we didn't, we didn't ever connect with management that way.

The 18-month contract negotiation deteriorated relationships between teachers, members, and non-union members, as well between teachers and their principals. In addition to broken relationships, some teachers faced more unintended consequences from unionization.

Repercussions for Union Involvement

Teachers at Hope Charter School believed that the charter school model could be sustainable for teachers if their concerns were addressed. They never intended to strain the relationship with management and they remained hopeful that even within a business school model, the union would gain some parity with the management. One consequence they did not expect was that doors would close for them in their future endeavors at Hope Charter School. Before the unionization, Kim, a founding member, had been in talks with the executive director to create a new position for herself outside of the classroom. At the end of that year, that option was no longer available. Kim described her experience, "After [unionization], it was as if doors closed for me in terms of what I could do within the school, and I wasn't happy staying, so I started to look [for another job]." Kim was never told that it could have been a result of unionization, but she felt that it was related.

Michelle, another founding member, faced closed doors when she applied to return as a teacher years after unionization. She recalled, "I tried to return, and applied for a job. It was my understanding that the hiring principal (who was not on staff when we founded [the union]) wanted to hire me but that was blocked by the executive director due to my history at the school." In fact, Michelle's friend, who applied at the same time, did get the job to teach fourth grade. Other teachers who founded the union had also tried to return to HCS and had not received a call back.

For other teachers, it was the question of whether they could move into administrative roles at HCS. Kelly, a founding member, believed that she would be rehired as a teacher if she chose to return, but she was not so confident about returning as an administrator. She stated:

I'm not sure that I would ever be considered for a principalship or any other type of administrative role because of my role in the union leadership. It's just a hunch, I don't have any evidence, but it's a hunch.

As of 2012, no one who was involved in the unionization efforts had been hired in a leadership capacity at HCS. In fact, even though teachers who founded the union were the most senior veterans at HCS, they had been passed up when positions in leadership opened up. Although there was no direct evidence suggesting a connection, the teachers interviewed noted the possibility of this being a consequence of their involvement in the union. Elisa, a current teacher, pondered, "It's hard to say at this point in the year for myself personally, but it has always been a concern. Based on what I have seen, it [unionization] does seem to have a negative consequence." Despite the broken relationships and the consequences teachers faced as a result of unionizing, teachers described that the most important value gained from the unionization efforts was the voice and presence of the union.

Voice and Presence

Before unionization, when teachers felt frustrated by their working conditions at Hope Charter School, they would opt to leave. Teachers unionized seeking job security, sustainability, and parity in the organization. They gained some rights, including clearer language for evaluations, two-year contracts, and other language that secured processes, but many teachers shared that the most valuable consequence from unionization became having a voice and presence as a union. Valeria, a founding member, recalled, "It [unionization] helped teachers feel that they had a voice and I think that prior to that, people would just leave. They didn't really continue because they didn't feel they had a voice." Even though the teachers had sought unionization as a vehicle towards job security, sustainability, and parity, they realized that having a voice could be an avenue to keep teachers at HCS.

The founding members of the union still believed that the presence of the union and the creation of collective bargaining was a successful consequence of unionization. Michelle, a founding member, stated, "I think that was a success, that we tried to incorporate as many viewpoints as possible and come up with an organic union that was true to ourselves. I think it's a success that it happened . . . that the contract continues." Teachers who founded the union expressed a value in having a collective bargaining agreement providing a process and voice for teachers.

Still, the contract was not the most important aspect of the unionization for all teachers. Some teachers saw it as a representation of the union, but they valued the presence of the union even more. When I asked Kelly, a founding member, if the values of the union were reflected in the contract, she declared:

I don't know that it has anything to do with the contract. It has to do with the presence of the union . . . It reflected the values in that our voices were heard and they hadn't been heard. The fact that there were site reps that would talk to the principals and talk about issues . . . I really feel like it was our biggest win. That spoke to our vision in unionizing. We wanted to be active participants.

Teachers described that the most important consequence from unionization was the voice that it gave to teachers. Before unionization, HCS paraded an ideal of being teacher-led, yet teachers considered it a façade. Teachers worked hard alongside school leaders and parents to make HCS a successful school, yet they held no power over their working conditions. Despite the gains in their collective bargaining agreement, their biggest gain was having a voice and presence in the organization.

Summary

The teachers in this study described their unique experiences of working within a charter school when they decided to unionize. The unionization created a backlash of broken relationships with their administration and repercussions for union involvement. Teachers discovered that they were considered a "third party" and were referred to as "bad apples" during negotiations. The teachers began to question why the social justice ideals that were part of the mission of the school did not apply to their rights as employees. Even after the broken relationships and contentious negotiation process, teachers believed that having a voice and presence in the organization was the biggest gain from unionizing.

Analysis

The experiences of HCS teachers, although unique, are part of a larger neoliberal movement that has transformed public education from a government service to a profit-making good (Davies & Bansel, 2007). Schools, like other public services, which were once essential to the collective well-being of the country, are now managed like any other private business. In addition, neoliberalism also blames unions and its large bureaucracies for spending money pleasing teachers rather than meeting the needs of families (Chubb & Moe, 1990). In the last 20 years, the ideals of neoliberalism have fueled a system where deregulated charter schools expand and public entities such as unions come under attack.

Even though charter schools were founded as places where autonomy and innovation flourish, the flexibility granted to charter school operators has not automatically been extended to teachers (Johnson & Landman, 2000). Because the power in charter schools goes to the governing board and to the principals, teachers have no guarantees about the nature of their workplace and whether it would be fair, responsive, and supportive (Johnson & Landman, 2000). In addition, when teachers have questioned their working conditions, it has fueled a suspicion regarding the teachers' loyalty to the organization (Johnson & Landman, 2000). School administrators, who are also employees of the board, take the responsibility to pressure teachers into maintaining their loyalty to the schools to the point where some teachers have given up their rights to unionize altogether (Sawchuck, 2009). Furthermore, because charter schools are managed by a typically conservative, business-oriented, non-educational, and non-elected governing board, they are wary of teacher unionization, seeing them as an external third-party entity (Gyurko, 2008). Charter schools have become a popular answer to reform movements seeking accountability, yet they have not shown that their environments are supportive to teachers.

Conclusion

This chapter provides a glimpse into the experiences of teachers within one charter school organization. Teachers described an environment where they worked alongside school leaders and families. Yet when they realized they had no say in their working conditions, they decided to unionize. The unionization efforts led to broken relationships with their school leaders and a contentious 18-month contract negotiation process against their governing board. Teachers found that their governing board had no desire to work with teachers, deeming them a "third party." Despite the damaged relationships, the union gained a voice and presence in the organization. It has been over 20 years since the charter school movement began and there is a need to look at the impact that this choice movement has on all stakeholders, including teachers and unions. Understanding the effects of charter schools on their employees is crucial if charter schools are determined to be a viable form of reform.

References

Blume, H. (2009, February 5). Teachers union organizes celebrated charter school. *Los Angeles Times*. Retrieved from http://latimesblogs.latimes.com/lanow/2009/02/teachers-union.html

Chubb, J. E., & Moe, T. M. (1990). *Politics, markets, and America's schools*. Washington, DC: The Brookings Institution Press.

Cohen, R. M. (2015, Summer). When charters go union. *The American Prospect*, 26(2). Retrieved from http://prospect.org/article/when-charters-go-union

Davies, B., & Bansel, P. (2007). Neoliberalism and education. *International Journal of Qualitative Studies in Education*, 20(3), 247–259. doi: 10.1080?0951839070 1281751

Guba, E. G., & Lincoln, Y. S. (1981). *Effective evaluation: Improving the usefulness of evaluation results through responsive and naturalistic approaches*. San Francisco, CA: Jossey-Bass.

Gyurko, J. (2008). The grinding battle with circumstance: Charter schools and the potential of school-based collective bargaining. Retrieved from http://www.ncspe.org/publications_files/OP152.pdf

Hatch, J. A. (2002). *Doing qualitative research in education settings.* Albany, NY: State University of New York Press.
Johnson, S. M., & Landman, J. (2000). "Sometimes bureaucracy has its charms": The working conditions of teachers in deregulated schools. *Teachers College Record, 102*(1), 85–124.
Kahlenberg, R. D. (2007). *Tough liberal: Albert Shanker and the battles over schools, unions, race and democracy.* New York, NY: Columbia University Press.
Kerchner, C. T., Menefee-Libey, D. J, Mulfinger, L. S., & Clayton, S. E. (2008). *Learning from L.A.: Institutional change in American public education.* Cambridge, MA: Harvard Education Press.
Lincoln, Y. S., & Guba, E. G. (1986). But is it rigorous? Trustworthiness and authenticity in naturalistic evaluation. In D. D. Williams (Ed.), *Naturalistic evaluation* (pp. 73–84). San Francisco, CA: Jossey-Bass.
Malin, M. H., & Kerchner, C. T. (2006). Charter schools and collective bargaining: Compatible marriage or illegitimate relationship? *Harvard Journal of Law and Public Policy, 30*(3), 885–938.
Malloy, C. L., & Wohlstetter, P. (2003). Working conditions in charter schools: What's the appeal for teachers? *Education and Urban Society, 35*(2), 219–241. doi:10.1177/0013124502239393
Margolis, J. (2005). "Every day I spin these plates": A case study of teachers amidst the charter phenomenon. *Educational Foundations, 19*(1/2), 87–111.
Montano, E. (2012). *Becoming unionized in a charter school: How charter school teachers navigate the culture of choice* (Doctoral dissertation). Retrieved from ProQuest Dissertations and Theses. (Accession Order No. AAT 3540408)
Montano, E. (2015). Becoming unionized in a charter school: Teacher experiences and the promise of choice. *Equity and Excellence in Education, 48*(1), 87–104. doi:10.1080/10665684.2015.991220
National Commission on Excellence in Education. (1983). *A nation at risk: The imperative for educational reform.* Washington, DC: U.S. Government Printing Office.
NewSchools Venture Fund. (2007). *Green dot public schools: Working in a union environment.* San Francisco, CA: NewSchools Venture Fund. Retrieved from www.newschools.org/files/GreenDotUnionCase.pdf
Ravitch, D. (2010). *The death and life of the great American school system: How testing and choice are undermining education.* New York, NY: Basic Books.
Sawchuck, S. (2009, June 10). Unions set sights on high-profile charter-network schools. *Education Week, 28*(33), 14–15.
Wells, A. S., Artiles, L., Carnochan, S., Cooper, C. W., Grutzik, C., Holme, J. J., & Vasudeva, A. (1998). Beyond the rhetoric of charter school reform: A study of ten California school districts. *UCLA Charter School Study.* Los Angeles, CA.

5 Discursive Violence and Economic Retrenchment

Chartering the Sacrifice of Black Educators in Post-Katrina New Orleans

Kevin Lawrence Henry, Jr.

A Prelude: Un-Buried Distortions

The year 2005 was painful. The residuals of that humid, sunny fall day when the levees broke and life as Joyce knew it was going to change reeked of old shrimp heads and oyster shells. The effects of the storm were present, a year and a half later; everyone knew it was going to take time to rebuild. The questions were, "how?" and "who?" The urgency of change and the vehemence of arrogance, of greed pillaged the atmosphere, impregnating it with a new (re)form and arrested or evacuated—disposed to be sure— anyone who uttered a murmur of resistance. It was clear, by now, that the water was easiest to recede, faster than injustice and certainly with more momentum than ideology.

Joyce's bedroom was lavender inspired. The lilac accent wall was her favorite. It adored all the memories she chose not to forget. She had just finished grading her students' papers and sat at the edge of the bed watching the 10 o'clock news. The flicker of the Saint Anthony candle was diminishing. She was practically asleep as the tease of the third story on the Recovery School District (RSD) crept into her subconscious, waking her.

With perspicuity, the anchor came on and said, "New news tonight on the Recovery School District's efforts to improve education." The screen then cut to a press conference that Superintendent Friedman, who came from Chicago Public Schools, had held earlier that day. As Joyce sat up, impatient to hear the new pronouncement from her boss and recalling that he could pretty much pronounce anything at this point—no one could really challenge him—she listened. "Before the hurricane, public schools here were uncontrollable, ill performing and ill preparing our students," he said. "There was very limited accountability and parental participation was needed. Now we have created a system of schools that offers choice to parents and holds us truly accountable. Today, I would like to share with you that we are authorizing a new charter school that will be staffed with the best and brightest educators that a child can have."

Joyce instantly turned off her television, tired of the political rhetoric, tired of the backhanded remarks and cavalier disregard that politicians, policy makers, and the media held for her as a 10th grade English teacher. "This shit is just disrespectful," Joyce pronounced. She picked up her cell phone to call her friend Janice, who taught geometry at the same school as she.

The phone rang. Janice picked up. And before Joyce could even say hello, Janice, like any best friend, had the precise words to say before they needed to be said.

"Girl, I'm so tired of these people. They really act like we *were* and *are* incapable of teaching these babies."

"Jay," Joyce said, "I know. I wonder what exactly was the point in RE-hiring us."

"They couldn't fire *all* of us Joyce."

"I know. It's just not right I tell you. They got all these new, *white*, ivy-leagued teachers who don't know what in da hell to do! Those children would lose their minds if some of us veterans weren't there—well, the few of us that are left!"

"Jay, you don't have to tell me. I know that's right. And *what* did he mean by accountability? I was always accountable to the most important people—parents and the children."

"Say it!" Janice blurted out.

"I mean. I taught and teach hard! I always saw and see my future in those children. So, I have no other option. No other." Joyce was becoming to get flustered with the dissonance between what she knew and did and what *they* said.

"I still just don't understand why they make us seem like the enemy, Joyce. It's like anyone who taught in a public school before the storm and wasn't from Harvard or Yale had a negative effect on the children's well-being."

Solemnly, Joyce said, "Talk about it, girl."

"This is so draining," Janice remarked. "And what's even sadder, they say all of this about 'reform' and nothing has gotten better, even with *their* new teachers. We're the ones holding the schools."

They had both become undone and the exasperation in their voices could only be subdued by changing the subject.

"Well, enough of that. What are you doing?" Janice inquired.

"Child," Joyce said, "I'm about to go and watch last week's episode of *Scandal* and hit the sack."

"Well, tell that man of yours he owes me and you a home-cooked meal. He kept talking smack during the game and his team left much to be desired." The laughter in Janice's voice was infectious.

"Yes, I'll tell him. You know he don't know a thing about sports."

"Clearly!"

"I'll see you tomorrow morning girl," said Janice.

With a smile in her voice Joyce excitedly proclaimed, "See you Jay!"

Introduction

> "If you are silent about your pain, they'll kill you and say you enjoyed it."
>
> —Zora Neale Hurston

The dominant narratives surrounding charter schools generally, and charters in New Orleans, specifically, caters to neoliberal ventriloquisms that offer empty promises of achievement, equity, justice, and democratic localism (Buras, 2014; Dixson, Royal, & Henry, 2014; Fabricant & Fine, 2012; Lipman, 2011). These narratives abstract, suppress, and conceal the harsh realities and protracted suffering—the le petite misère that Bourdieu (1999) explores—that students and teachers experience in these spaces (Dumas, 2014). And of course, while there are some charter schools that do provide an emancipatory, culturally relevant education, those schools are few and far between (Rofes & Stulberg, 2004; Stulberg, 2008). Hegemonic discourses about the "success" of charter schools buoy the institutional arrangements that attempt to both silence and mute the voices and perspectives of those on the margins. These are often voices of dissent. This chapter is a humble attempt to illuminate the everyday realities of African American educators in charter schools in post-Katrina New Orleans, offering their voices as counter to the narratives of dominance. In fact, the opening "fictional" chronicle of Joyce and Janice is an attempt to do such, providing a synoptic snapshot of the contents of this chapter. I use this counter-story to illustrate and underscore deeper racial animus and to, as Gloria Ladson-Billings (2013) urged, "advance larger concerns or help us understand how law or policy is operating" (p. 42). The aforementioned counter-story is an attempt to not be silent about racialized pain that is voiced by African American educators in post-Katrina New Orleans.

The voices of African American educators such as "Joyce and Janice" are significant in as much as they provide us with a "perspective advantage" and "minority criticism" from which to disenchant discourses and construct alternate epistemes that attempt to reconstitute the discursive cartographies and material realties that map onto, shape, and organize educational policy and schools (Ladson-Billings, 2000; Tillman, 2006; Wynter, 1992). Indeed, the perspectives of African American educators are often muted with respect to policy construction and implementation, with both researchers and policy makers, as Michael Dumas (2014) notes, "less concerned with how policy is lived and too often suffered" (p. 2).

African American educators have long been used as hosts for parasitic policies, in the name of justice, that sacrifice their being in service to camouflaged restructurings of the state. One need not look further than *Brown v. Board of Education* (1954) to realize the precarious positions of the African American educator in educational reform history. Scholars have documented that African American educators in the South were largely displaced after schools were desegregated (Fultz, 2004; Horsford, 2011; Tillman, 2004). Michael Fultz (2004) goes on to note, "displacement became the phase which subsumed the many policies and practices ... which sought to undermine the employment and authority of African American school staff: dismissals, demotions, forced resignations, 'nonhiring,' token promotions, reduced salaries, diminished responsibilities," and coercion in their teaching with respect to subject matter and grade (p. 14). The loss of Black educators was not only an attack on the pedagogical techniques and curricular subversions of Black teachers, but also an issue of labor and wealth accumulation. Even in northern locations prior to *Brown*, the Black teacher was an important figure for understanding and indexing civil rights. Jack Dougherty's (2004) historical work illustrated the ways various stakeholder groups, such as the Urban League in Milwaukee, worked to recruit and retain more Black teachers. Understanding that Black teachers are critical to our conceptualizations of justice in schools, but also beyond the school, those committed to justice-centered reforms should consider not only what impact these reforms have on students, but also on the "absent presence" embedded in these reforms: the teachers.

While Black educators have been central figures in reform, much of the current research on charter school reform has focused on the mixed to lesser academic gains of charter schools (Barr, Sadovnik, & Visconti, 2006; Bettinger, 2005; CREDO, 2013; Gleason, Clark, Tuttle, & Dwoyer, 2010; Ladd & Bifulco, 2004). There is a generous amount of research that shows that charter schools, when compared to their traditional public school counterparts, have fewer enrolled students that are English language learners and are in special education (Buckley & Sattin-Bajaj, 2010; Darling-Hammond, 2010; de la Torre & Gwynne, 2009; Frankenberg & Lee, 2003; Garcia, 2008; Wells, 2009). Additionally, while the rhetoric around charter schools bespeaks of innovation, extensive evidence of such innovation has yet to been seen. In fact, we see teachers with less experience, qualifications, and receiving lesser pay, all of which contribute to higher teacher turnover in these spaces (Barr et al., 2006; Bettinger, 2005; Darling-Hammond, 2010; Henig, 2008; Wells, 2009; Zimmer & Buddin, 2009).

As such, this chapter aims to center the Black teacher in charter school reform, situating them within the nexus of power relations that organize schooling policy and practices. I focus on the New Orleans case, as New Orleans is the most dramatic instance of charter school takeover, with the entirety of the district being comprised of charter schools. New Orleans is also significant because other districts have sought to emulate the "grand experiment." I argue that the proliferation and production of charter schools in New Orleans coincided with the discursive marginalization of Black educators and thus the retrenchment of Black labor rights. Said another way, Black teachers were sacrificed and used to lubricate the production of charter schools in New Orleans.

I will first provide an overview of the state takeover of New Orleans public schools. Then, I provide illustrations of the negative constructions of Black teachers—parasitic discourses that eat away at the humanity of Black teachers. These discourses create the necessary conflict and crisis to be resolved via neoliberal charter school reform. The narratives of African American veteran educators are next brought to bear to counter the master narrative. I then situate charter schools in the larger political economy. Ultimately, this analysis is in sharp contrast to the majoritarian narrative of New Orleans charter school reform, which argues that New Orleans is the model to follow for urban school reform and more specifically, the utilization of charter schools and teacher union dismemberment as the sine qua non of educational reform.

School Reform in the City That Care Forgot

Perhaps there is no place that best illuminates and illustrates market approaches in the form of charter schools than New Orleans. New Orleans as a site of school reform is both the "grand experiment" of educational restructuring and charter school reform as well as the miner's canary, cautioning us of the dangers of and pitfalls in neoliberal, market-based approaches to reform. On August 29, 2005, Hurricane Katrina's violent winds, which reached upwards of 127 miles per hour, slammed into New Orleans with unforgiving force and uncertain outcomes. As the hurricane left the city, the subsequent flooding practically decimated New Orleans and opened the floodgates for a reshaping of public schooling in New Orleans and, arguably, the United States writ large (Buras, 2007, 2012; Dixson, 2011; Dixson et al., 2014; Ladson-Billings, 2006; Lewis, 2010).

In this sense, New Orleans is the model of corporatist, market-based school reform. The progeny of *A Nation at Risk* and *No Child Left Behind*, New Orleans school reform due to the natural and man-made disaster of Hurricane Katrina provided neoliberals a host space for policy implementation. Some 40 years prior to Hurricane Katrina, the early architect of neoliberalism Milton Friedman (1962) bespoke of the need for crisis and disaster, stating that "only a crisis—actual or perceived—produces real change" (ix). The crisis of Hurricane Katrina lubricated policies that "rolled back" redistributive polices and institutions and "rolled out" capital accumulation markets to "remedy" such crises (Barnett, 2010; Harvey, 2005; Lipman, 2011). In New Orleans, this has taken root and form in the shrinkage of traditional school boards, thereby further removing democratic participation from youth, parents, and communities of color, the rise of venture philanthropy, the mass firing of African American educators, the legislative dissolving and dismemberment of the teachers union and collective bargaining, and the proliferation and expansion of charter schools (Buras, 2014; Dixson et al., 2014; Sondal, 2013). Significantly, New Orleans is the *first* entirely charter school district in the United States (Greenblatt, 2014; Kamenetz, 2014).

As Ladson-Billings (2006) clarified for us, "[Hurricane] Katrina reminds us that race still matters, property rights trump human rights and the intersections of race and property creates an analytic tool through which we can understand inequality" (p.vi). The significance of the New Orleans case is beyond the notions of its exceptionality that often surround it, but rather toward the properties and powers that aim to situate New Orleans as the norm, exemplar, and model. Hurricane Katrina provided the rational for racialized neoliberal restructuring in the form of disaster capitalism, which further muted the already marginalized voices of the Black community (Dyson, 2006; Klein, 2007), thus allowing for the enshrining of the current system.

In the New Orleans case, the ideological commitment to market approaches was buttressed by economic support and legislative policies. This can be seen, for instance, in the federal approach that helped to facilitate the state policy. Within a month after Hurricane Katrina, then-Secretary of Education under the Bush administration Margaret Spellings released federal funds to the tune of nearly $20 million dollars to help build charter schools (Cook & Dixson, 2013; Newmark & De Rugy, 2006), with no equivalency offered to traditional public schools. These funds could be categorized as "force" or "coercion." It set the stage for the primacy of charter schools in restructuring efforts.

Shortly after came the advent of executive fiats from Louisiana Governor Kathleen Blanco. Executive Orders 58 and 79 were central to the production of charter schools and the reengineering of democracy in post-Katrina New Orleans education. Executive Orders 58 and 79 subsequently eliminated stipulations that required parties desiring to operate conversion charter schools—charter schools that would take over existing public schools—to consult, collaborate, and obtain votes of approval from parents, faculty, and staff before a conversion into a charter school could take place; fiduciary responsibility and duty to parties impacted was constructed as juridically superfluous. These executive orders annihilated provisions that would ensure that charter schools remained democratic and responsive to the desires of those who would be most affected: students, parents, and educators. The initial charter school legislation was more in line with charter schools being sites of innovation and experimentation based on the collective interests, wisdom, and desires of veteran educators and communities, not venture philanthropists and corporations (Scott, 2009). Executive Orders 58 and 79 changed the charter school laws in the state to be more amendable to the creation of charter schools aligned with the interests of elite whites (Buras, 2012).

One month later, in November, Blanco held a special legislative session to put the final nail in the coffin of public schools in New Orleans. During this session, the passage of Legislative Act 35 (Act 35), which reconstituted the definition of a "failing" school and placed it in the state created-and-run RSD, took place. This legislatively contrived definition of failure shifted from the state cut-off score of 60 to 87.4. This nearly 30-point increase allowed for more schools in New Orleans to be subsumed under the Recovery School District. In fact, Act 35 enabled 107 schools to be included in the RSD's dossier. Prior to the shift in the definition of failing schools, the RSD operated only five schools in New Orleans. It is crucial to note that these legislative mandates took place while the African American residents of New Orleans were displaced due to the devastation of Hurricane Katrina. Twelve out of the fifteen Orleans Parish state legislators voted against the state takeover (Cook & Dixson, 2013). The policy approaches to school reform in New Orleans can best be understood as the shifting away of local, democratic autonomy in the name of market-based autonomy.

What is more, in the midst of the political maneuverings that created the chartering of traditional public schools in New Orleans, the overwhelmingly African American veteran teaching force was fired en mass. In November 2005, nearly 7,500 teachers and other professionals were notified that they were to be terminated with the loss of their health insurance. This firing marked one of the largest displacements of African American educators since *Brown v. Board of Education*. This mass firing significantly shifted the demographics of the teaching force in New Orleans. The demographics suggest that the majority African American teaching force, representing 73% of the teaching population pre-Katrina, was reduced by 20% in post-Katrina estimates. Moreover, while the number of African American teachers has been reduced, due to the chartering of New Orleans, one must also consider that present-day demographics are also infused with non-veteran African American teachers. That is it say, the number of veteran, unionized African American teachers has decreased significantly in post-Katrina New Orleans education reform and includes teachers alternatively placed via Teach for America (TFA) and teachNOLA. Pre-Katrina data illustrates that during the 2004–2005 academic year, less than 20% of the teaching force had less than three years of teaching experience. By the 2007–2008 academic year, over 50% of the teachers in New Orleans had less than three years of teaching experience (Dixson et al., 2014). As Buras (2012) noted, "Black veteran teachers possess intimate knowledge of the city's history, its culture, and its communities" (p. 179). This shift in teaching demographics changes the cultural and heritage knowledge of school personnel. This shift also makes it more difficult—not impossible—to engage in culturally relevant and responsive teaching.

While African American teachers were fired en mass, without due process, this firing created a necessary hole to be filled. To add insult to injury, teachers were recruited from out of state to fill this "void." Black teachers were replaced by overwhelmingly novice, Teach for America educators and other alternative placement initiatives. This, in reality, was an effective dismemberment of a powerful, Black union; this had economic consequences for African American teachers in New Orleans. By replacing veteran African American educators with novice, young, white educators who, essentially, serve in temporary positions—two-year contracts—issues of tenure, retirement, salary, and health care were nonessential to the rebuilding of public schools. While lower courts found that teachers in New Orleans had been wrongfully terminated, the Louisiana Supreme Court found in *Oliver v. Orleans Parish School Board et al.* (2014) that teachers in New Orleans had no "right" to return to their jobs and that teachers' due process rights were not violated. The court's ruling solidified the disposability of Black teachers and their labor, their lack of property rights, and the hegemonic, privileging nature of whiteness. Neoliberal charter schools were implicated in this process as many proactively sought to hire teachers outside of Black New Orleans via alternative programs (Buras, 2014). Let us now move to explore how the constructions of Black teachers by neoliberal charter advocates work to make possible the retrenchment of Black teachers' labor interests.

Constructing the Black Teacher: Discourses of White Abjectorship

Black teachers in New Orleans were subtly constructed as the abject other in a purposeful 'slip of the tongue.' This construction allowed discursive maneuverings to unfold into material realities. That is to say, simply, that constructing African American teachers as void, criminal, and lazy allowed for the siphoning of their rights. It is critical to understand the racial dynamics underplay in these particular constructions. Race as a signifier has power beyond the symbol. As Bonilla Silva (1997) reminds us, 'race' serves as a classificatory system and aids in reproducing and conserving inequitable social positions, relations, structures, and outcomes. By classifying teachers as abject, charter school reformers were able to deflect from their political machinations and create the necessary crisis of confidence.

The actions of reformers can be considered as part of *white abjectorship*. White abjectorship is embedded in Western regimes of truth. It is the way whiteness works to devalue, debase, and dispossess blackness for its own gain and profit. To take white abjectorship to its logical extent, it is the constituting of blackness as un-human. I will quote Broeck (2014) at length; she explores white abjectorship during the Enlightenment era. Broeck notes:

> To come into being, the European subject needed its underside, as it were: the crucially integral but invisible part of the human has been his/her abject, created in the European mind by way of racialized thingification: the African enslaved, an un-human species . . . The free human citizen of Europe gained . . . his (and eventually her) destiny by the creation of a mental, physical, political, and social borders around the free human, which was marked and maintained by the existence of the Black/slave . . . this thing species was structurally severed from human subjectivity, forcefully submitted to white use and benefit as laboring commodity . . . .
> (pp. 118–119)

Broeck reminds us that the construction of blackness is intimately tied to the construction of whiteness. The production of the abject black is needed for the "healthy" constitution of white identity and thus various white privileges. Whiteness creates fictions of race to maintain white supremacy (Harris, 1993; Martinot, 2010). And importantly, whiteness uses blackness to fund itself. Its parasitic appetite feasts on blackness as a way to maintain its might and survival (Woodard, 2014). White abjectorship is most clearly illustrated in charter school reform discourses surrounding African American teachers in New Orleans.

Ms. Charles, an African American veteran educator with over 30 years of teaching experience, commented, "I felt ashamed for feeling shamed. That shame they tried to put on us. I was starting to absorb that." Ms. Charles's words bespoke some of the sentiments many African American veteran educators held after the mass firing and public shaming of them. Negative constructions of Black educators in New Orleans deployed shame as a mode for not only garnering public support for the firing of educators, but also as a way to give "reason" to an unreasonable assault.

In an interview with PBS News Hour, James (Jimmy) Farenholtz, a former Orleans Parish school board member, and Bill Roberti and Sajan George of the New York firm Alvarez and Marsal, who handled the pre-Katrina turnaround of Orleans Parish schools, constructed the pre-Katrina school system as in need of the salvific grace of charter school reform.

Farenholtz: "Fraud, corruption, contract scams, flat-out-theft, people walking out with laptops, **anything you can imagine**. Any way you could steal, **they** were doing it."

Roberti: "Just years and years and years of **abuse**, and of people just doing what they wanted to do. I mean there was—there was **no discipline**."

George: "We had a person that has been on paid leave for 35 years. I joked with somebody, do we send them, you know, like a silver anniversary card? Thank you for 35 years of **non-service**? We had documented cases of people that were putting in 50 hours of overtime a week, 50 hours a week, every week of the year, including Christmas."

Taken together, these parasitic narratives negatively construct Orleans Parish schools and more precisely, the individuals within them, as menacing. Tacitly embedded within these narratives are dog-whistle politics that propel notions of black inferiority and criminality. Farenholtz's comments give the "necessary" allusion to the sinisterness of blackness. It tells a single narrative about African American teachers, painting them as serial offenders. Both Roberti's and George's statements, too, offer a glimpse into white abjector rationalities. These narratives evoke the always-ready notions of black savagery and shiftlessness. According to the dominant narratives, one might assume that all of the issues of public education can be collapsed into the figure of the black teacher. Deeply entwined and entrenched racism is removed from the conversation, while African American employees are seen as *the* problem. They are constructed as the abject.

The figure of the abject, according to Kristeva (1982), is that "which disturbs identity, system, order . . . what does not respect borders, positions, rules" (p.4). The overwhelmingly African American workforce is projected as incapable of adhering to the professional standards necessary for a "functioning" system. By constructing and classifying New Orleans educators as the abject other, the necessary conflict and crisis arises to be resolved via neoliberal charter school reform. One need not forget that the true chaos and crisis of structural racism is never addressed. These abjected, debased teachers and staff begin to stand in for the chaos that needs to be targeted and fixed, the 'crisis' of Hurricane Katrina and the "criminal" majority. The Black Orleans Parish staff were sacrificed and from that sacrifice made possible the introduction of neoliberal policies. (Barnett, 2010; Harvey, 2005; Lipman, 2011). These teachers were constructed to represent a pre-existing crisis and chaos that could be expunged via their removal. Farenholtz, again, makes the necessary historical, discursive linkage, alluding to these Black women's criminality and "dependency." Farenholtz states,

> I don't think you are going to see it, the 'old okey doke,' as a friend of mine used to say. Some of **those people aren't coming back**. The light's on them; **they can't do** the things they **used** to do with the kind of oversight that we have now.

The extermination of these teachers marks the dawn of a new day of reform. Farenholtz's statement sheds light on white abjectorship rationalities that debase African American educators. There is a presumed level of accountability, fairness, and justice that is already built into the restructuring of New Orleans via neoliberal charter schools. The success of neoliberal charter schools hinges, in part, on the "personnel." This "successful" personnel is made possible by the erasure and dismissal of the African American teacher—the abject other.

These teachers were constructed to be a symbol for bureaucratic malfeasance, and the projected protector of such malfeasance was the teachers' union. There is no need to protect the abject other, as the abject other is disposable in Western regimes of truth. As such, the shrinkage and hollowing of the teachers' union, which provided various hard-earned civil rights labor-related securities and protections, was an effect of the mass firing of the overwhelmingly African American female teaching population and the proliferation of charter schools. The majority African American workforce was signified as a population that was a "special problem in the gesture toward the interests of the whole" (Popkewitz, 2006, p. 123). As such, the constructed reformation of education and thus New Orleans literally comes at the expense of Black women educators.

Their voices tell a story of pain, frustration, and sacrifice with respect to charter schools in New Orleans. Ultimately, their perspectives provide a counter-narrative to white abjectorship logic and performances that claim, as Neerav Kingsland, former CEO of New Schools for New Orleans, a neoliberal charter incubator organization, stated, "the New Orleans story is really one of transferring power back to educators and parents" (Landrieu, 2012). These educators' narratives suggest, if anything, that power has been removed from them.

From Discursive Constructions to Material Realities, or When Life Becomes the Things You Teach

Solórzano and Yosso (2002) remind us that counter-stories come in various types and styles with varying purposes. One purpose of the counter-story is to challenge the taken-for-granted assumptions, perspectives, and systems of reasoning of those in power. Counter-stories are a mechanism to puncture and deflate narcissistic narratives of dominance. In the case of the African American veteran educators I have interviewed, their narratives of post-Katrina charter reform highlight the more insidious effect these reforms have had on teachers.

One veteran educator, Ms. Charles, provides us with what she understands to be the deeper rationale behind the restructuring of New Orleans public schools. Ms. Charles states, "It was a decision made hastily to wipe all the schools out because they knew we had a good union and that was a good way to get rid of it." For Ms. Charles, there exists a deep connection between the hostile state takeover of schools, their transmogrification into charter schools, and the elimination/weakening of the teachers union. By changing the governance and organizational structure of schools to the status of charter, charter school operators would no longer be required to negotiate or consider union-based policies. What this in effect means is that particular protections and quality of life standards were no longer available to educators. Charter school operators would be able to create schools as they pleased, with very little consideration of the livelihoods of their employees.

The below narratives of teachers reveal, contrary to the dominant narrative that positions charter takeover as ideal, that within these systems, teachers' labor rights are often curtailed significantly—eaten away.

> When Katrina came, we knew that the union we were under had been busted. And they [white power brokers] were glad to see that happen. They [white power brokers] took it away and when that happened (long pause) we had to come back and be interviewed again; we had to reapply for *our* jobs. I thought that was the most asinine thing I had ever heard

of. That really lowered my dignity. I vowed that I would not do that. We were under contract. We [the teachers at the school] had been successful. We were a very good school . . . our school always made it in the third or fourth spot in the city. We had some of the highest test scores. We were a Blue Ribbon school [tone in her voice changes, slightly demure, saddened]. I just couldn't see reapplying for my job. And I knew without a union what would happen under him [principal who was racist].

—Ms. Charles

Child, they didn't even want us to talk about salary issues. Either you were with it or not. No, negotiations, no asking about salaries of other teachers. You could get fired for that. It was like I was in *Animal Farm* or *Lord of the Flies* [rolls her eyes in frustration]. It was like being on a deserted island with folks who didn't know what they were doing . . . They were taking advantage of us. Folks were changing the rules. It was a mess.

—Ms. Battiste

Both of the narratives from these veteran, African American educators outline the contours of inequitable power relations. Ms. Charles and Ms. Battiste highlight the resulting chaos of the chartering of New Orleans schools and the ways in which disrespect manifests in these schools. We see in Ms. Charles's narrative how the abject other is debased. By voiding the union contract with schools and forcing teachers to reapply for jobs that were theirs prior to the catastrophic hurricane, Ms. Charles felt it was a way to demean and humiliate her. This, as we know, is not a new tactic of those in power. For Ms. Charles, the teachers union provided her various protections from a principal who she understood as tacitly racist. Ms. Charles later commented that as African American teachers in her former school, they had to fight for equity in hiring, promotions, and curriculum. Ms. Charles relays a story of what took place once the school reopened post-Katrina without the union:

[An] incident [occurred] when they were hiring what they call a 'master teacher' and some of these people had been in the school quite a many number of years who applied. A teacher applied to become a master teacher [master teachers monitored other teachers and evaluated them]. There was a particular Black teacher who had applied and she was *very* good. And all of the four lead teacher positions . . . he decided [the principal] would go to whites. Some of the whites were people who had just walked into the school . . . These are the types of things that were swept under the rug.

Becoming a master teacher provided teachers with more power to influence the culture of schools organizationally and pedagogically, as well as provided teachers with an increased salary. Ms. Charles's comments about the hiring of the all-white 'master teachers' that had inferior teaching experience and skill highlights the capricious hiring practices and deeper issues of institutional racism that have a bearing on not just issues of labor, but also on students' learning. What can be essentially deduced from Ms. Charles's comments is that Black teachers' upward mobility was stifled in this school due to union protections being weakened via white dominance run amuck.

Ms. Charles's comments corroborate with Ms. Battiste's comments. Ms. Charles did not want to return to her former school because she believed that the principal would create a hostile working environment without union protections. She believed he would be less equitable in his practices without the union oversight and protections. Ms. Battiste's comments illustrate the chaotic environment inside her charter school and the ways in which power crystallized for those in authority. As a middle school English educator, Ms. Battiste alludes to two classic texts—*Animal Farm* by George Orwell and *Lord of the Flies* by William Golding. Both of the dystopian texts illuminate how power, corruption, and deceit become normalized aspects of our social organization. Louise B. draws that connection to charter school reform in post-Katrina New Orleans. Most striking is the top-down, authoritarian nature of these organizations. Without the support and backing of the teachers union, labor issues for teachers were reduced to a simple market based dichotomy—work here or leave/"exit." The negotiatory protections teachers had prior to Katrina were washed away and replaced with practices of submission, compliance, and silencing.

Ms. Battiste goes on to note the devastating economic and emotional effect of the chartering of New Orleans schools and the effective elimination of collective bargaining. She states,

> After teaching in this system for over 20 years, I lost pretty much everything. Everything I earned, everything I worked for . . . all of my vestedness. Just lost. [pause] It was like the storm [Hurricane Katrina] hit me all over again. I still can't believe that. I mean thank God I was rehired—I know folks who weren't—so I guess . . . I mean . . . I know I'm fortunate. But, I came in making less than a first-year teacher from one of those private schools. I mean I just couldn't believe that. It was like a . . . like a slap in the face, humiliating. I never understood why they would do that us.

Ms. Battiste's reflection brings into sharp relief how the restructuring of New Orleans public schools into charters sacrificed the basic protections and hard-earned entitlements of the overwhelmingly African American teaching staff. Ms. Battiste's narrative highlights not only how some teachers were unable to return to work because of new hiring rationales that valued majority white, alternatively certified teachers associated with TFA or TeachNOLA, but also the realities of being "fortunate" to return to work. Those fortunate enough to be rehired had, in some instances, their dignity stripped and economic well-being reduced. With the dissolving of the collective bargaining agreement and the effective dismemberment of the teachers union, African American educators in New Orleans lost wealth in terms of both pay—either fired or never rehired or reduced pay—as well as having to pay higher insurance premiums. As Ms. Armstrong commented, "I wanted to go back to work in New Orleans, but it was just too expensive. My insurance premiums would have been really high with some of the charter schools."

These compacting issues left little room for economic justice and dignity for these teachers. The movement to create charter schools in New Orleans was made possible, in part, by the sacrificing of Black educators and their teachers union. These educator narratives speak back to majoritarian narratives about the success of the New Orleans reform. These educators' voices illuminate the retrenchment of their labor and economic rights.

Un-Concluding Thoughts for an Unending Nightmare

What I have attempted to do, thus far, is elucidate the 'hows' of school reform. I have attempted to illustrate how black teachers are constructed in various white abjector discourses and rationalities. I have also attempted to link these discursive constructions to the material realities of African American veteran educators, illuminating how they are situated in neoliberal charter reform, essentially, the effects of the age-old Du Boisian question, 'How does it feel to be a problem?' What I now want to do is explore the 'why' of these reforms. That is to say, the remainder of this chapter is dedicated to locating the abjection of African American educators and the retrenchment of their labor rights within larger forces of white domination and on topographies of stratification.

Veteran African American educators from New Orleans in the aftermath of Hurricane Katrina not only lost their homes, property, community, and sense of homeplace, but they also had to experience the additional parasitic policy assault against their being—ontological and economical feastings on and against them. It is crucial to understand that the debasing of and white abjectorship discourses on African American female educators, first, is rooted in a larger Western (il)logic about the intellectual and corporeal performances of Black people and Black women, specifically. Second, these racialized constructions provide a canvas to make legible the excising of African American women from the realities of humanity, toward their reconstitution as property and as libidinal-speculative material/commodities for capital accumulation. To be clear, Black women, historically and presently, have been understood as desirous sites for the reproduction of property and wealth for white patriarchal capitalism (Davis, 1981). In the case of African American veteran educators in New Orleans, their mass firing and reduction in salary and benefits is part of capitalism's austerity measures (Brewer, 2012).

The racialized-gendered assault on African American teachers and their union in New Orleans is a constitutive element of capitalism's restructuring. Because Blacks have historically been understood as laboring property, as "subpersons" as Charles Mills (1997) notes, "it is possible to get away with doing things to subpersons that one could not do to persons, because they do not have the same rights as persons" (p. 56). Such is the case for New Orleans educators. This discursive construction is intimately tied to the materiality of their existence. In this neoliberal period, Black labor is seen as less necessary for the operation of capitalism (Brewer, 2012; Gržinić, 2014). As such, this should be a red flag for all issues of labor, as the displacement of Black workers suggests a reworking of labor dynamics more generally. Here one can easily note the assault on teacher unions post-Katrina in cities such as Chicago, Philadelphia, Detroit, Washington, D.C., and next, I suspect, Atlanta—due to the Georgia legislature's desire to charter, becoming more like New Orleans.

Teachers and their unions are a central focus of neoliberal reform as they stand as a challenge to market-driven reform initiatives and larger neoliberal mandates. If the basic underlying principal of capitalism is profit for the "owners of the world," then inhibitors to profit must be weakened or eliminated. For neoliberal reform advocates, traditional/veteran teachers and their unions are one such obstacle. A core mechanism utilized by neoliberal reformers is that of accumulation by dispossession (Harvey, 2005; Lipman, 2011). Accumulation by dispossession is the feasting on, utilization of, and profiting from assets that were for one group by another more powerful group. As Brewer (2012) reminds us, there exists two major efforts at ensuring austerity and guaranteeing of profitable returns for market-driven, neoliberal reformers: cutting educational budgets and eliminating teachers unions. Obviously, due to space limitations, the former cannot be discussed in a chapter of this size. Yet, it is vitally important to understand that the mass firing, lessening of pay, higher insurance premiums, and loss of union protections all are part of larger processes of capital accumulation. By dispossessing teachers of their economic and labor rights, reformers are able to increase administrator salaries while simultaneously running schools "like businesses," offering investors and charter management organization profits and lower operational costs.

Yet, we must also be clear in our understanding that there is a specific racial dynamic underway with such initiatives. It not *just* about capitalism's efforts at restructuring and accumulation, but precisely capitalism's desire to restructure on the bridge of women of color's backs that is most insidious (Moraga & Anzaldúa, 1984), and white women's culpability and acquiesces in such efforts (Leonardo & Boas, 2013). As Leonardo and Boas (2013) remind us, "white women have done the work of [w]hite supremacy specific to their own place in the hierarchy, producing their own contradictions in the process" (p.315). Following the mass termination of African American veteran educators in New Orleans, white teachers affiliated with TFA were networked into the reform and seen as the salvific laboring personnel needed to bring about the New Orleans renaissance. While the largely African American female staff is constructed as criminal and experienced an amplified loss of wages and benefits, in fewer words, dispossessed, younger white women are offered those African American women's jobs and access to capital streams that once built black wealth. As a result, these parasitic policies rooted in white dominance aid in the reproduction and conservation of white supremacy. All of this is done in the name of reform and equity.

Coda

The African American educator, historically and presently, stands as an important figure for indexing issues of educational (in)justice. While African American educators' voices are often muted by those who maintain racialized hierarchies—either tacitly or explicitly, consciously or dysconsciously, but maintained nonetheless—African American educators' perspectives are instructive. In the case of New Orleans veteran educators, they were sacrificed by neoliberal charter reformers. Constructed as malefactors and then dispossessed, these educators became the standing symbol of bureaucratic inertia and pre-Katrina educational chaos, the abject. As such, their "toxicity" would need to be expunged and eliminated. However, their voices are like that of the canary in the mine (Guinier & Torres, 2003). Their critiques offer us incisive insights into the racial dynamics that operate in schools and educational policy. And while those in power often pathologize the canary, the canary warns all of us of ensuing danger, of the *true* toxicity—the structure, conditions, and atmosphere of the mine (Guinier & Torres, 2003).

Unfortunately, neither new nor unprecedented, the sacrificing of African American educators in New Orleans is part of a long history of using black bodies and labor, particularly female, as props for white profit accumulation and power solidification. Although such parasitic policies take veneers of neutrality and are heralded as promoting racial opportunity, they often reproduce and reinvent the violence of white dominance. The restructuring of New Orleans public schools into charter schools and in tandem the dismemberment of the majority African American teachers' union is part of a much larger neoliberal policy approach that advances the interests of elites.

I am reminded that we are perpetually, as Saidiya Hartman (2007) comments, haunted by the "afterlife of slavery." This afterlife—slavery's past in the present—is made manifest in the various forms of racial suffering and oppression that organizes our schools and society. The violence, dispossession, silencing, and foreclosing of upward mobility that has been enacted upon African American educators in New Orleans is yet another iteration of the afterlife of slavery. This perpetual haunting must be continually exorcized. The sacrifice of African American educators is one we must dare to know, yet one that we can no longer bear.

References

Barnett, C. (2010). Publics and markets: What's wrong with neoliberalism? In S. Smith, S. Marston, & J. P. Jones, III (Eds.), *The Sage handbook of social geographies* (pp. 269–296). London and New York: Sage.

Barr, J. M., Sadovnik, A. R., & Visconti, L. (2006). Charter schools and urban education improvement: A comparison of Newark's district and charter schools. *Urban Review, 36*(4), 291–312.

Bettinger, E. P. (2005). The effects of charter schools on charter students and public schools. *Economics of Education Review, 24*(2), 133–147.

Bonilla-Silva, E. (1997). Rethinking racism: Toward a structural interpretation. *American Sociological Review, 62*(3), 465–480.

Bourdieu, P. (Ed.). (1999). *The weight of the world: Social suffering in contemporary society.* Stanford, CA: Stanford University.

Brewer, R. M. (2012). 21st century capitalism, austerity, and black economic dispossession. *Souls: A Critical Journal of Black Politics, Culture, and Society, 14*(3–4), 227–239.

Broeck, S. (2014). Legacies of enslavism and white abjectorship. In S. Broeck & C. Junker (Eds.), *Postcoloniality-decoloniality-Black critique* (pp. 109–128). Frankfurt and New York: Campus Verlag.

Buckley, J., & Sattin-Bajaj, C. (2010). *Are ELL students underrepresented in charter schools?* New York: National Center for the Study of Privatization in Education.

Buras, K. L. (2007). Benign neglect? Drowning yellow buses, racism, and disinvestment in the city that bush forgot. In K. Saltman (Ed.), *Schooling and the politics of disaster* (pp. 103–122). New York: Routledge.

Buras, K. L. (2012). "It's all about the dollars": Charter schools, educational policy, and the racial market in New Orleans. In W.H. Watkins (Ed.), *The assault on public education: Confronting the politics of corporate school reform* (pp. 160–188). New York, NY: Teachers College Press.

Buras, K. L. (2014). *Charter schools, race, and urban space: Where the market meets grassroots resistance.* New York: Routledge.

Center for Research on Education Outcomes [CREDO]. (2013). *National charter school study.* Stanford, CA: Stanford University Press.

Cook, D. A., & Dixson, A. D. (2013). Writing critical race theory and method: A composite counterstory on the experiences of black teachers in New Orleans post-Katrina. *International Journal of Qualitative Studies in Education, 26*(10), 1238–1258.

Darling-Hammond, L. (2010). *The flat world and education: How America's commitment to equity will determine our future.* New York: Teachers College Press.

Davis, A. (1981). *Women, race, and class.* New York: Vintage Books.

De la Torre, M., & Gwynne, J. (2009). *When schools close: Effects on displaced students in Chicago public schools.* Chicago, IL: Consortium on Chicago School Research.

Dixson, A. D. (2011). Democracy now? Race, education and Black self-determination. *Teachers College Record, 113*(4), 811–830.

Dixson, A. D., Royal, C., & Henry, K. L., Jr. (2014). School reform and school choice. In H. R. Milner, IV & K. Lomotey (Eds.), *Handbook of urban education* (pp. 474–503). New York: Routledge.

Dougherty, J. (2004). *More than one struggle: The evolution of black school reform in Milwaukee.* Chapel Hill: University of North Carolina Press.

Dumas, M. J. (2014). "Losing an arm": Schooling as a site of Black suffering. *Race Ethnicity and Education, 17*(1), 1–29.

Dyson, M. E. (2006). *Come hell or high water: Hurricane Katrina and the color of disaster.* New York: Basic Civitas.

Fabricant, M., & Fine, M. (2012). *Charter schools and the corporate make over of public education: What's at stake?* New York: Teachers College Press.
Frankenberg, E., & Lee, C. (2003). Charter schools and race: A lost opportunity for integrated education. *Education Policy Analysis Archives, 11*(23). Retrieved from epaa.asu.edu/epaa/v11n32/.
Friedman, M. (1962). *Capitalism and freedom*. Chicago: University of Chicago.
Fultz, M. (2004). The displacement of Black educators post-Brown: An overview and analysis. *History of Education Quarterly, 44*(1), 11–45.
Garcia, D. R. (2008). Academic and racial segregation in charter schools: Do parents sort students into specialized charter schools? *Education and Urban Society, 40*(5), 590–612.
Gleason, P., Clark, M., Tuttle, C. C., & Dwoyer, E. (2010). *The evaluation of charter school impacts: Final report* (NCEE 2010–4029). Washington, DC: National Center for Education Evaluation and regional Assistance, Institute of Education Sciences, U.S. Department of Education.
Greenblatt, A. (2014). New Orleans district moves to an all-charter system. *National Public Radio*. Retrieved May 30, 2014, from http://www.npr.org/blogs/ed/2014/05/30/317374739/new-orleans-district-moves-to-an-all-charter-system
Gržinić, M. (2014). Europe's colonialism, decoloniality, and racism. In S. Broeck & C. Junker (Eds.), *Postcoloniality-decoloniality-Black critique* (pp. 129–144). Frankfurt and New York: Campus Verlag.
Guinier, L., & Torres, G. (2003). *The miner's canary: Enlisting race, resisting power, transforming democracy*. Cambridge, MA: Harvard University Press.
Harris, C. (1993). Whiteness as property. *Harvard Law Review, 106*(8), 1707–1791.
Hartman, S. (2007). *Lose your mother: A journey along the Atlantic slave route*. New York: Farrar, Straus, and Giroux.
Harvey, D. (2005). *A brief history of neoliberalism*. New York: Oxford University Press.
Henig, J. (2008). *Spin cycle, how research is used in policy debates: The case of charter schools*. New York: Russell Sage Foundation.
Horsford, S. D. (2011). *Learning in a burning house: Educational inequality, ideology, and (dis)integration*. New York: Teachers College Press.
Kamenetz, A. (2014). The end of neighborhood schools. *National Public Radio*. Retrieved September 2, 2014, from http://apps.npr.org/the-end-of-neighborhood-schools/
Klein, N. (2007). *The shock doctrine: The rise of disaster capitalism*. New York: Picador.
Kristeva, J. (1982). *Powers of horrors*. New York: Columbia University Press.
Ladd, H., & Bifulco, R. (2004). *The impacts of charter schools on student achievement: Evidence from North Carolina*. Working Paper SAN04–01. Durham, NC: Terry Sanford Institute of Public Policy, Duke University.
Ladson-Billings, G. (2000). Racialized discourses and ethnic epistemologies. In N. Denzin & Y. Lincoln (Eds.), *Handbook of qualitative research* (2nd ed., pp. 257–277). Thousand Oaks, CA: Sage Publications.
Ladson-Billings, G. (2006). They're trying to wash us away: The adolescence of critical race theory in education. In A. D. Dixson & C. Rousseau (Eds.), *Critical race theory in education: All God's children got a song* (pp. v–xiii). New York: Routledge.
Ladson-Billings, G. (2013). Critical race theory—What it is not! In M. Lynn & A. D. Dixson (Eds.), *Handbook of critical race theory in education* (pp. 34–47). New York: Routledge.
Landrieu, M. (2012). Landrieu hosts education panel and launches New Orleans-systole education reform: A guide for cities (press release). Retrieved February, 2013, from https://votesmart.org/public-statement/673302/landrieu-hosts-

education-panel-launches-new-orleans-style-education-reform-a-guide-for-cities#.VaPfvZNViko

Leonardo, Z., & Boas, E. (2013). Other kids' teachers: What children of color learn from white women and what this says about race, whiteness, and gender. In M. Lynn & A. D. Dixson (Eds.), *Handbook of critical race theory in education* (pp. 313–324). New York: Routledge.

Lewis, N. (2010). After Katrina: Poverty, politics, and performance in New Orleans public schools. *Loyola Journal of Public Interest Law, 11*(2), 285–318.

Lipman, P. (2011). *The new political economy of urban education: Neoliberalism, race, and the right to the city.* New York, NY: Routledge.

Martinot, S. (2010). *The machinery of whiteness: Studies in the structure of racialization.* Philadelphia, PA: Temple University Press.

Mills, C. W. (1997). *The racial contract.* Ithaca, NY: Cornell University Press.

Moraga, C., & Anzaldúa, G. (Eds.). (1984). *This bridge called my back: Writings by radical women of color.* New York: Kitchen Table, Women of Color Press.

Newmark, K. G., & DeRugy, V. (2006). Hope after Katrina: Will New Orleans become the new city of choice? *Education Next, 6*(4), 12–21.

Oliver v. Orleans Parish School Board et al. (2014).

Popkewitz, T. S. (2006). Hopes of progress and fears of the dangerous: Research, cultural theses, and planning different human kinds. In G. Ladson-Billings & W. F. Tate (Eds.), *Education research in the public interest: Social justice, action, and policy* (pp. 119–140). New York: Teachers College Press.

Rofes, E., & Stulberg, L. M. (Eds.). (2004). *The emancipatory promise of charter schools: Towards a progressive politics of school choice.* Albany, NY: SUNY.

Scott, J. (2009). The politics of venture philanthropy in charter school policy and advocacy. *Educational Policy, 23*(1), 106–136.

Solórzano, D. G., & Yosso, T. (2002). Critical race methodology: Counter-storytelling as an analytical framework for education research. *Qualitative Inquiry, 8*(1), 23–44.

Sondal, B. (2013). Raising citizens or raising test scores? TFA and "no excuse" charter schools in post-Katrina New Orleans. (Unpublished dissertation).

Stulberg, L. M. (2008). *Race, schools & hope: African Americans and school choice after Brown.* New York: Teachers College Press.

Tillman, L. C. (2004). (Un)intended consequences?: The impact of the Brown v. Board of Education decision on the employment status of Black educators. *Education and Urban Society, 36*(3), 280–303.

Tillman, L. C. (2006). Researching and writing from an African American perspective: Reflective notes on three research studies. *International Journal of Qualitative Studies in Education, 19*(3), 265–287.

Wells, A. S. (2009). The social context of charter schools: The changing nature of poverty and what it means for American education. In M. G. Springer, H. J. Walberg, M. Berends, & D. Ballou (Eds.), *Handbook of research on school choice* (pp. 155–179). Philadelphia: Lawrence Erlbaum.

Woodard, V. (2014). *The delectable Negro: Human consumption and homoeroticism within U.S. slave culture.* New York: New York University Press.

Wynter, S. (1992). *Do not call us "Negros": How "multicultural" textbooks perpetuate racism.* San Francisco: Aspire Books.

Zimmer, R., & Buddin, R. (2009). Is charter school competition in California improving the performance of traditional public schools? *Public Administration Review 69*(5), 831–845.

6 Struggling for Community and Equity in New Orleans Public Schools

Lessons from a First-Year Charter School

Joseph L. Boselovic

Introduction

Recent decades have seen an increase in the presence of white, middle-class constituencies in urban education reform in the United States. As more and more white families and well-educated young adults have chosen to live in cities, public discourse has begun to evolve around how this has or can affect public education (Carr, 2012; Monroe, 2014; Rogers, 2009; Smith, 2009). Similarly, this period shows a transition in the ways in which parent and family engagement in schooling is understood more broadly. Research on different aspects of this phenomenon has shown both risk and potential (Cucchiara, 2008, 2013a, 2013b; Cucchiara & Horvat, 2009, 2014; McGinn & Ben-Porath, 2014; Posey, 2012; Posey-Maddox, 2014; Reay et al., 2007). The risk for reproducing social and economic inequalities in new forms comes from the concern that the arrival of young, white professionals and middle-class families in cities signals gentrification, displacement, and the further marginalization of disadvantaged students both in and outside of school. The potential for these phenomena is grounded in the fact that more advocates for improving public education—advocates with the necessary social, economic, and symbolic capital—will increase educational funding (and improve city tax revenues) and bring about benefits for disadvantaged and privileged families alike.

In this chapter, I examine the phenomenon of parent engagement as it has developed in post-Katrina New Orleans and analyze this risk and potential in how the white middle class is engaging in the institution of public education. To do this, I focus specifically on the Homer A. Plessy Community School (henceforth referred to as the Plessy School). This charter school came into existence largely because of the persistent advocacy of white, middle-class parent and community advocates and arose in the downtown neighborhoods of the city—Bywater, Marigny, St. Roch, and St. Claude— that have been significantly gentrified in the years before and following Hurricane Katrina (Campanella, 2013).

I begin by exploring the changing role and significance of parent engagement in public schooling in order to frame the Plessy School as a case study. I complement this review with a brief overview of the local context in which the school has its roots. From there, I provide a portrayal of the movement to open the Plessy School. I rely primarily upon detailed notes from my experiences working at the Plessy School during its first year as well as research conducted with Brian Beabout (Beabout & Boselovic, 2015). In this portrayal, I also draw upon historical documents, newspaper reports, and census data. I then focus upon two central, interrelated contradictions evident in the Plessy case study: the creation of a charter school premised upon parent engagement that functioned to stratify parent engagement, and the creation of a charter school as an effort to create a new neighborhood public school in the context of a market-based education reform policy regime. I argue that the Plessy case study reveals a fundamentally new dynamic in parent engagement in public schooling. In concluding, I expand upon the findings of this case study to discuss the implications of white, middle-class engagement for education policy.

My goal in developing this argument is to contribute to the developing bodies of work around public education, the middle class, and charter schools within their socio-political context. While much of the literature around this kind of engagement focuses on an existing school, the dynamics of a new charter school provide a distinct and informative perspective. Additionally, while New Orleans is unique in light of the significant social and demographic changes following Hurricane Katrina, the city's stature as a focal point for many current education reform initiatives positions it as a beneficial case study to analyze the ways in which the white middle class is and could shape public education in the future.

Literature Review

Parent and Family Engagement and the Changing Relationship Between Schools and Families

The concept of parent and community engagement as it pertains to education focuses on the dynamics of how families interact with teachers, administrators, and school officials to influence the organizational and educational functioning of schools. In schools where engagement is an explicit goal, personal connections are formed between families and school staff as families take on specific, active roles in school life. Although the term engagement is often used interchangeably with the term 'involvement,' Warren, Hong, Rubin, and Uy (2009) argue that 'engagement' articulates a more active, nuanced role for families not only in the education of their children, but in school life more generally.

While the relationship between school and family life has been a perennial concern of education, more recent research suggests that seeking to bring together the "spheres of influence" (Epstein, 1995/2010) of school, family, and community can have substantial, positive impacts within each of these areas (Beabout & Boselovic, 2015; Cucchiara & Horvat, 2009; Epstein, 1995/2010; Mapp, 2003; Warren, 2005; Warren et al., 2009).

In her foundational framework of school, family, and community engagement, Epstein (1995/2010) highlights six types of caring that shape engagement: parenting, communicating, volunteering, learning at home, decision-making, and collaborating with community. These are rooted, she argues, in conceptions of trust and respect that serve as the root for positive educational change in students, families, teachers, and administrators alike at any kind of school.

The way in which each of these six steps of engagement do or do not take place can have substantial impacts on the experiences of students. In order for such forms of engagement to take place and to benefit students, schools must be deliberate in their engagement strategies. At the same time, students and families bring many different experiences, expectations, and communicative styles to schools (Horvat, Weininger, & Lareau, 2003; Lareau, 1987, 2003/2011; Lareau & Horvat, 1997). From the perspective that schools are sites of social and cultural reproduction, some communicative styles and forms of parent and family engagement are valued over others (Bourdieu, 1979/1984; Bourdieu & Passeron, 1977; Lareau, 2003/2011; MacLeod, 1997/2008). In consequence, while much of the language and rhetoric around diversity in schooling is progressive, it can also entail the privileging of more middle-class families over their peers with less social, cultural, and economic capital (Ben-Porath, 2012; Gofen & Blomqvist, 2014; McGrath & Kuriloff, 1999; Reay et al., 2007; Roda & Wells, 2013).

While the initial calls for increased freedom and school choice that arose in educational policy discourse in the 1990s (Epstein, 1995/2010) articulated an understanding of parents and families as being rational actors, deliberately choosing schools for explicit reasons, Cucchiara and Horvat (2014) have shown the significance of school choice by middle-class parents as an act that contains specific meaning for families and ramifications for public schools. Identifying their parent study participants in a large American city as politically liberal, Cucchiara and Horvat found, "By using an urban public school [parents] saw themselves as living their beliefs, tying their choice of a school to their politics and activism" (2014, p. 497). Cucchiara (2013a) has also noted the sort of group psychology that develops in diverse schooling situations, where parents either feel particular forms of isolation or group anxiety over navigating the school choice process in a diverse public school context. Reay et al. (2007) show how white middle-class families experience a "privilege trap" in urban schools, which can lead to frustration, guilt, and insecurity as parents try to navigate their way through a school context that they recognize as rife with historical inequalities. Examining the dynamics of colorblind school choice policy frameworks, Roda and Wells (2013) similarly show that without more proactive, coordinated attempts to integrate schools along racial and economic lines at the district level, the presence of parents with differing levels of affluence and influence can, despite a sense of critical self-awareness or good intentions, function to exacerbate and reproduce existing social inequalities that shape public schooling.

The work of Lynn Posey-Maddox (Posey, 2012; Posey-Maddox, 2014) builds on this literature to provide significant detail regarding the context in which middle-class parents are engaging in public schools. She uses the concept of "free-market diversity" to describe the sources of privilege as well as strain that middle-class parents face in a variety of situations as they are choosing to engage in urban public schools. She observes,

> [M]iddle-class parents are . . . positioned by many civic and educational leaders as *both valued customers and agents of change*: they are encouraged to enroll their children in urban public schools and are also asked to ensure that these schools become or remain high quality. They are treated by civic and educational leaders as a key driver of urban school reform and are also asked to fill the gaps left by state and local governments.
>
> (2014, pp. 29–30)

In consequence, just as policy makers position parents to 'choose' to engage in urban public schools, these families are engaging with a public institution that bears the vestiges of structural inequality and poor funding. The conclusion that Posey-Maddox (2014) ultimately draws, in line with Roda and Wells (2013), is that while the return of predominantly white middle-class constituencies to public school brings with it significant possibilities for improvement, sustaining such changes and ensuring educational equity is difficult absent any organized effort by local or state-level educational authorities.

The depiction of white, middle-class families that comes into focus in the literature on engagement highlights a more active constituency than in previous forms of educational leadership and policy making, altering the efficacy and influence of such families as they pursue educational opportunities. Concurrent with this changing nature of parent and family engagement, the reliance upon school choice policies has put more responsibility upon parents *qua* consumers. How this engagement actually takes place in particular schools provides the foundation for a more macro-level analysis of how such a change in engagement affects and can affect public schooling more generally.

Hurricane Katrina, Years of Recovery, and the "New" New Orleans

Following Hurricane Katrina in 2005, the dynamics of parent engagement in public education in New Orleans were radically altered as initiatives at the local, state, and federal levels led to the development of charter schools and school governance shifted from the previously dominant and locally elected Orleans Parish School Board (OPSB) to the state-level Recovery School District (RSD) (Mirón, Beabout, & Boselovic, 2015). Instead of serving as the "blank slate" that some policy makers and business leaders saw in post-Katrina New Orleans, struggles for civic progress after the storm were characterized by a vacuum of social trust between the city's historically white population and the Black constituency of the city (Cowan, 2008).

The charter schools were quickly developed as the solution to improving schooling in New Orleans, which would eventually result in a city with 91% of students in charter schools by 2012, operating under the valence of public schooling but run by nonprofit, private entities (Cowen Institute for Public Education Initiatives, 2014). Within this power dynamic of educational policy making, Black citizens—dispersed or not—were largely left out in a policy making process that went beyond the bounds of democratic deliberation (Buras, 2011; Cook, 2010; Dixson, 2011; Huff, 2013; Orfield, 2010). The constituency of public education has changed noticeably in the post-Katrina years as well: While the percentage of Black students in the city's public schools declined from 94% in 2005 to 85% in 2013, the percentage of white students in public schools rose from around 3% to 7% during the same time period (Cowen Institute for Public Education Initiatives, 2014). Beyond the public schools, the city's historically prominent private schools faced instability following Katrina, with enrollments declining steadily over the past decade (Dreilinger, 2014).

The History of the Homer A. Plessy Community School Through a Personal Lens

The parents and community members that led the effort to create the Plessy School in New Orleans sought to form a new school that reflected the diversity and history of the downtown neighborhoods of Marigny, Bywater, St. Roch, and St. Claude (see Figure 6.1). A coalition formed to realize these objectives at community meetings that were held in the years after Katrina where a master plan for school rebuilding was considered. Although the group would gain and lose members over the time it took to open the school, it would remain largely white throughout this process and consisted mainly of residents of the gentrified Marigny and Bywater neighborhoods. None of those most active in the group—a deacon and community organizer, a university staff member, an art teacher, an architect, and other professionals—had previous experience, involvement, or connections to the post-Katrina education reform movement (Beabout & Boselovic, 2015). In developing a stronger portrayal of the efforts to open the school and its first year in existence, it is important to first look briefly at recent demographic changes in Marigny and Bywater specifically and to see how these trends relate to changes in the city more generally.

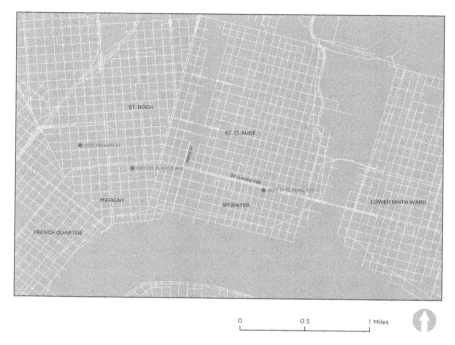

Figure 6.1 Map of the downtown neighborhoods of New Orleans. Included are three particular locations relevant to the Plessy School: 2300 St. Claude Ave. marks the site of the proposed school site, the Colton building; 3820 St. Claude Ave. marks the school's location during the 2013–2014 school year, the Frederick Douglass Building (originally known as the Francis T. Nicholls Building); and 2021 Pauger St. marks the school's location during the 2014–2015 school year [map created by Gene Stroman, 2015].

Creating a New Charter School in Changing Neighborhoods

Both Marigny and Bywater contain what geographer (and Bywater resident) Richard Campanella (2013) has argued are the geographic prerequisites for gentrification in New Orleans: the presence of historic housing stock (such as the city's iconic shotgun houses) and proximity to neighborhoods that have already gone through gentrification or never suffered sustained economic hardship. In this scheme, he argues, the bohemian French Quarter became gentrified in the 1970s, with a slower pace of gentrification moving through Marigny. The incoming individuals that moved to the city following the storm functioned, in part, to accelerate that process throughout Bywater, which is sometimes referred to (in a pejorative sense) as "the Williamsburg of the South," due to its bohemian reputation, a visible constituency of transplant residents, an abundance of artists and creative professionals, and chic, new restaurants (Campanella, 2013).

Demographic trends provided by the U.S. Census align with this narrative. In Bywater, the ratio of Black to white residents went from 61% and 32.4% in 2000 to 33.1% and 56.1% in 2010. In Marigny, this same ratio went from 17.7% and 72.7% in 2000 to 12.7% and 75.5% in 2010. During this time, both neighborhoods saw increases in residents with bachelor's degrees as well as increases in average income, by 144% in Bywater and 129% in Marigny (United States Census Bureau, 2010).

This shift was facilitated, in large part, by developments in housing policy in the city, which saw the demolition of all public housing following Katrina and the use of federal HOPE VI funds to provide tax incentives to developers specifically targeting new housing opportunities for more middle-income (or "market-rate") renters, rather than concerted support for low-income housing. The Bywater Arts Lofts, a refurbished factory targeting artist-type renters, is just one example of this development, one that has indeed had a part in developing the image of the neighborhood that Campanella (2013) describes.

In kind, while the objective of the school's founders was to bring together a diverse constituency, the status and demographics of the neighborhoods in question were experiencing significant social and economic changes. Many of the Bywater and Marigny parents and residents that built the school routinely discussed the border of St. Claude Avenue (which demarcates the beginning of the St. Roch and St. Claude neighborhoods) as a powerful social barrier. Discussions around community engagement and diversity at the school often came back—both in the school's creation and in its first year of operation—to a predominantly white group of parents and community members discussing the lack of engagement or connection they were often able to bring about with those "on the other side." This implicit bias, however, belies the experience of the many attempts made by predominantly Black community groups, families, and educators to form neighborhood schools following Katrina that were denied by education officials at the city and state levels.

In order to get a better understanding of the concrete aims of the Plessy School's founders—and the attraction felt by particular families—it is useful to look at the vision statement from the school's charter:

> The vision for Homer A. Plessy Community School is a school that offers children an opportunity for excellence; is rooted in the St. Roch, Bywater, St. Claude and Marigny neighborhoods; has students, teachers, and parents that reflect the racial and cultural diversity of the area; teaches students about the importance of citizenship and community engagement; attracts dedicated educators by creating a professional environment in which teachers can develop their full potential; fosters creative and divergent thinking; draws on the resources of a community eager to help; recognizes the importance of meaningful engagement with parents; serves as a focal point for the community and has a sense of place.
> (OPSB, 2013, p. 23)

While many of the charter schools that had opened following Katrina often emphasized a longer school day, a curriculum focused around student achievement data and college prep, and were operated largely by younger, less experienced educators and administrators (Sondel, 2013, 2015), Plessy stood out. Additionally, the school's tagline, "Arts Infused, Reggio Inspired," offered something that was different from other schools and that also resonated with some middle-class residents in Bywater and Marigny. An oft-heard comment of parents at the school during the first year was the fact that Plessy was the first school in the neighborhoods of downtown New Orleans that offered a curriculum focused on the whole child and arts education and that consciously rejected the thinking of the controversial "No Excuses" model.

It was this issue of choice that lay at the roots of the school's founding and the dynamics of engagement. Following Katrina, the Colton School building on St. Claude Avenue was home to an artist's colony until discussions on the renovation of the school took place. Parents and community members in the immediate neighborhoods of Marigny and St. Roch gathered, along with other concerned parties, to discuss plans for the city's School Facilities Master Plan and the fate of the school building. The parents and community members that would come together to articulate the mission provided above gathered first in coffee shops and a local church to discuss what the public school in their neighborhood should look like. Parents, future parents, and interested community members alike would become involved in this process.

Political Contestation over a Community-Oriented Charter School

This group, however, was not alone in looking to shape the future of the Colton building, as Knowledge is Power Program (KIPP) New Orleans also developed plans for the school site. Accounts from local news sources recount a contentious battle between an established national charter management organization (CMO) and, as the New Orleans *Times-Picayune* put it, "the more bohemian sensibilities of the mostly white neighborhood group" (Chang, 2011). Another city news source referred to the battle for the Colton building as one between "KIPPsters" and "hipsters" (Cannon, 2011). As this struggle unfolded in early 2011, it quickly became clear that while both groups participated in public forums, the decision was all but confirmed in favor of KIPP. In addition to being an established CMO in the city, leaders in the organization also held favor with the then-superintendent of the RSD, Paul Vallas.

After the RSD moved forward with this decision, the neighborhood group decided not to pursue further options with the state-level agency, but to try instead with the local OPSB. It was at this point that they also transformed from a loosely organized group of parents and community members advocating for a public school model to a group of united individuals who realized that if this school as they had envisioned it was to become a reality, they would have to build it themselves. Unable to find a CMO suitable to their needs and without a traditional school option in the neighborhood, these parents and community members decided that opening a charter school of their own was their only choice.

Whereas most charter schools that opened in the city post-Katrina have developed largely along particular academic or pedagogical models, the founders of the Plessy School advocated for not only the richness but the necessity of a form of schooling that was situated—geographically and culturally—in the history of downtown New Orleans. The school's namesake, the figure of the historic United States Supreme Court case *Plessy v. Ferguson* (1896), was arrested on a train on Press Street (one of the commonly understood boundaries between Bywater and Marigny today). Additionally, it was in the downtown neighborhoods of New Orleans that William Frantz Elementary and McDonogh No. 19 received the first black students into the previously all-white public schools of New Orleans on November 14, 1960. Furthermore, Marigny was also home to the *Institute Catholique*, a school opened in 1840 that was the first in the nation to provide a free public education to Black boys and girls. The relevance and importance of these historical precedents in the minds of the school's founders is perhaps most evident in the fact that the nonprofit organization that the school established to apply for a charter took the name the Citizens' Committee for Education. This is a direct homage to the *Comité des Citoyens*, one of the nation's pioneering civil rights groups, whose members largely lived and worked in the downtown neighborhoods of New Orleans.[1]

The school's organizers were eventually successful in receiving a charter from OPSB in early 2012 and being allocated space in the Frederick Douglass Building on St. Claude Avenue.[2] It would be this building that KIPP would leave once the newly renovated Colton School was opened.

From Parent Advocacy Group to Fledgling Charter School

A white transplant resident of Bywater, I joined the school's founding staff in the summer of 2013 in a position that held both administrative and teaching responsibilities. This position allowed me to work with teachers in different classrooms and observe the educational development of students as well as the dynamics of the relationships between families and the school leadership on a daily basis.

The excitement of the school's leaders and founders was tangible when the school finally opened in August 2013, serving students and families in Pre-K through second grade. The reality of the situation, however, came about quickly, as the school faced significant shortfalls in both student enrollment and, partially in consequence, the school's budget. Whereas the charter agreement that the Citizen's Committee for Education signed with the OPSB listed a projected enrollment of 273 students (OPSB, 2013, p. 1), the actual enrollment of the school fluctuated around 125 students throughout the course of the first year. While a single cause for this chasm between the expectation and the reality is hard to discern, many families and staff speculated that while any first-year school will have more difficulty recruiting parents and families than established schools, the expectation that the school would attract a higher number of middle-class students was unfounded.[3] In contrast to these expectations, more than 80% of the student body qualified for free and reduced-price lunch status. This was felt perhaps most acutely in the school's Pre-K classes, which could only function depending on the school's ability to bring in enough middle-class parents to pay tuition and subsidize the program. In terms of other enrollment objectives, though, the school was somewhat more successful. The ratio of Black to white students was roughly 60% to 30%,[4] and nearly two-thirds of the students enrolled at the school lived within the downtown neighborhoods (including the nearby Lower Ninth Ward) that the school aimed to be a part of and to serve.

The school's leader and charter board had to make difficult decisions in regards to personnel and school resources as a result of the budget shortfall. The difficulty in managing this situation led to significant changes in parent and family engagement and in the school's organizational dynamics more generally. As a few teachers and staff members (including the school counselor) were let go, parents in the school pushed to get the school the resources it needed and to support staff positions. At the same time, some of the relatively few white, middle-class families that the school had managed to enroll but who were able to pursue other public or private school options left the school over the course of the long first semester over concerns of school leadership, classroom management, and the long-term stability of the school.

At the level of school leadership, amidst this financial and organizational turmoil, the board moved to fire the school's founding principal. With the guidance of the Orleans Parish School Board, the founders of the Plessy School chose to recruit an assistant principal from a selective admissions school in the city that was highly regarded for its academic program but which served a substantially different student population than the Plessy School. While the new principal had extensive experience at her previous school, she had little knowledge of the arts integration or Reggio philosophies that characterized Plessy.

Amidst this change, parents and families were still struggling to support the school's existence and to make it work for their children. As the school's development had been marked by community engagement efforts that did not often make it across the symbolic divide of St. Claude Avenue, the parental community of the school, committed as it generally was to the school's success, was largely fractured along the lines of race and class. While it was largely white, middle-class parents and families that were able to support the school the most through time in the school and added resources, this sometimes served to further separate parents rather than to bring them together. Students themselves, however, did a much better job of navigating the diverse school environment, and the friendships they formed with new friends outside their own neighborhood brought together families of different backgrounds in some cases.

As I had been asked to serve as standing principal for the days and weeks when the school's first principal was away, I had gained an even greater knowledge of the teachers, students, and families at the Plessy School than my previous role had afforded. However, given the organizational change that often comes with any change in leadership, I no longer felt that I had a place at the school and that if I did stay through to the end of the year, I would not be hired the following year. As I had expected would be the case for myself and my colleagues at the school, all but a few of the original staff that made it through the difficult first year were let go at its conclusion.

As of the conclusion of the school's second year, the Plessy School has now moved (temporarily) into a school building in St. Roch. Partially through the efforts of parents with resources and time, it has been fortunate to receive multiple grants and continued support from the Orleans Parish School Board and is no longer in the state of crisis that it faced in its first year. But while most of the school's founders and the new principal remain at the school, many of the families from the school's first year (including a few of the school's board members) have left to pursue other schooling options—public and private—for their children. Perhaps more significantly for its future, the school—originally opposed to much of the education reform that characterized the city following Katrina—is starting to get more local and national media and policy attention as an innovative charter school with a goal of diversity.

Discussion

In exploring the dynamics of white, middle-class engagement in the development of the Plessy School, two significant, interrelated contradictions must be examined in greater depth to understand what is a fundamentally new role of parent engagement in schooling. The first is the fact that while the school was premised upon and indeed brought into existence largely by the efforts of engaged parents, the model of engagement that developed over the course of the school's first year functioned, in some ways, to stratify parents' actual roles within the school. The second is the goal of developing a diverse neighborhood school as a charter school in the policy framework of school choice. After interrogating these questions in concert, I will conclude by returning to the dilemma with which I began this study: the possibility of risk and potential alike in the relatively recent phenomena of white, middle-class engagement in urban public schooling.

Stratification Through Intensive Parent Engagement

What is perhaps most significant about the Plessy School as a case study of white, middle-class engagement in urban public education is the fact that while the school's mission emphasized parent and community engagement in a thoughtful and deliberate manner, the mechanisms by which the school was brought into existence and by which it operated on a daily basis worked, in many ways, against these goals. The parents with the time and resources to be at the school during the day, to volunteer to advocate or write grant proposals for the school, pay to support the school's Pre-K program, or to donate funds more generally were those that gained the most influence and attention at the school. Consequently, rather than serving as a successful, diverse school in practice, the school could often be a segregated space in and of itself, with different constituencies demonstrating different social, symbolic, and financial capital and different epistemological frameworks for understanding the purpose of the school.

In line with Posey-Maddox's (2014) broader assessment of the return of white, middle-class constituencies to public education, those parents and families with the resources and time to support a school struggling financially and organizationally were sometimes in a position of greater influence over those parents who were not able to provide support in these specifically defined forms. The burden of responsibility for this inequitable model was not entirely on the school's leadership, however, as the school did not receive many of the same public and philanthropic dollars that other start-up charter schools in the city had received. On a similar note, the reliance upon such a small group of individuals to achieve broad educational and social goals was unrealistic and unjust. It is not surprising that many of the parents who became intensively involved in the school described it as having a second full-time job (Beabout & Boselovic, 2015) and that some of these parents ultimately chose to leave the school in the middle or at the end of the first school year.

In a similar manner to the divisions along the lines of parent engagement, the school itself—founded upon an educational and civic mission of serving as a community institution and providing citizenship education—exhibited little sense of long-standing unity or solidarity of parents and families that was not born out of racial and social difference. This was a result of both the organizing model as well as the educational policy framework by which it came into existence as a new charter school. From the implicit bias of being unable to transcend the boundary of St. Claude Avenue and the crucial misperception of the amount of children within the respective downtown neighborhoods, the school had an uphill battle in terms of school-wide engagement as its first school year had just begun. This sense of a fractured community came about in the specific practices that parents and families developed around supporting the school, occupying the social spaces of the school (morning meetings, school drop off and pick up, and school events), and engaging with one another. As multiple individuals would openly recount over the course of the school year, while the Plessy School was moderately successful in bringing together a racially and economically diverse body of students and families, social divisions remained in how particular students and their families experienced the school. As the school will likely stabilize now that it is past its first year, it is possible that this sense of fractured community might be alleviated as families and staff at the school form more sustained forms of engagement and trust that are only possible in time.

These divisions of the first year were perhaps most evident in the inevitable paths that brought different children and families to a school that was intended to be community-based but is part of a colorblind, city-wide open enrollment policy framework that preferences more privileged families and provides little means for the school to actually function as a neighborhood entity in the traditional terms of student enrollment and community engagement. Although a not insubstantial minority of parents and families chose the Plessy School on philosophical grounds (such as investment in diverse and public forms of schooling, desiring a diverse education for their children, and belief in the arts-based educational model), many more families came to the school simply because of its location or, since it was an untested first-year school, its empty seats for enrollment that other desired schools may not have had. In consequence, in addition to those with resources and time, parents who had a strong emotional and personal investment in the school's mission (beyond the education of their children) were often seen as more dedicated, reliable, or likely to come through with resources in comparison to students and families that may have entered the school mid-year, without a strong, explicit interest in the model of parent and family engagement articulated by the school's founders and mission statement.

Finally, the trust that Epstein (1995/2010) highlights as foundational to parent and community engagement and that was largely lacking in the city's civic culture at this time (Cowan, 2008) was also largely absent across different constituencies at the school. Echoing the findings of Cucchiara (2008, 2013a, 2013b) and Cucchiara and Horvat (2009, 2014), the school's white and middle-class leaders and parents often felt anxiety and difficulty in navigating the dynamics of the school in an equitable and effective way. In day-to-day interactions, this social context often functioned as a barrier to building such trust, explicit as a goal as this was throughout the school's development.

From the district level, all those involved in the school were exposed to the dynamic that Posey-Maddox (2014) refers to as "free market diversity," where the ability of parents of privilege to compensate for what the school and district struggle to provide leaves the school perhaps more engaged with particular families, but in a way that can be socially divisive and—absent any sustained, equitable policy framework or change in funding—precarious.

Risk and Potential: Lessons Learned

As a case study of a first-year charter school, the Plessy School provides an illuminating experience of how parental engagement in urban public schooling is going beyond the traditional models of engagement as outlined by Epstein (1995/2010), with parents not only choosing the schools where their children will attend but creating —through political contestation—and struggling to sustain a school choice of their own. As the precarious situation of the school from its origins through to its second year proves, the efficacy of such a model of parental engagement is potentially unsustainable in certain ways and sets up dynamics within the school that may serve to reproduce, rather than alleviate, the very social inequities that such white, middle-class parents articulated as part of their mission.

Situated in the context of the extreme makeover of public education in post-Katrina New Orleans and in line with much of the recent scholarship on white, middle-class parent engagement, this case study demonstrates how such schools are not outliers, but can and do develop within the context of contemporary market-based education reforms. It is this reconciliation of the principles of diverse schooling and parent engagement with school choice that should serve as an area of focus in continued research. Furthermore, the organizing and effort that went into the creation and maintenance of this school should also serve as an indication of the social significance and influence of a constituency in public education that had long been absent. Whether or not organizing around equitable approaches to parent engagement in diverse schooling can go beyond the school level and bring together the multiple constituencies needed to lessen the precarity and stratification as outlined in this study is still to be seen. If recent demographic trends in the downtown neighborhoods of New Orleans and across the city are any indication, it is likely that increased engagement from white, middle-class families—whether in incremental enrollment in particular public schools or in more efforts such as the Plessy School—is likely to take place and affect the experiences of all students in public education, for better or for worse.

Conclusion: Placing the White, Middle Class in the New Landscape of Urban Public Education

I began this study by raising the question of the potential for risk and potential alike in the return of white, middle-class constituencies to American cities such as New Orleans. I explored the concept of parent and community engagement—how families interact with teachers, administrators, and school officials to influence schooling—to show how within the rise of educational policy making aligned with school choice and market-based reform, the role of parents and families is changing.

With the understanding of the development and first-year experience of the Plessy School as a case study of this phenomenon, I then presented an overview of the school's development. From this perspective, I discussed two central contradictions. First, I outlined the predicament of a public school not only premised upon parent and community engagement, but actually *run* by a particular group of parents and community members. Then I analyzed the Plessy School case study as an attempt to create a neighborhood school within the context of market-based education reform. Exploring these contradictions allowed me to highlight the classroom-, school-, and city-level dynamics that shaped how white, middle-class engagement at the Plessy School influenced the trajectory of the school. It is on the question of the possibilities for meaningful engagement around public education that I will conclude.

Just as years of racial, economic, and social history is mapped onto the geography of New Orleans (Boselovic, 2015), the move toward a universal choice system in the city takes place on contested geographic terrain. It was from this foundation that the Plessy School developed and—despite the progressive vision and persistence of its leaders and families—faced obstacles to its progressive goals; it was from this foundation that the school was also forced to confront the policy dynamics of market-based reform shaping education in the city following Hurricane Katrina. In short, while the Plessy School aimed to provide something radical in the downtown neighborhoods of New Orleans, it was inevitably tangled up in the structures of power that characterize education policy.

As my review of the literature and this case study have shown, the lessons of the Plessy School and New Orleans more generally have significant value for understanding the dynamics of white, middle-class engagement in urban public education as well as in education reform more generally. Cucchiara and Horvat (2014) note, "In cities across the US (including Chicago, Boston, and New York) and in Europe (including Paris and London), groups of middle-class parents are making similar choices in growing numbers" (p. 487). As I argued above regarding the uncertain future role of this constituency in the public schools of New Orleans, the stratification and precarity of such schools across the country is likely to continue absent any concerted efforts to sustain and support such schools in an equitable manner. Policy frameworks posit individuals in different positions of power and perspective within society (Ball, 2007), and as Cucchiara and Horvat (2014) and others have shown, the position of power and perspective starting to be occupied by white, middle-class families is significant. While it is clear that the role of white, middle-class engagement is changing within the nation's public schools to have greater influence, the ultimate impact of such a move toward this new, intensive form of parent engagement, however, is still to be seen.

Notes

1 A contradiction to this focus on community-based, neighborhood schooling appears, however, in the school's initial charter agreement with OPSB. In laying out the school's long-term goals, the first item listed is as follows: "Create *a replicable model* of a community-based school that meets the needs of the full range

of learners and produces civically engaged citizens" (OPSB, 2013, p. 5, emphasis mine).

2 For more on the history of different schools at the Douglass Building, see Dixson, Buras, and Jeffers (2015), and Michna (2009).

3 While approximately two-thirds of students came from downtown neighborhoods, as noted subsequently, a substantial portion of this number came from St. Roch and St. Claude. Census data also validates this line of thought. As of 2010, there were only 383 individuals under age 18 in Bywater and only 132 in Marigny. In contrast, there were 1,528 individuals under age 18 in St. Claude and 1,637 in St. Roch (The Data Center, 2014).

4 For a general standard of comparison, the ratio of Black to white students in public schools in New Orleans in 2013 was 85% to 7%. The percent of public school students eligible for Free or Reduced-Price Lunch was 85%—the highest of any city in the nation (Cowen Institute for Public Education Initiatives, 2014).

References

Ball, S. J. (2007). *Education plc: Understanding private sector participation in public sector education*. New York, NY: Routledge.

Beabout, B. R., & Boselovic, J. L. (2015). Urban charter schools prioritizing community engagement. In M. Evans & D. Hiatt-Michael (Eds.), *The power of community engagement for educational change* (pp. 41–63). Charlotte, NC: Information Age Publishing.

Ben-Porath, S. (2012). School choice and educational opportunity: Rationales, outcomes, and racial disparities. *Theory and Research in Education*, *10*(2), 171–189.

Boselovic, J. L. (2015). Education and the public sphere in New Orleans, 1803–2005: Conflicts over public education, racial inequality, and social status in pre-Katrina New Orleans. In L. Mirón, B. R. Beabout, & J. L. Boselovic (Eds.), *Only in New Orleans: School choice and equity post-Hurricane Katrina* (pp. 17–35). Rotterdam, The Netherlands: Sense Publishers.

Bourdieu, P. (1979/1984). *Distinction: A social critique of the judgment of taste* (Trans. Richard Nice). Cambridge, MA: Harvard University Press.

Bourdieu, P., & Passeron, J.-C. (1977). *Reproduction in education, society, and culture* (Trans. Richard Nice). Thousand Oaks, CA: Sage Publications.

Buras, K. (2011). Race, charter schools, and conscious capitalism: On the spatial politics of whiteness as property (and the unconscionable assault on Black New Orleans). *Harvard Educational Review*, *81*(2), 296–330.

Campanella, R. (2013, March 1). Gentrification and its discontents: Notes from New Orleans. *New Geography*. Retrieved from www.newgeography.com

Cannon, C. W. (2011, February 9). KIPPsters vs. Hipsters: Why so little choice in Downtown schools? *The Lens*. Retrieved from www.thelensnola.org

Carr, S. (2012, August 20). The integrationists: Diverse cities need diverse schools. How do we get there? *Next City*. Retrieved from www.nextcity.org

Chang, C. (2011, February 7). KIPP, neighborhood group both covet old Colton Middle School building. *The Times-Picayune*. Retrieved from www.nola.com

Cook, D. A. (2010). Disrupted but not destroyed: Fictive-kinship networks among Black educators in post-Katrina New Orleans. *Southern Anthropologist*, *35*(2), 1–25.

Cowan, M. A. (2008). Elbows together, hearts apart: Institutional reform, economic opportunity, and social trust in post-Katrina New Orleans. *Seattle Journal for Social Justice*, *7*(1), 205–234.

Cowen Institute for Public Education Initiatives. (2014). *State of public education in New Orleans, 2014*. New Orleans, LA: Tulane University.

Cucchiara, M. (2008). Re-branding urban schools: Urban revitalization, social status, and marketing public schools to the upper middle class. *Journal of Education Policy, 23*(2), 165–179.

Cucchiara, M. B. (2013a). "Are we doing damage?" Choosing an urban public school in an era of parental anxiety. *Anthropology & Education Quarterly, 44*(1), 75–93.

Cucchiara, M. B. (2013b). *Marketing schools, marketing cities: Who wins and who loses when schools become urban amenities*. Chicago, IL: University of Chicago Press.

Cucchiara, M. B., & Horvat, E. M. (2009). Perils and promises: Middle-class parental involvement in urban schools. *American Educational Research Journal, 46*(4), 974–1004.

Cucchiara, M. B., & Horvat, E. M. (2014). Choosing selves: The salience of parental identity in the school choice process. *Journal of Education Policy, 29*(4), 486–509.

The Data Center. (2014). *Bywater District 7 (Planning District 7)*. New Orleans, LA: The Data Center.

Dixson, A. (2011). Whose choice? A critical race perspective on charter schools. In C. Johnson (Ed.), *The neoliberal deluge: Hurricane Katrina, late capitalism, and the remaking of New Orleans* (pp. 130–151). Minneapolis, MN: University of Minnesota Press.

Dixson, A. D., Buras, K. L., & Jeffers, E. K. (2015). The color of reform: Race, education reform, and charter schools in post-Katrina New Orleans. *Qualitative Inquiry, 21*(3), 288–299.

Dreilinger, D. (2014, February 13). Private school enrollment falls 5% in Louisiana, even more in New Orleans, Baton Rouge areas. *The Times-Picayune*. Retrieved from www.nola.com

Epstein, J. L. (1995/2010). School/family/community partnerships: Caring for the children we share. *Phi Delta Kappan, 92*(3), 81–96.

Gofen, A., & Blomqvist, P. (2014). Parental entrepreneurship in public education: A social force or a policy problem? *Journal of Education Policy 29*(4), 564–569.

Horvat, E. M., Weininger, E. B., & Lareau, A. (2003). From social ties to social capital: Class differences in the relations between schools and parent networks. *American Educational Research Journal, 40*(2), 319–351.

Huff, A. (2013). Reforming the city: Neoliberal school reform and democratic contestation in New Orleans. *The Canadian Geographer, 57*(3), 311–317.

Lareau, A. (1987). Social class differences in family-school relationships: The importance of cultural capital. *Sociology of Education, 60*(2), 73–85.

Lareau, A. (2011/2003). *Unequal childhoods: Class, race, and family life* (2nd ed.). Oakland, CA: University of California Press.

Lareau, A., & Horvat, E. M. (1997). Moments of social inclusion and exclusion: Race, class, and cultural capital in family-school relationships. *Sociology of Education, 72*(1), 37–53.

MacLeod, J. (1987/2008). *Ain't no makin' it: Aspirations and attainment in a low-income neighborhood* (3rd ed.). Boulder, CO: Westview Press.

Mapp, K. L. (2003). Having their say: Parents describe why and how they are engaged in their children's learning. *The School Community Journal, 13*(1), 35–64.

McGinn, K. C., & Ben-Porath, S. (2014). Parental engagement through school choice: Some reasons for caution. *Theory and Research in Education, 12*(2), 172–192.

McGrath, D. J., & Kuriloff, P. J. (1999). "They're going to tear the doors off this place": Upper-middle-class parent school involvement and the educational opportunities of other people's children. *Educational Policy, 13*(5), 603–629.

Michna, C. (2009). Stories at the center: Story circles, educational organizing, and the fate of neighborhood public schools in New Orleans. *American Quarterly, 61*(3), 529–556.

Mirón, L., Beabout, B. R., & Boselovic, J. L. (Eds.). (2015). *Only in New Orleans: School choice and equity post-Hurricane Katrina*. Rotterdam, The Netherlands: Sense Publishers.

Monroe, D. (2014, January 19). When elite parents dominate volunteers, children lose. *The New York Times*. Retrieved from www.nytimes.com

Orfield, M. (2010, May 15). *The state of public schools in post-Katrina New Orleans: The challenge of creating equal opportunity*. Minneapolis, MN: Institute on Race and Poverty.

Orleans Parish School Board. (2013). *Type 3 charter school operating agreement between Citizens Committee for Education, Inc. and the Orleans Parish School Board*. New Orleans, LA: Orleans Parish School Board.

Plessy v. Ferguson, 163 U.S. 537, 539 (1896).

Posey, L. (2012). Middle- and upper-middle-class parent action for urban public schools: Promise or paradox? *Teachers College Record, 114*, 1–43.

Posey-Maddox, L. (2014). *When middle-class parents choose urban schools: Class, race, & the challenge of equity in public education*. Chicago, IL: The University of Chicago Press.

Reay, D., Hollingworth, S., Williams, K., Crozier, G., Jamieson, F., James, D., & Beedell, P. (2007). "A darker shade of pale?" Whiteness, the middle classes and multi-ethnic inner city schooling. *Sociology, 41*(6), 1041–1060.

Roda, A., & Wells, A. S. (2013). School choice policies and racial segregation: Where white parents' good intentions, anxiety, and privilege collide. *American Journal of Education, 199*, 261–293.

Rogers, T. K. (2009, April 5). The sudden charm of public school. *The New York Times*. Retrieved from www.nytimes.com

Smith, R. S. (2009, August 26). Affluent parents return to inner-city schools for educational opportunities. *Edutopia*. Retrieved from www.edutopia.org

Sondel, B. (2013). *Raising citizens or raising test scores? Teach for America and "no excuses" charter schools in post-Katrina New Orleans*. (Unpublished doctoral dissertation). Madison, WI: The University of Wisconsin-Madison.

Sondel, B. (2015). Market-based pedagogies: Assessment, instruction, and purpose at a "no excuses" charter school. In L. F. Mirón, B. R. Beabout, & J. L. Boselovic (Eds.), *Only in New Orleans: School choice and equity post-Hurricane Katrina* (pp. 109–128). Rotterdam, The Netherlands: Sense Publishers.

United States Census Bureau. (2010). *Profile of general demographic characteristics: 2010 census*. Washington, DC: U.S. Department of Commerce.

Warren, M. R. (2005). Communities and schools: A new view of urban education reform. *Harvard Educational Review, 75*(2), 133–173.

Warren, M. R., Hong, S., Rubin, C. L., & Uy, P. S. (2009). Beyond the bake sale: A community-based relational approach to parent engagement in schools. *Teachers College Record, 111*(9), 2209–2254.

7 Segregated by Choice?
Urban Charter Schools and Education Choices for Black Students and Disadvantaged Families in the United States

Erling E. Boe, Shaun R. Harper, and Katherine M. Barghaus

Among the several strategies for creating parental choice among schools in the United States, the charter school movement has been by far the most successful (Gill, Timpane, Ross, Brewer, & Booker, 2007). After the first charter school opened in Minnesota in 1992, a period of rapid growth ensued, with approximately 4,200 charter schools operating as of 2007 (Center for Education Reform, 2009). This growth required enabling legislation in each state with charter schools, and was facilitated by financial support under the 1994 Federal Charter School Program (a component of the Elementary and Secondary Education Act of 1965).[1]

The National Alliance for Public Charter Schools (NAPCS) recently published the results of their analysis of relevant state legislation to identify the original goals to be attained by charter schools (Smarick, 2005). As of 2005, 40 states and the District of Columbia had enacted charter school laws, 32 of which had a preamble or purposes section that defined goals. The *predominant* goal in 94% of these 32 state laws was to provide *all families* with expanded education choices. Likewise, the Federal Charter Schools Program was intended to provide *all parents* with more choices among public schools (United States of Education [USDE], 2004).[2,3]

This predominant legislative goal for charter schools nationally entails two distinct components—to expand education *choices*, and to provide such choices to *all families* (instead of to special populations, such as the economically disadvantaged). The research reported here focuses on attainment of the "all families" component of this goal.[4]

More specifically, Smarick (2005) stated this goal as expanding "education choices to all families, regardless of geography, income, race, or prior achievement" (p. 2). This statement is equivalent to the intent of the Federal Charter School Program that "every student should have an equal opportunity to attend a charter school" (USDE, 2004, p. 2). These state-level and federal legislative intents to bring the benefits of expanded school choices to all families are certainly consistent with non-discrimination policies for charter schools. They are also politically astute. The enactment of charter school legislation has been facilitated by securing wide support from constituencies that are devoted to improving educational opportunities for all families.

The implementation of charter schools, however, may not have conformed to established public policy about providing charter school access to all families. According to the Chief Operating Officer of NAPCS, a disproportionate number of charter schools have been established in urban areas, with a desire by many (if not most) charter school leaders "to close the achievement gap and provide low-income and minority students a higher quality education than they've received under the traditional system" (Smarick, 2005, p. 6). Apparently, the goal of charter school leaders to focus on selected student groups is in conflict with the goal of policy makers to serve all families regardless of geography, income, prior achievement, or race. Some state- and national-level research on this issue has been published, but the results are not always consistent, as reviewed below.

At the state level, Rapp and Eckes (2007) studied the voluntary segregation of minority students in 32 specific states that enrolled at least 1,000 charter school students as of the 2002–03 school year. Although some states enrolled a somewhat higher percentage of White students in charter schools than in regular schools, the predominant finding was that charter schools were much more likely to enroll a higher percentage of *minority* students than White students. In other state-level data, evidence of racial segregation of *Black* students in charter schools has been found (d'Entremont & Gulosino, 2008, for New Jersey; Miron, Cullen, Applegate, & Farrell, 2007, for Delaware). Since these studies did not compare segregation between charter and regular schools, it is not known whether charter schools were particularly prone to segregate Black students. However, segregation was not found in Michigan in 1998–99 when urban charter school enrollment of Black students was compared with the urban regular school enrollment of Black students (close to 40% in both types of schools) (Miron & Nelson, 2002).[5]

Little research has been reported at the state level about the enrollment of economically disadvantaged students in charter schools versus regular schools. Based on data from Michigan in 2000–01, Miron and Nelson (2002) found that an equivalent percentage of economically disadvantaged students were enrolled in charter and regular schools in host districts (about 53%). In a study from Delaware, Miron et al. (2007) did not compare charter and regular schools, but instead examined the variability of charter school students. They reported high variability among charter schools in the percentage of low-income and special education students enrolled. It appears that, in Delaware at least, charter schools (as a group) did not avoid the enrollment of low-income students and students with disabilities.[6]

With respect to national-level research, data from the National Assessment of Education Progress (i.e., the 2003 Mathematics Charter School Pilot Study) were used to examine enrollment by race/ethnicity of fourth grade students (National Center for Education Statistics [NCES],

2005). The percentage of Black students enrolled in charter schools (31%) was higher than the percentage of Black students in regular schools (17%). Conversely, the percentage of White students enrolled in regular schools (58%) was higher than the percentage of White students in charter schools (45%). Equivalent percentages of Hispanic students were enrolled in charter and regular schools, as were equivalent percentages of low-income students. Furthermore, a substantial difference was seen between the percentages of charter versus regular school students enrolled in urban schools (50% vs. 29%, respectively).

Another national study of charter versus regular school enrollments was based on data from the U.S. Department of Education's 2003–04 NCES Schools and Staffing Survey (SASS) (Strizek, Pittsonberger, Riordan, Lyter, & Orlofsky, 2006). Results also demonstrated a tendency for charter schools to enroll a relatively high percentage of Black students, a low percentage of White students, and an equivalent percentage of Hispanic students, in comparison with regular schools. In addition, these charter schools seem to have enrolled a disproportionately high percentage of economically disadvantaged students and a disproportionately low percentage of students with disabilities.

A third national study used NCES's Common Core of Data for 2000–01 to compare enrollments in charter and regular schools in 15 states with at least 5,000 charter students (Frankenberg & Lee, 2003). They found that a majority (56%) of charter students were enrolled in urban schools. Charter schools enrolled a relatively high percentage of Black students (33%) in comparison with regular schools (17%), whereas a relatively low percentage of White students (43%) were enrolled in charter schools in comparison with regular schools (59%). Equal percentages of Hispanic students constituted the enrollment of charter and regular schools (19% in each).

Beyond this, only Frankenberg and Lee (2003) also analyzed the degree to which Black students were intensely segregated in charter and regular schools (i.e., schools with 90–100% *minority* student enrollment). Over 70% of Black charter students attended such highly segregated charter schools, while only 34% of their regular school counterparts did so. Hispanic students were found to be less segregated than were Black students in charter schools and no more segregated in charter schools than in regular schools. However, Frankenberg and Lee's analysis did not examine the degree to which Black students were concentrated in charter and regular schools with high percentages of Black students (as distinguished from all minority students), and the degree to which Hispanic students were concentrated in charter and regular schools with high percentages of Hispanic students. Therefore, much more remains to be known about segregation effects by race/ethnicity in charter versus regular schools. Based on the results of their analyses, Frankenberg and Lee concluded that charter schools had not addressed the issue of racial segregation.

In comparison with regular schools, these three national-level studies have shown that charter schools enroll a higher percentage of Black students, a lower percentage of White students, and equivalent percentages of Hispanic students. The results of these studies have been inconsistent regarding differences between charter and regular schools in terms of other student characteristics such as economic disadvantage, learning disabilities, and limited English proficiency.

Also, national-level research has consistently shown that a majority of charter school students have been enrolled in charter schools located in urban areas as compared with all non-urban areas (Frankenberg & Lee, 2003; NCES, 2002, 2005; Smarick, 2005). However, no study has examined differences in student enrollment patterns between charter and regular schools specifically in urban areas, or whether differences between charter and regular school enrollments by student characteristics varies with school location (i.e., urban vs. non-urban).

As Strizek et al. (2006) note, "more sophisticated analyses can be conducted with the restricted-use version of the SASS data" (p. 2). Fortunately, such SASS data includes extensive national-level information of high quality about the characteristics of students enrolled in charter and regular schools as of the 2003–04 school year. With these data, it is possible to: 1) Compare charter school enrollment patterns with regular school enrollment patterns only in states with charter schools; 2) Examine in greater detail the extent to which White, Black, and Hispanic students become segregated in schools with predominant enrollment of the same racial/ethnic group; and 3) study these enrollment patterns in both urban and non-urban schools. Thus, much remains to be learned about the degree to which state and federal policy objectives have been attained by charter schools with respect to equality of opportunity to attend charter schools.

Accordingly, we used the most recent restricted-use data from the 2003–04 SASS to investigate, in national perspective, three central research questions:

1) To what extent have charter schools, in comparison with regular schools, provided *all families* (regardless of location, income, prior achievement, or race/ethnicity) with expanded education choices?
2) To what extent have charter schools, in comparison with regular schools, become segregated by race/ethnicity?
3) To what extent do enrollment patterns in charter schools, in comparison with regular schools, vary by urban versus non-urban location?

Methods

Data Source

This chapter is based on data from the School Questionnaire of the 2003–04 SASS, which is the largest survey in the United States of public (including public charter), private, and Bureau of Indian Affairs schools. The School

Questionnaire included items on school type, grade levels, student enrollment, and programs offered. SASS produced a large national-probability sample of 7,991 public schools available for analysis, with a weighted response rate of 81%. Tourkin et al. (2007) provide detailed technical information about the SASS.

Definitions of School Contexts

According to definitions used by SASS (Tourkin et al., 2007), a regular school has an assigned principal, receives public funding as primary support, provides free public elementary and/or secondary schooling, and is operated by a local education agency or a contracted education program. A charter school is a public school that, in accordance with an enabling state statute, has been granted a charter exempting it from selected state or local rules and regulations. A charter school may be a newly created school or it may previously have been a regular public or private school.

School Samples

As of 2003–04, about 3,200 charter schools were operating in 37 states and the District of Columbia (Center for Education Reform [CER], 2004). Of these, SASS collected school information from a national probability sample of 233 charter schools located in 27 states and the District of Columbia. For this research, we selected states with at least three charter schools in the sample, yielding a study sample of 220 charter schools located in 17 states plus the District of Columbia. These charter schools were compared with the full sample of 2,859 regular schools in these same states. The 17 states providing these samples of charter and regular schools were Arizona, California, Colorado, Florida, Hawaii, Massachusetts, Michigan, Minnesota, New Jersey, New York, North Carolina, Ohio, Oregon, Pennsylvania, South Carolina, Texas, and Wisconsin.

Schools were further classified into three categories by locale: urban (including large and mid-sized central city), suburban (including the urban fringe of large and mid-sized cities), and rural (including small towns and rural areas). The sample of 220 charter schools analyzed was distributed as follows: 122 urban, 72 suburban, and 26 rural. The sample of 2,859 regular schools analyzed was distributed as follows: 778 urban, 1,425 suburban, and 656 rural.

Research Design

This research was designed to quantify and analyze, from the perspective of states with charter schools, the extent to which charter schools have attained one of their most prominent legislative goals—to provide all families (regardless of location, income, prior achievement, or race) with expanded education choices. Accordingly, we analyzed charter schools in terms of several relevant characteristics of enrolled students, as described below, and compared charter schools with regular schools in these respects.

These analyses were performed separately for public schools located in urban areas and in non-urban areas. Included in SASS data are the following characteristics of students enrolled in charter and regular schools:

> **Economic Disadvantage.** As the index of economic disadvantage, we identified students who were approved for free or reduced-price lunches under the National School Lunch Program.
> **Individualized Education Programs (IEP).** As the index of disability, we identified students who have an IEP because they have special needs.
> **Limited English Proficiency (LEP).** As the index of LEP, we identified students whose native or dominant language was not English, and who had sufficient difficulty speaking, reading, writing, or understanding the English language that it denied them the opportunity to learn successfully in an English-speaking-only classroom.
> **Race/Ethnicity.** As the index of race/ethnicity, we identified students as White (not of Hispanic background), as Black (not of Hispanic background), and as Hispanic (regardless of race).

Data Analysis

Based on the samples of charter and regular schools completing the SASS School Questionnaire, we computed weighted national estimates of the numbers of schools and numbers of students enrolled in these schools of each type included in the design (along with associated percentages and standard errors) using special procedures developed by NCES for complex sample survey data (Tourkin et al., 2007). Because SASS data are subject to design effects due to the stratification and clustering of the sample, we computed standard errors for the national estimates and tests of statistical significance by the method of balanced repeated replications with statistical software (WesVar 4.2). We used a logistic regression analysis to compute an effect size statistic (odds ratio) of the differences observed between charter and regular schools and to test the statistical significance of these differences (May, 2004).

Limitations

Since our results are based on large national-probability samples of schools and of estimates of students enrolled in these schools, they should *not* be interpreted as directly applicable to the state or local levels unless supported by other data from the relevant level. For example, the attainment of legislative goals for charter schools might be greater in some states than in other states—a topic for further research. In addition, the SASS data analyzed are from self-reports of school personnel, and therefore are subject to errors of recall and bias. Finally, as with all sample data such as SASS, the estimates reported are subject to sampling error as well as to measurement and recording error. All estimates should therefore be interpreted as approximate.

For the past decade, the CER has ranked states based on the strength of their charter school laws. Each state's laws receive a grade based on a dozen criteria, including the ability for charters to operate without burdensome legal, operational, and fiscal controls (CER, 2006). The majority of states (14 states and the District of Columbia) in our sample are considered to have strong charter school laws. Overall, 22 states have strong charter school laws, while 19 states have weak laws. Thus, it is possible that the effects found here are not be representative of those states with weaker laws.

Results

Enrollment by Location

Charter schools were located predominantly in urban areas (55%) in comparison with regular schools (28%) (OR = 3.6, $p < .001$). It follows that most charter school students attended urban charter schools (57%), while few (6%) attended rural charter schools (see Figure 7.1). Charter school

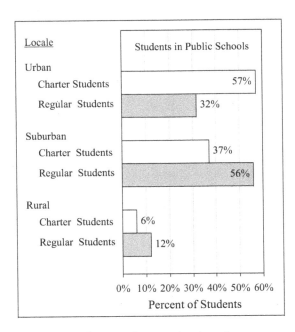

Figure 7.1 Percentage of students in charter schools and percentage of students in regular public schools by locale in states with charter schools. Based on data from the 2003–04 Schools and Staffing Survey, NCES, USDE.

students were almost three times more likely to attend an urban school than were regular school students (OR = 2.8, $p < .001$). Conversely, most regular school students attended suburban schools (56%) (see Figure 7.1). Regular school students were about twice as likely to attend a suburban school or a rural school as were charter school students (OR = 2.1, $p < .001$ for suburban; OR = 2.2, $p < .02$ for rural).

Based on these findings, it is apparent that urban students had much greater access to charter schools than did students living in suburban and rural areas. In view of this finding, further analyses of the attributes of students attending charter and regular schools were made separately for urban and non-urban schools (i.e., suburban and rural schools combined to assure sufficient sample size) so that comparisons could be made between student enrollment variables in these two locales.

Enrollment by Economic Disadvantage

As shown in Figure 7.2, a somewhat higher percentage of students enrolled in urban regular schools were economically disadvantaged than were students enrolled in urban charter schools (58% vs. 48%, respectively; OR = 1.5, $p < .01$). However, this phenomenon was not found in *non-urban* areas,

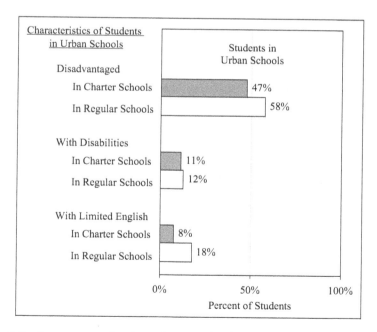

Figure 7.2 Percentages of urban charter school students and of urban regular school students by slected student characteristics. Based on data from the 2003–04 Schools and Staffing Survey, NCES, USDE.

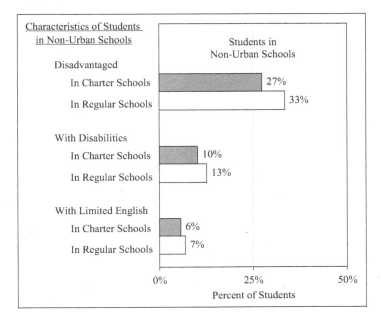

Figure 7.3 Percentages of non-urban charter school students and of non-urban regular school students by slected student characteristics. Based on data from the 2003–04 Schools and Staffing Survey, NCES, USDE.

where the difference between the enrollment of disadvantaged students in regular and charter schools was small (OR = 0.8) and not statistically significant (see Figure 7.3).

Enrollment by Prior Achievement

SASS provides information about the enrollment of students with disabilities (IEP) and (separately) with LEP—two populations generally with below average academic achievement. Urban charter and regular schools enrolled equivalent percentages of IEP students (see Figure 7.2). The same finding was observed for non-urban regular and charter schools (see Figure 7.3). The differences shown in Figures 7.2 and 7.3 between charter and regular schools in the enrollment of IEP student populations are not statistically significant.

However, with respect to the enrollment of LEP students, urban regular schools were over two and a half times more likely to enroll LEP students than were urban charter schools (as shown in Figure 7.2, 18% vs. 8%, respectively; OR = 2.6; $p < .01$). This phenomenon was not observed in non-urban areas, where the enrollment of LEP students in charter and regular schools was not statistically significant (Figure 7.3).

Enrollment by Race/Ethnicity

As shown in Figure 7.4, urban charter and regular schools enrolled White students at nearly equivalent percentages (30% vs. 31%, respectively; difference not statistically significant). However, urban charter schools were more than twice as likely to enroll Black students as urban regular schools (42.7% vs. 25%%, respectively; OR = 2.1, $p < .001$). By contrast, urban regular schools were almost twice as likely to enroll Hispanic students as urban charter schools (36% vs. 24%, respectively; OR = 1.8, $p < .001$). Thus, Black students were overrepresented in urban charter schools (in proportion to their numbers), while Hispanic students were underrepresented.

The same type of analyses for *non-urban* schools showed that the enrollment differences between charter and regular schools in the percentages of White, Black, and Hispanic students were all small, and none approached a conventional level of statistical significance (see Figure 7.5). Contrary to the results of similar analyses for urban charter schools reported above, students of various races/ethnicities were represented to equivalent degrees proportionately in non-urban charter schools.

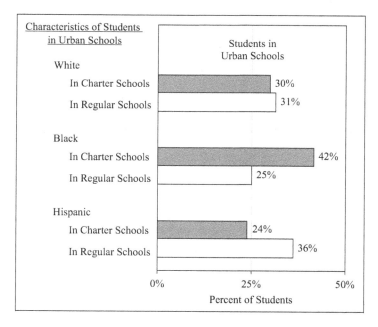

Figure 7.4 Percentages of urban charter school students and of urban regular school students by race/ethnicity. Based on data from the 2003–04 Schools and Staffing Survey, NCES, USDE.

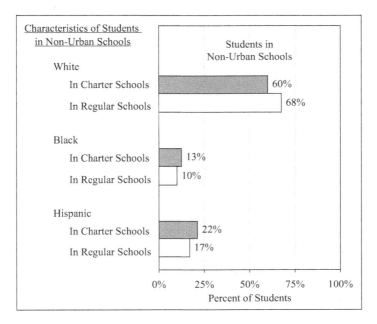

Figure 7.5 Percentages of non-urban charter school students and of non-urban regular school students by race/ethnicity. Based on data from the 2003–04 Schools and Staffing Survey, NCES, USDE.

Concentrated Enrollment by Race/Ethnicity

The relatively high percentage of Black students (41.7% from Figure 7.4) enrolled in urban charter schools as compared with White and Hispanic students suggested a further analysis to explore the extent to which students might be concentrated in charter schools with the majority of enrolled students representing particular racial/ethnic populations. Accordingly, we identified the specific urban charter and regular schools with a majority (51–100%) of their enrollment accounted for by a concentration of White students, a concentration of Black students, and a concentration of Hispanic students.

After identifying schools with such concentrated enrollment, we computed for each of the three racial/ethnic populations the percentages of urban charter school students and regular school students enrolled in these schools. As shown in Figure 7.6, the percentages of White students enrolled in urban charter and regular schools with concentrations of 51–100% White students were comparably high (73% vs. 64%, respectively; OR = 1.52; $p > .10$). Thus, urban charter and regular schools differed little in this respect.

Likewise, there was little difference in the percentages of Hispanic students enrolled in urban charter and regular schools with concentrations

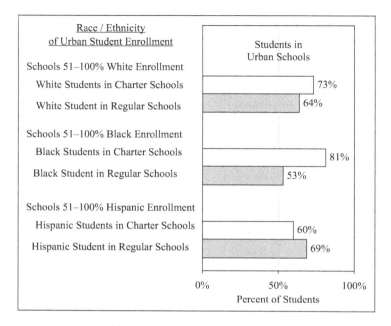

Figure 7.6 Percentages of urban charter school students and of urban regular school students by race/ethnicity attending schools with 51–100% enrollment by students of the same race/ethnicity. Based on data from the 2003–04 Schools and Staffing Survey, NCES, USDE.

of 51–100% Hispanic students (60% vs. 69%, respectively; OR = 0.68; $p < .10$).

However, as also shown in Figure 7.6, the percentage of Black students enrolled in urban charter schools with a concentration of 51–100% Black students was substantially higher than the percentage of Black students enrolled in regular schools with such a concentration of Black students. Urban charter schools were almost four times more likely to have a high level of enrollment of Black students (81%) than urban regular schools (53%) (OR = 3.70; $p < .001$). In view of this finding, we extended this type of analysis to examine urban schools with even higher concentrations of Black students (i.e., schools with 76–100% and schools with 91–100% enrollment of Black students).

As shown in Figure 7.7, we continued to find remarkably high concentrations of Black students in highly segregated charter schools. For example, 75% of Black charter students were enrolled in urban charter schools with 76–100% enrollment by Black students. The corresponding percentage (34%) was much lower for Black students enrolled in regular schools with 76–100% enrollment of Black students (OR = 5.65; $p < .001$).

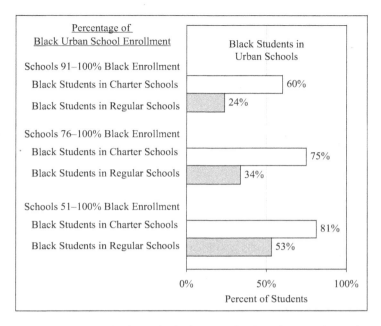

Figure 7.7 Percentages of urban Black charter school students and of urban Black regular school students attending schools with 51–100%, 76–100%, and 91–100% enrollment of black students. Based on data from the 2003–04 Schools and Staffing Survey, NCES, USDE.

As also shown in Figure 7.7, 60% of Black charter students were enrolled in urban charter schools with 91–100% enrollment by Black students. The corresponding percentage (24%) was much lower for Black students enrolled in regular schools with 91–100% enrollment of Black students (OR = 4.67; $p < .001$).

It is possible that the high concentration of Black students in urban charter schools (much more so than in urban regular schools) is confounded by school size because such concentrations may more readily occur in small schools. In fact, urban charter schools in our SASS sample have much smaller enrollment on average than urban regular schools (medians of 180 vs. 568, respectively). To control for school size, we created a binary variable with a small school defined as a student enrollment of less than 409 and a large school defined as an enrollment of 409 or greater. Including both the school size variable and the student concentration variable in a multivariate logistic regression model to predict school type (i.e., urban charter vs. regular school), the OR for the student concentration variable was reduced to 3.2 from the unadjusted 4.7. Although the greater percentage of urban charter schools with high concentrations of Black students than observed in regular schools was partly confounded with school size, a strong association remained after controlling for school size (i.e., the adjusted OR of 3.2).

Regarding schools in *non-urban* areas, we did not find statistically significant differences between percentages of charter and regular schools with concentrations of 51–100% Black students (or like concentrations of White or of Hispanic students). Nonetheless, substantial percentages of non-urban White students were enrolled in both charter and regular schools (26% and 33%, respectively) with high concentrations (91–100%) of White students. This might be accounted for, to a considerable extent, by non-urban schools serving geographic areas with a homogeneous White population.

Economically Disadvantaged Black Students

As shown in Figure 7.2, urban charter schools were somewhat less likely to enroll students who were economically disadvantaged than were urban regular schools (OR = 1.5). We performed further analyses of the enrollment of disadvantaged students in urban charter schools with a high concentration of Black students (schools with 76–100% Black student enrollment). Such schools enrolled 75% of Black students in urban charter schools (see Figure 7.7).

Urban charter schools with a high concentration of Black students (schools with 76–100% Black student enrollment) were more than twice as likely to enroll students who were *not* economically disadvantaged than those who were disadvantaged (OR = 2.24). We found virtually the same result for urban charter schools with even higher concentrations of Black students (schools with 91–100% Black student enrollment).

Thus, neither charter schools with high concentrations of Black student enrollment nor charter schools as a whole had an emphasis on enrolling economically disadvantaged students. This is not to imply that charter schools serve only a small percentage of disadvantaged students. Almost half (48%) of all urban charter students were classified as economically disadvantaged, while urban charter schools with a high concentration of Black students (76–100% Black student enrollment) enrolled an even higher percentage (61%) of disadvantaged students.

Discussion and Implications

In comparison with regular schools, three previous national-level studies have shown that charter schools enrolled a higher percentage of Black students (and a correspondingly lower percentage of White students) (Frankenberg & Lee, 2003; NCES, 2005; Strizek et al., 2006). Their results were inconsistent regarding other student characteristics such as family income and academic achievement prior to charter school entry. Except for

Frankenberg and Lee, these studies did not examine the extent to which charter schools may have become highly segregated by race/ethnicity.

To investigate these issues more precisely, our methods differed in two important ways that exploited the capabilities of restricted-use SASS data. First, we compared charter schools with regular schools located only in states with charter schools. Second, we analyzed the characteristics of charter and regular school students enrolled in urban and non-urban schools separately and found striking differences between these two locations. Students in *urban* charter schools differed considerably from students in urban regular schools in terms of family income, certain indicators of prior achievement, and race/ethnicity. By contrast, students in *non-urban* charter schools did *not* differ from students in non-urban regular schools in these three respects.

Thus, location (urban vs. non-urban) is a critical variable in investigating the characteristics of students enrolled in charter schools in comparison with regular schools. Since our methods are different in this respect from prior published research, the findings from our investigation are not comparable to findings from research that did not disaggregate analyses by location.

Access to Urban Charter Schools

Compared with urban regular schools, our results demonstrated that urban charter schools enrolled a higher percentage of Black students and a lower percentage of disadvantaged, LEP, and Hispanic students. What are the implications of these findings for access to the benefits of an urban charter school education for students? Are urban charter schools located in neighborhoods that created better access for certain groups and less access for others, or are selection standards biased in favor of certain groups and biased against others? Since these questions could not be investigated with SASS data, our research does not provide evidence about equal or unequal access to charter schools by students of any particular characteristic.

d'Entremont and Gulosino (2008) suggested that urban charter schools might have been placed in locations that provide equal access to all groups of students and that admission decisions have not been biased for or against particular groups. Alternatively, the disproportionate enrollment (either high or low) in urban charter schools of certain groups could be driven by disproportionate numbers of applications for admission (either high or low) submitted by parents of students who were more strongly attracted to special programs offered by charter schools or who were more determined to avoid troubled regular schools—a trend observed by Rapp and Eckes (2007). Our study demonstrated a phenomenon (i.e., the disproportionate enrollment of students with certain characteristics in urban charter schools), but it did not provide answers as to why this happened. This should be investigated in future research.

Policy Implications

This research was designed to examine the extent to which charter schools have provided *all families* (regardless of location, income, prior student achievement, or race) with expanded education choices as intended by state and federal charter school legislation and in accordance with federal non-discrimination policies. Contrary to legislative intent, a substantial majority of charter schools has been established in urban areas—well out of proportion to the substantial majority of public school students who reside in suburban and rural areas. Thus, urban students had much greater access to charter schools than did non-urban students.

This outcome was of concern to the Chief Operating Officer of NAPCS, who wrote, "Given that an overwhelming purpose of charter schools was to provide more options to all families, what should we make of the fact that most charter schools are serving urban areas? Have we given insufficient attention to the benefits charter could provide to suburban and rural areas?" (Smarick, 2005, p. 6). It appears so, and especially for rural students in proportion to their numbers.

In the aggregate (as distinguished from particular schools), our findings show that charter schools in non-urban areas enrolled students without regard to family income, certain indicators of prior achievement, or race/ethnicity. In particular, we found no evidence that non-urban charter schools overall have been established to segregate White students from minority students more so than has occurred in non-urban regular schools. In fact, our results suggest the possibility that the enrollment of White students in non-urban charter schools was lower than in non-urban regular schools (60% vs. 68% respectively; $p < .06$, not significant). In these respects, non-urban charter schools have been implemented successfully in accordance with legislative intents, but not in accordance with the preference of charter school leaders to focus on low-income and minority students in order to reduce the achievement gap. These findings about characteristics of charter school students in non-urban areas, as compared with regular school students, are unique because other research has not been reported on such comparisons.

By contrast, we found that characteristics of students enrolled in *urban* charter schools were not in accord with the intent of charter school legislation to serve all families without regard to income, prior achievement, or race/ethnicity. With respect to income, it appears that urban regular schools enrolled a somewhat higher percentage of low-income students than did charter schools. At the least, there was no evidence that charter schools assumed more responsibility for educating low-income students than have regular schools. As with other studies, we have necessarily used eligibility for free or reduced-price school lunches as an imperfect proxy for family income. Until better measures of family income are available for charter school research, final judgment should be reserved about the enrollment of low-income students in these and regular schools.

As to prior achievement, urban charter schools enrolled an equivalent percentage of IEP students as did regular schools, but enrolled a much lower percentage of LEP students. Unfortunately, no national study (including ours) has been able to report data on prior achievement based on standardized tests. Until such data are available, judgment should be reserved regarding how well charter schools in comparison with regular schools enroll students without regard to prior achievement.

The race/ethnicity of urban charter schools students represented the greatest departure from state and federal legislative intents to serve all families evenhandedly. Compared with urban regular schools, we found that *urban* charter schools enrolled a much higher percentage of Black students and a much lower percentage of Hispanic students. In addition, Black students have become remarkably segregated in urban charter schools.

Contrary to state and federal charter school legislation about serving all families, charter school leaders have sought to address the achievement gap by providing a higher-quality education for low-income and minority students than they have received under the traditional system (Smarick, 2005). Our results suggest that charter school leaders have been successful in creating an emphasis on serving Black students in urban charter schools, but have been unsuccessful in creating an emphasis on serving Hispanic students or on serving low-income students. In fact, urban charter schools in comparison with regular schools have underserved Hispanic students and low-income students. Thus, with regard to populations of students to be served, neither the objectives of state and federal policy nor the objectives of charter school leaders have been entirely achieved in urban charter schools.

These findings raise issues about managing the further development of charter schools and the possible need for revising the policy of serving all families. Regarding the management and further development of charter schools, our results provide charter school leaders and policy makers with reliable information about charter school success in providing all families with expanded education choices in non-urban areas and the extent of failure in this respect in urban areas. This information can be used in the further development of charter schools if those responsible wish to serve all geographic areas and all racial/ethnic groups equitably in accordance with legislative intents.

Our findings suggest that charter school leaders have been more influential than have state and federal policy makers in determining the location of charter schools predominantly in urban areas and in fostering the disproportionate enrollment of students with certain characteristics in urban charter schools. In this respect, Rapp and Eckes (2007) similarly concluded that "state statutory admissions and enrollment plans may not be enforced" (p. 629). These findings demonstrate a need to reconsider relevant policies, the outcome of which could either lead to changes that recognize and support the kind of enrollment inequalities observed in urban charter schools (including the voluntary segregation of Black students), or confirmation of current policy with establishment of a regulatory process to assure implementation as intended.

Results pertaining to the representation of Black students in urban charter schools are simultaneously laudable and troubling. Such high concentrations of these students are evidence that many Black parents have become well aware of charter schools as alternatives to urban regular schools. Conant (1961) described a host of problems that unfortunately continue to plague many contemporary urban schools, including overcrowding, inadequate resources, high dropout rates, insufficiently motivated teachers, and environmental factors that stifle academic achievement. Other researchers (e.g., Fordham, 1996; Henig, 1996; Henig, Hula, Orr, & Pedescleaux, 2001) have documented Black parents' dissatisfaction with the urban public school conditions in which their children are often forced to learn. Thus, our study demonstrates how the intent of state charter school legislation to provide parents with expanded educational choices appears to have been fulfilled for a disproportionately high percentage of Black families in urban contexts.

Although investigating curricular content offered by charter schools was not possible with SASS date used in our research, the considerable voluntary segregation observed of Black students in urban charter schools could be partially explained by the appeal and availability of culturally responsive curricula and pedagogies (Bulkley & Wohlstetter, 2003; Murrell, 1999; Rapp & Eckes, 2007). Ladson-Billings (1994) described preferences among Black parents for schools that recognize their cultures and teachers who facilitate learning in ways that are perceived as relevant by Black students in those schools. It is possible that charter schools, especially those in urban areas with high concentrations of Black residents, offer these features more so than do urban regular schools. This would contradict Wells's (1996) argument that Black students who transfer from urban regular schools do so because they and their parents adopt "white is right" viewpoints and perceive predominantly white school alternatives as better. Notwithstanding the conjecture regarding culturally appealing school features, our findings do make clear that parents perceived charter schools, even those that were predominantly Black, as attractive alternatives to urban regular schools.

Moreover, some single-sex charter schools (e.g., the Urban Prep Charter Academy for Young Men in Chicago)[7] offer gender-affirming educational experiences for students (Bulkley & Wohlstetter, 2003). As Rapp and Eckes (2007) note, most students in such schools are of a particular race by nature of locale as well as the culture that has been created in the school. To some extent, the existence of such charter schools accounts for the voluntary segregation trends observed here, but the effects of their cultural and pedagogical features on Black parents' school choices warrant further study.

In addition to Black parents being attracted to urban charter schools offering culturally relevant and gender-affirming educational experiences, it is also possible that the high concentration of Black students seen in such schools has been driven by the preferences of White (and perhaps Hispanic) parents. Based on their review of relevant research, Rapp and Eckes (2007) suggested that White parents avoid high-minority charter schools.

According to Orfield (2001), "one of the least studied and perhaps most important transformations in the nation's schools in recent decades has been the steadily increasing isolation of Latino students" (p. 46). He observed that all states with significant Latino populations had experienced increased segregation. Despite this, Frankenberg and Lee (2003) found that Hispanic charter school students were less segregated than were their Black counterparts, a trend also revealed in our analyses. The comparatively low representation of Hispanic students in urban charter schools is noteworthy and signifies the need for more aggressive outreach to Hispanic parents, who may not be fully aware of their educational choices. It could be that they are not afforded equitable access to information about the availability, features, and possible benefits of charter schools, as noted throughout Fuller, Elmore, and Orfield's (1996) book. Given this, resources should be provided to develop informational campaigns about charter schools that are targeted to Hispanic families in urban areas.

Implications for Future Research

The appearance of differential access to urban charter schools by student characteristics (such as race/ethnicity) is a prime topic for further research. First, accurate measures of family income and student academic achievement in multiple core subjects are needed to establish accurately whether, and to what extent, family income and prior achievement are factors favoring, or impeding, enrollment in charter schools. Using the best measures available for family income, prior academic achievement, and race/ethnicity, more incisive studies are needed to ascertain the extent to which variation in school funding, educational programs offered, location, selection biases, and family initiative (to secure admission) are factors in the disproportionate representation (either more or less) of students with certain characteristics.

In light of the relatively high percentage of Black students enrolled in urban charter schools, more evidence is needed to develop sociopolitical explanations for the voluntary segregation phenomenon. In addition, the consequences (both positive and adverse) for their academic and social development should be investigated. Also, the benefits and liabilities for Black students who become substantially segregated by choice in urban charter schools need to be examined and taken into account in policy deliberations.

Our study was based on cross-sectional data on school enrollments during one year. As recommended by Gill (2005), longitudinal data are needed to examine the effects of *introducing* charter schools on the voluntary segregation or integration of students in all schools in a community, taking into account the voluntary segregation or integration effects on other forms of school choice, such as private schools, change in district of residence, intradistrict choice, and home schooling. The voluntary segregation of Black students in urban charter schools observed in our research is but one element in a wider perspective of school choice effects.

Notes

1 The second most frequently stated goal (90% of states) was to improve the achievement of all students. See Hill, Angel, and Christensen (2006) for a review of research on the attainment of this goal. Of the 18 distinct goals identified, other prominent goals were to give teachers more ownership of their schools, to generate more accountability, and to increase school autonomy. Research about attainment of goals such as these can be found in Barghaus and Boe (2009) and Gawlik (2007).
2 With respect to charter schools providing "expanded educational choices," one review of published research has shown that charter schools indeed provide alternatives to regular public schools "in areas such as class size, technology, and programmatic options" (Lubienski, 2003, p. 418). A recent national study has shown that charter schools, in comparison with regular schools, are considerably more likely to offer programs with special emphases (e.g., science/math schools and foreign language immersion schools) and to adopt classroom innovations such as special instructional approaches (e.g., Montessori and ungraded classrooms).
3 As stated by the USDE (2004), charter schools must comply "with the Age Discrimination Act of 1975, Title VI of the Civil Rights Act of 1964, Title IX of the Education Amendments of 1972, Section 504 of the Rehabilitation Act of 1973, Title II of the Americans with Disabilities Act of 1990, and Part B of the Individuals with Disabilities Education Act" (p. 7).
4 The sum of White, Black, and Hispanic student percentages in regular schools in Figures 7.4 and 7.5 (separately) does not equal 100% because we excluded other race/ethnicity groups due to small sample size. The same pertains to the sum of race/ethnicity percentages of students enrolled in charter schools.
5 We would have selected an index of concentration greater that 51–100% of enrollment by one racial/ethnic group (e.g., an index of 76–100%), but this was precluded due to a limit of charter school sample size for the Hispanic students.
6 This cut-off point was selected to ensure a sufficient sample of large charter schools. One-third of charter schools and three-quarters of regular schools had enrollments of 409 or greater.
7 See http://www.urbanprep.org.

References

Bulkley, K. E., & Wohlstetter, P. (2003). *Taking account of charter schools: What's happened and what's next?* New York: Teachers College Press.
Center for Education Reform. (2004). National Charter School Directory, (9th ed.). Retrieved July 8, 2008, from http://www.edreform.com/index.cfm?fuseAction=document&documentID=1757
Center for Education Reform. (2006). *Charter schools: Changing the face of American education. Part 2: Raising the bar on charter school laws 2006 ranking and scorecard* (9th ed.). Washington, DC: Author.
Center for Education Reform. (2008, July). Annual survey of America's charter schools. Retrieved August 22, 2008, from http://www.edreform.com/_upload/CER_charter_survey_2008.pdf

Conant, J. B. (1961). *Slums and suburbs.* New York: McGraw-Hill.
d'Entremont, C., & Gulosino, C. (2008). *Circles of influence: How neighborhood demographics and charter school locations influence student enrollments* (Paper No. 160). New York: Columbia University, Teachers College, National Center for the Study of Privatization in Education.
Fordham, S. (1996). *Blacked out: Dilemmas of race, identity, and success at Capital High.* Chicago: University of Chicago Press.
Frankenberg, E., & Lee, C. (2003). *Charter schools and race: A lost opportunity for integrated education.* Cambridge, MA: Harvard University, Harvard Civil Rights Project.
Fuller, B., Elmore, R. F., & Orfield, G. (Eds.). (1996). *Who chooses? Who loses? Culture, institutions, and the unequal effects of school choice.* New York: Teachers College Press.
Gawlik, M. A. (2007). Beyond the charter schoolhouse door: Teacher-perceived autonomy. *Education and Urban Society, 39,* 524–553.
Gill, B. (2005). School choice and integration. In J. B. Betts & T. Loveless (Eds.), *Getting choice right: Ensuring equity and efficiency in education policy* (pp. 130–145). Washington, DC: Brookings Institution Press.
Gill, B., Timpane, P. M., Ross, K. E., Brewer, D. J., & Booker, K. (2007). *Rhetoric verse reality: What we know and what we need to know about vouchers and charter schools* (Rev. ed.). Santa Monica, CA: RAND Corporation.
Henig, J. R. (1996). The local dynamics of choice: Ethnic preferences and institutional responses. In B. Fuller, R. F. Elmore, & G. Orfield (Eds.), *Who chooses? Who loses? Culture, institutions, and the unequal effects of school choice* (pp. 95–117). New York: Teachers College Press.
Henig, J. R., Hula, R. C., Orr, M., & Pedescleaux, D. S. (2001). *The color of school reform: Race, politics, and the challenge of urban education.* Princeton, NJ: Princeton University Press.
Hill, P. T., Angel, L., & Christensen, J. (2006). Charter school achievement studies. *Education Finance and Policy, 1,* 139–150.
Ladson-Billings, G. (1994). *The dreamkeepers: Successful teachers of African American children.* San Francisco: Jossey-Bass.
Lubienski, C. (2003). Innovation in education markets: Theory and evidence on the impact of competition and choice in charter schools. *American Educational Research Journal, 40,* 395–443.
May, H. (2004). *JACKREG.sas macro for use with the SAS System* (Version 4.0) [Computer Software]. Philadelphia, PA: Author. Retrieved January 13, 2008, from http://www.gse.upenn.edu/~hmay/
Miron, G., Cullen, A., Applegate, B., & Farrell, P. (2007). *Evaluation of the Delaware charter school reform final report.* Kalamazoo, MI: The Evaluation Center at Western Michigan University.
Miron, G., & Nelson, C. (2002). *What's public about charter schools? Lessons learned about choice and accountability.* Thousand Oaks, CA: Corwin.
Murrell, P. C., Jr. (1999). Class and race in negotiating identity. In A. Garrod, J. Ward, T. L. Robinson, & R. Kilkenny (Eds.), *Souls looking back: Life stories of growing up Black* (pp. 3–14). New York: Routledge.
National Center for Education Statistics. (2002). *Schools and Staffing Survey, 1999–2000: Overview of the data for public, private, public charter, and Bureau of Indian Affairs elementary and secondary schools* (NCES 2002-313). Washington, DC: U.S. Department of Education, Institute of Education Sciences, National Center for Education Statistics.
National Center for Education Statistics. (2005). *America's charter schools: Results from the NAEP 2003 pilot study* (NCES 2005-456). Washington, DC: U.S. Department of Education, Institute of Education Sciences, National Center for Education Statistics.

Orfield, G. (2001). *Schools more separate: Consequences of a decade of resegregation*. Cambridge, MA: Harvard Civil Rights Project, Harvard University.

Rapp, K. E., & Eckes, S. E. (2007). Dispelling the myth of "white flight": An examination of minority enrollment in charter schools. *Educational Policy, 21*(4), 615–661.

Smarick, A. (2005). *Original intent: What legislative history tells us about the purposes of chartering*. Washington, DC: National Alliance for Public Charter Schools.

Strizek, G. A., Pittsonberger, J. L., Riordan, K. E., Lyter, D. M., & Orlofsky, G. F. (2006). *Characteristics of schools, districts, teachers, principals, and school libraries in the United States: 2003–04 schools and staffing survey* (NCES 2006-313 Revised). Washington, DC: U.S. Department of Education, National Center for Education Statistics. U.S. Government Printing Office.

Tourkin, S. C., Warner, T., Parmer, R., Cole, C., Jackson, B., Zukerberg, A., Cox, S., & Soderberg, A. (2007). *Documentation for the 2003–04 schools and staffing survey* (NCES 2007-337). Washington, DC: U.S. Department of Education, National Center for Education Statistics.

U.S. Department of Education. (2004). *Non-regulatory guidance, title V, part B, charter schools program*. Jessup, MD: ED Pubs.

Wells, A. S. (1996). African American students' view of school choice. In B. Fuller, R. F. Elmore, & G. Orfield (Eds.), *Who chooses? Who loses? Culture, institutions, and the unequal effects of school choice* (pp. 25–49). New York: Teachers College Press.

Westat Inc. (2002). *WesVar* (Version 4.2) [Computer software]. Rockville, MD: Author.

Afterword
Schools of Education as Stakeholders in the Charter School Debate

Virginia L. McLaughlin

Each chapter in this edited volume has addressed a particular aspect of the charter school puzzle. For this Afterword, I was invited to comment on charter school issues from the perspective of an education school dean. Having served in that role for 18 years, until 2013, I readily apply that perspective to educational issues. Undoubtedly, my career-long experiences as a special educator and my four-year term on a state board of education influence my views as well. I will consider charter school issues as they intersect with the core teaching and research mission of universities and explain why schools of education have reason to be concerned about—and engaged in—the charter school movement.

The Teaching Mission

Today's schools of education often house a diverse range of programs, such as kinesiology, counseling psychology, and human services, yet educator preparation remains our central purpose. Our primary reason for being is to prepare teachers, specialists, and administrators for work within the P-20 educational system. Through baccalaureate and master's degree programs, as well as alternative routes, schools of education are heavily involved in the initial preparation of P-12 teachers. As charter schools have evolved, they impact the preparation of teachers in at least two important ways. In this Afterword, I first will examine the role of charter schools in clinical partnerships with schools of education, then reflect upon the creation of standalone charter school teacher education programs.

Clinical Preparation of Teachers

While many aspects of teacher education are hotly debated, there is a solid evidence base (National Research Council, 2010) and general consensus on the importance of clinical experiences for the preparation of effective teachers. In 2010, the National Council for Accreditation of Teacher Education (NCATE) reaffirmed the importance of clinically based programs through the work of a Blue Ribbon Panel on Clinical Preparation and Partnerships for Improved Student Learning that was comprised of state officials, P-12 and higher education leaders, teachers, teacher educators, union representatives, and critics of teacher education. Similarly, the Council for Accreditation of Educator Preparation (CAEP), recently formed through the merger of NCATE and the Teacher Education Accreditation Council, includes *Clinical Partnerships and Practice* as one of its five major standards for preparation programs. Standard 2 states: "The provider ensures that effective partnerships and high-quality clinical practice are central to preparation so that candidates develop the knowledge, skills, and professional dispositions necessary to demonstrate positive impact on all P-12 students' learning and development" (CAEP, 2016).

Schools of education may shy away from clinical placements in charter schools for several reasons. First, schools of education tend to select school settings that are representative of the broader public school context and provide experiences with diverse learners, curricula, and pedagogies. They may perceive placements in particular charter schools as too narrow in scope, limiting the range of experiences for pre-service teachers. Furthermore, many higher education faculties share the serious concerns about equity and social justice that have been discussed in the preceding chapters of this text. Believing that the charter school movement is a threat to America's public system of education, many teacher educators will not promote charter schools by placing their teacher candidates in those settings.

A second reason that schools of education may not pursue placements in charter schools relates to the criteria for the selection of clinical faculty (formerly known as cooperating teachers). The American Association of Colleges for Teacher Education (AACTE) recommends that clinical faculty should have at least three years of teaching experience, be matched to their novice teachers by subject and grade level, and be selected jointly by preparation program and school faculty on the basis of the clinical faculty's interest and ability to guide the specific candidate through the clinical practice program (AACTE, 2010, p. 12). Given documented turnover rates, teachers in charter schools tend to be younger and less experienced (Stuit & Smith, 2012), and may not meet the selection criteria. Additionally, most states require their teacher education programs to place candidates with licensed (i.e., certified) clinical teachers. Since regulations in many states exempt charter schools from teacher licensure requirements (Education Commission of the States, 2015), it can be challenging to find qualified clinical faculty in charter schools.

Finally, many schools of education have established professional development schools to provide rich professional learning communities for experienced teachers, university faculty, and pre-service candidates. Schools of education may perceive the culture and working conditions of charter schools as a mismatch for this type of intensive clinical partnership for teacher preparation. In an earlier chapter, Stitzlein and Smith characterized charter school working environments that deprofessionalize teachers with long and unpredictable work hours, extreme pressure to ameliorate the achievement gap, evaluations and raises dependent on test scores, lack of autonomy, and forced adherence to pedagogical and disciplinary practices that violate teachers' own professional knowledge and beliefs.

More models of positive clinical partnerships between schools of education and charter schools might counter these apprehensions. Stanford University, for example, has received recognition for its professional development school at East Palo Alto Academy, in collaboration with the Ravenswood School District and Aspire Public Schools in a low-income, all-minority community near the university that had lacked a public high school. Stanford faculty from the education school, medical school, law school, and college work with the Academy to provide students with quality education, health care, and other support services (AACTE, 2010). It is likely that many universities, especially those in areas with high concentrations of charter schools, have developed successful clinical partnerships with charter schools. The field of teacher education could benefit from additional evaluation and dissemination of effective charter school-university clinical partnerships.

Charter Teacher Preparation

As noted above, teacher licensure has been among the flexibilities granted to charter schools in the 42 states that have enacted charter school laws. No licensure is required in Arizona, Louisiana, Texas, and the District of Columbia. Fifteen states require charter schoolteachers to be licensed, and the remaining 23 allow some provision for waivers and/or a certain percentage of teachers to be unlicensed (ECS, 2015). Many teachers in charter schools have come through alternate routes to licensure, whether these have been stand-alone programs or affiliated with universities. Stitzlein and Smith discussed the long-standing relationship between charter schools and Teach for America (TFA), with TFA serving as a pipeline into charter schools in many areas. From its early years, TFA has partnered with local colleges and universities to offer the coursework required for licensure, at least partially paid for with the stipends provided to corps members. Other teacher preparation partnerships developed, such as Teacher U, a partnership among Uncommon Schools, Knowledge is Power Program (KIPP), and Achievement First that prepares teachers for their own networks and for other New York City district and charter schools. Teacher U was designed as a two-year preparation program leading to a master's degree through Hunter College (NCATE, 2010, p. 14). In 2011, Teacher U became independent, was renamed the Relay Graduate School of Education, was granted a charter by the New York State Board of Regents, and became the first stand-alone graduate school of education to emerge in the States (Relay GSE, 2015).

Other teacher preparation programs have emerged through charter schools with loose university affiliations. Match Beyond, for example, explains on its website that it was incubated within Match Education and remains one of their operating units, which also includes a network of charter schools and an innovative graduate school of education that trains teachers and school leaders for urban schools. Match Beyond lists 17 charter schools and the College for America at Southern New Hampshire University as their current partners (Match Education, 2015).

Schools of education have good reason to be concerned about these new versions of "graduate school." During this time when the teaching profession has been greatly devalued, such programs contribute further to the critics' belief that teaching is merely a vocational skill that can be mastered quickly without an academic foundation. Stitzlein and Smith note that, with the exception of High Tech High Graduate School of Education, these programs avoid teaching educational theory, educational psychology, or the research base undergirding professional practice (2016).

Schools of education, our accrediting body (CAEP), and our professional associations such as AACTE face a true dilemma in responding to these emerging preparation programs. On the one hand, we in the teacher education profession would like to distance ourselves from such programs of highly questionable quality. On the other hand, we have argued strongly as a profession that *all* teacher preparation programs—university- and non-university-based—should be held to the same national and state standards. Should these stand-alone teacher preparation programs be allowed to seek national accreditation? Should they be accepted as members of established professional associations? Schools of education cannot afford to be silent on these issues, for the integrity of the teacher education profession is at stake.

The Research Mission

Although the intensity of the scholarship focus varies greatly from Research I universities to baccalaureate, liberal arts colleges, schools of education in all higher education institutions share a fundamental commitment to the production and application of research as a defining characteristic of the profession. In this section, I will review concerns about the quality of charter school efficacy research and the need for schools of education to be actively engaged in both conducting and critiquing this research. I will also revisit the expectation for innovation in charter schools and emphasize the need for rigorous independent evaluations of charter school programs.

Charter School Efficacy

Each of the earlier chapters in this text have reviewed the relevant research literature, and most have acknowledged the need for more and better studies on charter schools. Despite the inflated claims of some advocates, the overall evidence on charter school effectiveness is decidedly mixed (Finn & Manno, 2015; Toma & Zimmer, 2012). Some charter schools outperform, others underperform, and most charter schools perform similarly to their traditional public school peers (Aldis & O'Leary, 2015; Cheng, Hitt, Kisida, & Mills, 2015; Center for Research on Education Outcomes [CREDO], 2013, 2015; Crew & Anderson, 2003; Lubienski & Lubienski, 2014; Weil, 2009; Welch, 2010/2011).

By cherry-picking results of complex studies, both proponents and opponents find ample evidence to support their already entrenched positions. The misuse of research further stems from methodological shortcomings, such as confusion of correlation with causation, failure to account for selection or attrition bias, and long-distance leaps from evidence, to causal conclusions, and then to unsupported recommendations (Welner, Hinchey, Molnar, & Weitzman, 2010). Schools of education have an important role to play in helping, not only their own students, but also policy makers and the public at large to interpret the quality and nuanced findings of the research base on charter schools.

I applaud the open debates on charter school research methodology currently led by the National Education Policy Center (NEPC) within the School of Education at the University of Colorado. Toward their goal of providing high-quality information in support of democratic deliberation about education policy, NEPC conducts expert third-party reviews of major studies, including think tank reports (NEPC, 2015). NEPC has been deeply engaged with studies of charter schools, critiquing major reports, such as the widely cited studies completed by the Center for Research on Education Outcomes (CREDO) at Stanford University (CREDO, 2013, 2015), as well as others by the University of Washington's Center on Reinventing Public Education (Betts & Tang, 2014), and the University Of Arkansas, Department of Education Reform (Cheng, Hitt, Kisida & Mills (2014). Although not all of these university-based centers are housed in schools/colleges of education, the debates rightfully are taking place within an academic context. The back-and-forth discussion between NEPC (Maul, 2015a, 2015b) and CREDO (CREDO, 2015) on methodology and conclusions of the CREDO study of charter schools in 41 urban regions provides an excellent example of the scholarly discourse that is needed to make sense of reported findings and, more importantly, to craft more rigorous research methodologies for studying highly complex issues like charter school efficacy.

Charter School Innovation

Beyond the efficacy studies that investigate the aggregate effect charter schools have on student achievement, there is also a need for more research and rigorous program evaluations of specific charter school models. If charter school performance varies widely, we need to know more about the important attributes of different charter school programs that contribute to their relative success. As Welch has noted, "What should concern observers of charter schools and all public schools in general, is not whether or not charter schools are uniformly moving to a radically different form of schooling, but how the pockets of quality the movement has produced can be grown at scale and sustained over time" (Welch, 2010/2011, p. 63).

Identifying the key features of charter school programs for study or replication has not been easy. A large percentage of charter schools are operated by education management organizations (EMOs) that offer a standard school model, centralized management teams, and economies of scale (CRPE, 2007). Whether these are for-profit or nonprofit EMOs, they are likely to be proprietary regarding the specifics of their products. When constructing yearly profiles of EMOs comprised of basic data such as numbers of school operated, numbers of students enrolled, and Adequate Yearly Progress ratings, Miron and Urschel (2010) found that the nature of the industry and the lack of public information made the process of collecting and updating data difficult. In 2010, for example, only 11% of nonprofit EMOs responded to their requests for participation. A parallel study of for-profit EMOs elicited an 18% response rate (Molnar, Miron, & Urschel, 2010). Little is known about the effectiveness of EMO programs on student achievement, parental satisfaction, parental involvement, or school climate, because few studies have been conducted (Government Accountability Office [GAO], 2002). Much of the information about specific charter schools comes from their websites and published reports that are often geared more toward marketing than substantive program description. KIPP, for example, is one of the largest and most established charter school networks, currently operating 183 KIPP schools in 20 states and the District of Columbia (KIPP, 2015). While KIPP widely documents their operating principles, the Five Pillars, they provide little public information on the ways those principles translate into actual program practices across all KIPP sites. Without more specific programmatic information, it is impossible to judge the real contributions of charter schools.

Early proponents of charter schools touted the benefits of innovation and experimentation not only to increase student learning, but also to stimulate improvements in the overall K-12 education system. In tracing the origins of charter schools in the late 1980s, Ravitch described how Albert Shanker argued for teacher-led autonomous schools that would be highly experimental, "tasked with solving important problems of pedagogy and curriculum and expected to produce findings that would help other schools" (Ravitch, 2010, p. 123). In the same year as No Child Left Behind (NCLB, 2001) was signed into law, the National Education Association adopted a resolution in support of charter schools citing that one of their intended purposes was to serve as experimental laboratories for field testing curricular and instructional innovations with an eye to whether these innovations could be incorporated into mainstream public schools (Weil, p. 66). Current advocates for charter school expansion continue to emphasize the R&D potential of charter schools. Freed from the bureaucracy, regulations, and collective bargaining that stifle innovation in public schools, charters can incubate new and more effective ventures, what Hess refers to as the "greenfield" of schooling (Hess, 2010, p. 51).

The current knowledge base indicates that charter schools are not living up to their potential for innovation. In a study of differences between charter schools and traditional public schools based on the Schools and Staffing Survey, Preston, Goldring, Berends, and Cannata (2012) found that, with the exception of teacher tenure, charter schools were not more innovative in terms of student support services, staffing policies, organizational structures, and governance. Charter schools have been less likely to experiment with curricular and instructional models new to public education (Lubienski & Lubienski, 2014), but they have been able to package practices in new ways and bring them to diverse communities and learners (Lake, 2008). With few exceptions, such as High Tech High in San Diego (Neumann, 2008), charter schools have begun to resemble the district schools they were originally designed to disrupt (Danzig & Mathis, 2015; Hassel, Locke, Kim, Hargrave, & Losoponkul, 2015; Renzulli, Barr, & Paino, 2014). Even advocates for greater expansion and deregulation have noted that specialized schools (e.g., no excuses or STEM) have tended to morph into homogenized general schools (McShane & Hatfield, 2015). In Hess's view, charter schools have typically succeeded by hiring extraordinary teachers, extending the school day, and creating disciplined cultures—what good schools have always aspired to do (Hess, 2010, p. 50).

Once again, proponents and opponents of charter schools draw different implications from the limited evidence base. Proponents of choice advocate for greater deregulation and increased funding to stimulate further innovation, while opponents argue that charter schools are failing to produce the intended program diversity and models for change. The common ground is recognition of the need for additional rigorous research and evaluation. Schools of education are well positioned to conduct high-quality studies of specific charter schools that further our understanding of program design, implementation, outcomes, and relevant context (Crew & Anderson, 2003; Hughes & Silva, 2013; McDonald, Ross, Bol, & McSparrin-Gallagher, 2007). This is the information we need to make more informed decisions about charter school effectiveness and the potential for replication and scaling up.

Conclusion

Schools of education need to be actively engaged in the charter school debate. Despite the lack of efficacy evidence and serious social justice concerns, charter schools have a strong foothold in American education. As they increase in number, more of our education school graduates are likely to be employed in charter schools. It only makes sense for more schools of education, particularly those in areas with high concentrations of charter schools, to pursue selective clinical partnerships with the stronger programs. Continuing to monitor the growth of the charter teacher preparation enterprise and advocating for consistent application of accreditation and licensure standards are critical to our professional identity. Perhaps most importantly, schools of education have the expertise to contribute substantially to research and evaluation of charter schools. Although the intent of many charter school advocates has been disruption of the "traditional" education system, those of us in schools of education must recognize the opportunity for the profession to influence the charter school movement as well.

References

Aldis, C., & O'Leary, J. D. (2015, November 4). *Virtual charter school students are not learning nearly enough*. Washington, DC: Thomas B. Fordham Institute.

American Association of Colleges for Teacher Education (AACTE). (2010). The clinical preparation of teachers: A policy brief. Retrieved from https://aacte.org/pdf/Government_Relations/Clinical%20Prep%20Paper_03-11-2010.pdf

Betts, J. R., & Tang, Y. E. (2014). *A meta-analysis of the literature on the effect of charter schools on student achievement* (Working Paper). Seattle, WA: Center on Reinventing Public Education University of Washington. Retrieved from http://www.crpe.org/publications/meta-analysis-literature-effect-charter-schools-student-achievement

Center for Research on Education Outcomes. (2013). *National charter school study*. Stanford, CA: University Press. Retrieved from http://credo.stanford.edu/documents/NCSS%202013%20Final%20Draft.pdf

Center for Research on Education Outcomes. (2015a). *Urban charter school study report on 41 regions*. Stanford, CA: University Press. Retrieved from https://urbancharters.stanford.edu/download/Urban%20Charter%20School%20Study%20Report%20on%2041%20Regions.pdf

Center for Research on Education Outcomes. (2015b, June). *CREDO response to Maul and Gabor*. Stanford, CA: University Press. Retrieved from http://credo.stanford.edu/pdfs/CREDOResponsetoMaulandGabor3.pdf

Center on Reinventing Public Education. (2007). *Quality counts: The growth of charter school management organizations*. Seattle, WA: National Charter School Research Project. Retrieved from http://www.crpe.org/sites/default/files/pub_ncsrp_quancount_aug07_0.pdf

Cheng, A., Hitt, C., Kisida, B., & Mills, J. N. (2014). *No excuses charter schools: A meta-analysis of the experimental evidence on student achievement* (EDRE Working paper No. 2014–11). New Orleans, LA. Retrieved from http://www.uaedreform.org/downloads/2014/12/no-excuses-charter-schools-a-meta-analysis-of-the-experimental-evidence-on-student-achievement.pdf

Cheng, A., Hitt, C., Kisida, B., & Mills, J. N. (2015). *No excuses charter schools: A meta-analysis of the experimental evidence* (Occasional paper No. 226). New York, NY: National Center for the Study of Privatization in Education. Retrieved from http://www.ncspe.org/publications_files/OP226.pdf

Council for the Accreditation of Educator Preparation [CAEP]. (2016). *Standard 2: Clinical partnerships*. Retrieved from http://caepnet.org/standards/standard-2

Crew, R. E., Jr., & Anderson, M. R. (2003). Accountability and performance in charter schools in Florida: A theory-based evaluation. *American Journal of Evaluation, 24*(2), 189–213.

Danzig, A., & Mathis, W. J. (2015, September 1). *Review of measuring diversity in charter school offerings*. Boulder, CO: National Education Policy Center. Retrieved from http://nepc.colorado.edu/thinktank/review-charter-diversity

Education Commission of the States (ECS). (2015). Charter schools: Do teachers have to be certified? Retrieved from http://ecs.force.com/mbdata/mbquestNB2?rep=CS1425

Finn, C. E., Jr., & Manno, B. V. (2015, August 27) Charter schools: Taking stock. *Education Next*. Retrieved from http://educationnext.org/charter-schools-taking-stock/

Government Accountability Office. (2002, October). *Insufficient research to determine effectiveness of selected private education companies*. Washington, DC: United States General Accounting Office. Retrieved from http://www.gao.gov/new.items/d0311.pdf

Hassel, B. C., Locke, G., Kim, J., Hargrave, E., & Losoponkul, N. (2015). *Raising the bar: Why public charter schools must become even more innovative* (The Mind Trust). Indianapolis, IN: The Mind Trust. Retrieved from http://www.themindtrust.org/files/file/themindtrust-raisingthebar-final.pdf

Hess, F. (2010). The transformative promise of "Greenfield" schooling. *Phi Delta Kappan, 91*(5), 49–53.

Hughes, K. B., & Silva, S. A. M. (2013). Charter schools best practices: Authentic leadership and context matter. *Advances in Educational Administration, 18*, 156–171.

KIPP. (2015). About KIPP. Retrieved from http://www.kipp.org/about-kipp

Lake, R. J. (2008). In the eye of the beholder: Charter schools and innovation. *Journal of School Choice, 2*(2), 115–127. doi:10.1080/15582150802136090

Lubienski, C. A., & Lubienski, S. T. (2014). *The public school advantage: Why public schools outperform private schools*. Chicago, IL: University Press.

Match Education/Match Beyond. (2015) About us. Retrieved from http://www.matchbeyond.org/update/

Maul, A. (2015a). *Review of "urban charter school study 2015."* Boulder, CO: National Education Policy Center. Retrieved from http://nepc.colorado.edu/thinktank/review-urban-charter-school

Maul, A. (2015b, September 28). *Rejoinder of Andrew Maul to response from CREDO*. Boulder, CO: National Education Policy Center. Retrieved from http://nepc.colorado.edu/files/maul-credo-response.pdf

McDonald, A. J., Ross, S. J., Bol, L., & McSparrin-Gallagher, B. (2007). Charter schools as a vehicle for education reform: Implementation and outcomes at three inner-city sites. *Journal of Education for Students Placed at Risk, 12*(3), 271–300.

McShane, M. Q., & Hatfield, J. (2015, July). *Measuring diversity in charter school offerings*. Washington, DC: American Enterprise Institute. Retrieved from https://www.aei.org/wp-content/uploads/2015/07/Measuring-Diversity-in-Charter-School-Offerings.pdf

Miron, G., & Urschel, J. L. (2010). *Profiles of nonprofit education management organizations: 2009–2010*. Boulder, CO: National Education Policy Center. Retrieved from http://nepc.colorado.edu/publication/EMO-NP-09–10

Molnar, A., Miron, G., & Urschel, J. L. (2010). *Profiles of for-profit education management organizations: Twelfth annual report—2009–2010*. Boulder, CO: National Education Policy Center. Retrieved from http://nepc.colorado.edu/publication/EMO-FP-09–10

National Council for Accreditation of Teacher Education (NCATE). (2010). *Transforming teacher education through clinical practice: A national strategy to prepare effective teachers*. Washington, DC: National Council for Accreditation of Teacher.

National Education Policy Center [NEPC]. (2015). *Home*. Retrieved from http://nepc.colorado.edu/

The National Research Council. (2010). *Preparing teachers: Building evidence for sound policy*. Washington, DC: The National Academies Press.

NCLB Act of 2001, Pub. L. No. 107–110, 20 U.S.C. § 115, Stat. 1425 (2002).

Neumann, R. (2008). Charter schools and innovation: The high tech high model. *American Secondary Education, 36*(3), 51–69.

Preston, C., Goldring, E., Berends, M., & Cannata, M. (2012). School innovation in district context: Comparing traditional schools and charter schools. *Economics of Education Review, 31*, 318–330.

Ravitch, D. (2010). *The death and life of the great American school system: How testing and choice are undermining education.* Philadelphia, PA: Basic Books.

Relay Graduate School of Education. (2015) About. Retrieved from http://www.relay.edu/about/institution

Renzulli, L. A., Barr, A. B., & Paino, M. (2014). Innovative education? A test of specialist mimicry or generalist assimilation in trends in charter school specialization over time. *Sociology of Education, 80*(1), 83–102.

Stuit, D., & Smith, T. (2012). Teacher turnover in charter schools. *Economics of Education Review, 31*, 268–279.

Toma, E., & Zimmer, R. (2012). Two decades of charter schools: Expectations, reality, and the future. *Economics of Education Review, 31*, 209–212.

Weil, D. (2009). *Charter school movement: History, politics, policies, economies, and effectiveness* (2nd ed.). Amenia, NY: Grey House.

Welch, M. J. (2010/2011). Eight year study and charter legitimacy. *Journal of Education, 191*(2), 55–65.

Welner, K. G., Hinchey, P. H., Molnar, A., & Weitzman, D. (2010). *Think tank research quality: Lessons for policy makers, the media, and the public.* Charlotte, NC: Information Age.

About the Editors

Tara L. Affolter is an Assistant Professor in the Education Studies Program at Middlebury College. She has over 15 years of experience teaching high school English and theatre while working for social justice within the public schools. Her research and teaching focus revolves around antiracist teaching, inclusive education, and social justice. Her recent publications include chapters in various anthologies, including *Intersectionality & Higher Education: Theory, Research, and Praxis* (Peter Lang) and *Volume 6, RIP Jim Crow: Fighting Racism through Higher Education Policy, Curriculum, and Cultural Interventions* (Peter Lang).

Jamel K. Donnor is an Assistant Professor in Curriculum and Instruction in the School of Education at the College of William and Mary. His recent publications include: *Is the Post-Racial Still Racial?: Understanding the Relationship between Race and Education* published by Teachers College Record, and *The Resegregation of Schools: Race and Education in the Twenty-First Century*, from Routledge. He is currently working on the co-edited volumes *Scandals in College Sports: Legal, Ethical, and Policy Case Studies*, and the second edition of *Critical Race Theory in Education: All God's Children Got a Song*, both with Routledge. His forthcoming peer-reviewed article in *Urban Education*, "Lies, Myths, Stock Stories, and Other Troupes: Understanding Race and Whites' Policy Preferences in Education," examines the anti-diversity arguments articulated in the U.S. Supreme Court case *Fisher v. University of Texas*.

About the Contributors

Wayne Au is an Associate Professor in the School of Educational Studies at the University of Washington Bothell. Dr. Au's academic interests broadly encompass critical education theory and teaching for social justice. More specifically, his research focuses on educational equity, high-stakes testing, curriculum theory, educational policy studies, and social studies education.

Michael W. Apple is the John Bascom Professor of Curriculum and Instruction and Educational Policy Studies at the University of Wisconsin-Madison. A former elementary and secondary school teacher and past president of a teachers union, he has worked with educational systems, governments, universities, unions, and activist and dissident groups throughout the world to democratize educational research, policy, and practice. Professor Apple has been selected as one of the fifty most important educational scholars in the 20th century. *Knowledge, Power, and Education* and *Can Education Change Society?* are among his recent books.

Katherine M. Barghaus is a Research Associate in the Graduate School of Education at the University of Pennsylvania.

Erling E. Boe is a Professor of Education in the Graduate School of Education and Co-Director of the Center of Research and Evaluations in Social Policy at the University of Pennsylvania. Dr. Boe's research interests include the supply, demand, shortage, qualifications, and turnover of U.S. teachers (K-12); charter schools; academic achievement in science and mathematics of U.S. students (K-12) from a cross-national perspective; and educational reform strategies based on incentives for academic performance.

Joseph L. Boselovic is the Associate Director of the Institute for Quality & Equity in Education at Loyola University New Orleans. He is the co-editor of *Only in New Orleans: School Choice and Equity Post-Hurricane Katrina* (Sense Publishers, 2015). Boselovic's work is based around understanding the contexts of education and the relationship of education reform to social change, with a particular focus on New Orleans. With experience as a researcher, administrator, and teacher, his work and research is also focused on the dynamics of family and community engagement in K-12 schooling and academic-community partnerships.

Shaun R. Harper is the founding Director of the Center for the Study of Race and Equity in Education at the University of Pennsylvania. He is author of over 90 peer-reviewed journal articles and other academic publications. Dr. Harper has been interviewed on CNN, ESPN, and NPR, and featured or quoted in the *New York Times, Los Angeles Times, Wall Street Journal, Sports Illustrated, Chronicle of Higher Education, Inside Higher Ed*, and over 400 other media outlets. In 2015, he was appointed to President Barack Obama's My Brother's Keeper advisory council and recognized in *Education Week* as one of the 50 most influential professors in the field of education.

Kevin Lawrence Henry, Jr. is a native of New Orleans. He received his PhD in Curriculum and Instruction from the University of Wisconsin-Madison. He currently is an Assistant Professor of Educational Policy Studies and Practice at the University of Arizona. Kevin's teaching and scholarship revolves around social stratification, the politics of education, racial and ethnic inequality, educational policy—particularly market-based/neoliberal reforms—and counter-hegemonic theories and practices.

Virginia L. McLaughlin is Dean Emerita and the Chancellor Professor of Education in the School of Education at the College of William & Mary. Her areas of specialization are special education and education policy.

Elizabeth Montaño is an Assistant Professor of Teacher Education at Saint Mary's College in California. She taught in charter schools for 11 years in both Oakland and Los Angeles. Her areas of interest include sociocultural approaches to language and literacy across the content areas, culturally and linguistically diverse learners, teacher education and development, teacher induction, teachers in charter schools, teacher unions, and qualitative research.

Eleni Schirmer is currently a PhD student at University of Wisconsin-Madison in Educational Policy Studies and Curriculum and Instruction. She is currently working on a project looking at civil rights activists' influence on teachers unions. Her writing has appeared in *Jacobin, The Progressive, LaborNotes*, and *Education Review*.

Barrett A. Smith graduated from Middlebury College in 2013 with a Bachelor of Arts in Classics. He entered the field of education by teaching at Breakthrough Cincinnati. Barrett has since spent time as a Match Corps member, taken classes at the University of Cincinnati, and gained an alternative teaching certification. He currently teaches Latin at Walnut Hills High School in Cincinnati, Ohio.

Sarah M. Stitzlein received her PhD in Educational Policy Studies from the University of Illinois in 2005. She is currently an Associate Professor of Education and Philosophy at the University of Cincinnati. As a philosopher of education, she works to explore key aspects of education from the perspective of political philosophy. She is especially interested in issues of political agency, educating for democracy, and equality in schools.

Index

AACTE *see* American Association of Colleges for Teacher Education
Achievement First 54, 141
Act 10 32, 34
Allen, Paul 3–4
Alliance Public Schools 65
Alvarez and Marsal 88
American Association of Colleges for Teacher Education (AACTE) 140, 142
American Federation of Teachers 62
American Legislative Exchange Council (ALEC) ix, 1, 7–9, 14
American Motors Corporation 23
Americans for Prosperity 22, 33, 34, 35, 36
Andersson, A. 31
Apple, M. W. ix, 28
Aspire Public Schools 141
Au, W. viii–ix, 46

"bad apples" 74, 77
Ballmer, C. 4
Ballmer, S. 4
Barghaus, K. M. x, 136n1
Beabout, B. 100
Bezos, Jackie 4
Bezos, Jeff 4
Bezos, M. 4
Bezos family 3, 5
Bezos Family Foundation 5
Bill and Melinda Gates Foundation *see* Gates Foundation
Black educators in post-Katrina New Orleans 60–98; absent presence 83; counter-stories 90–3; Executive Order 58 85; Executive Order 79 85; Legislative Act 35 85–6; neoliberalism 84, 87, 89, 90, 93, 94, 95; Recovery School District (RSD) 80, 85–6, 103, 106; school reform 84–7; un-concluding thoughts for unending nightmare 93–5; white abjectorship 87–90, 93
Blanco, K. 85
Blue Ribbon Panel on Clinical Preparation and Partnerships for Improved Student Learning 91, 140
Boas, E. 94
Boe, E. E. x, 136n1
Bonilla-Silva, E. 87
Boselovic, J. L. x
Bourdieu, P. 82
Brewer, R. M. 94
Brighouse, H. 21
Brizard, J.-C. 26
Broad, E. 4
Broad Foundation 4, 5, 26
Broeck, S. 87–8
Brown v. Board of Education 82–3, 86
Bureau of Indian Affairs 120
Bywater 99, 103, 104, 105–6, 107, 114n3
Bywater Arts Lofts 105

California Charter Law 61
California Public Schools Accountability Act of 1999 65
California Teachers Association 62, 63, 70
Campanella, R. 104, 105
Center on Reinventing Public Education (CRPE) 3, 4, 5, 143, 144
Chapman, T. vii
charter management organizations (CMOs) 10, 64, 65, 94, 106–7
Charter Schools Act of 1992 61
Charter Schools USA 48
choice, school; democracy and rightist

mobilizations 21–2; politics 19–40; urban charter schools and education choices for Black students and disadvantaged families in the United States 117–38; *see also* Kenosha, WI; lottery
Chrysler Corporation 23–4
Citizen's Committee for Education 107–8
civil rights 41, 42, 83, 89, 107
closures, school 10, 11, 14, 55
CMOs *see* charter management organizations
Cochran-Smith, M. 56, 57
Colas, J. 32, 34, 35
collective bargaining 30, 31, 32–5, 37, 47, 62, 63, 64, 65, 66, 68, 69, 71, 76–7, 84, 92, 93, 144
Colton School 106, 107
Comité des Citoyens 107
common schools 10, 14
Conant, J. B. 134
Council for Accreditation of Educator Preparation (CAEP) 140, 142
CRPE *see* Center on Reinventing Public Education
Cucchiara, M. B. 101, 111, 113

Democrats for Education Reform (DFER) 3, 4, 5
d'Entremont, C. 131
de Sa Campos, T. 2, 7
DFER *see* Democrats for Education Reform
Dinning, A. 5
Donnor, J. K. vii
Dougherty, J. 83
Dumas, M. J. 82
Duncan, A. viii, 41

East Palo Alto Academy 141
Eckes, S. E. 118, 131, 133, 134, 135
Edison Learning 48
education management organizations (EMOs) 48–9, 51, 54, 144
Education Reform Now! Advocacy 4
Education Reform Now! Inc. 4, 5
efficiency 26, 28, 46, 55
Eli and Edythe Broad Foundation *see* Broad Foundation
EMOs *see* education management organizations
employment 41–60; philosophical foundations 42–7; precariat 47–53; teacher pipelines 51–3; teacher training 54–7
English language arts 50
English language learners vii, 12, 13, 27, 65, 83
Epstein, J. L. 101, 111, 112

Farenholtz, J. 88–9
Federal Charter Schools Program 117
Ferrare, J. J. 2
First Place Scholars 11–13, 14
Fisher, D. 5
Fladeboe, D. 34
Frankenberg, E. 119, 131, 135
free market vii, viii, 1, 6, 10, 11, 13, 14, 33; diversity 102, 111
Freire, P. 41, 44
Friedman, M. 80, 84
Fultz, M. 83

Gates, B., Jr. 3, 4, 6
Gates Foundation ix, 4, 5
GDPS *see* Green Dot Public Schools
George, S. 88
Gill, B. 135
Golding, W. 92
Green Dot Public Schools (GDPS) 64, 69
Gulosino, C. 131

Hanauer, N. 3, 4
Hancock, M. 26–7, 28–30, 31
Harper, S. R. x
Hartman, S. 95
Hastings, R. 4
HCS *see* Hope Charter School
HCSTA *see* Hope Charter School Teachers Association
Heineke, A. 53
Henry, K. L., Jr. x
High Tech High Graduate School of Education 54, 55, 142
High Tech High in San Diego 145
Hill, P. 3, 136n1
Hispanic students x, 65, 119–20, 122, 126, 127, 128, 130, 131, 133, 135, 136nn4–5
Homer A. Plessy Community School *see* Plessy School
Hong, S. 100
Hope Charter School (HCS) 61, 65–71, 73, 74, 75–6, 77
Hope Charter School Teachers Association (HCSTA) 66
Horvat, E. M. 101, 111, 113

Hujik, M. 25
Hunter College 141
Hurricane Katrina 84, 85, 86, 89, 92, 93, 99, 100, 102–3, 113
Hurston, Z. N. 82

IEP *see* individualized education programs
individualized education programs (IEP) 122, 125, 133
Ingersoll, R. 50
innovation vii, 51, 52, 77, 83, 85, 136n2, 142, 143–5
Institute Catholique 107
Investing in Innovation 51, 52

Kenosha, WI: Act 10 32, 34; capitalism and democracy fact off 23–4; economic crisis meets education reformer 26–9; financialization of Unified School District 24–6; ideological mobilizations and clash in school board elections 33–6; layoffs 26–7, 29, 31; neoliberal agenda 28, 29–33; The Transformation Plan 26, 27, 29, 31
Kingsland, N. 90
KIPP *see* Knowledge is Power Program
Knowledge is Power Program (KIPP) 42, 48, 54, 64–5, 106, 107, 141, 144
Koch brothers 22, 33, 35, 36
Kopp, W. 41
Kristeva, J. 89

LaCroix, K. 34, 35, 36
Ladson-Billings, G. 82, 85, 134
LAUSD *see* Los Angeles Unified School District
League of Education Voters (LEV) 2, 3, 5, 7
Lee, C. 119, 131, 135
Leonardo, Z. 94
LEP *see* limited English proficiency
limited English proficiency (LEP) 122, 125, 131, 133
Los Angeles Unified School District (LAUSD) 61, 63, 67
lottery 21, 28, 29
Louisiana *see* Black educators in post-Katrina New Orleans, LA
Louisiana Supreme Court 87

The Madison Project 32
MAP test 43, 44

Margolis, J. 64
Marigny 99, 103, 104, 105, 106, 107, 114n3
Marx, K. ix, 41, 42, 44, 47
Match Charter Public School 54; Beyond 141–2; Education 142; partnership 55
Mazza, B. 53
McDonogh No. 19 107, 145
Microsoft 3, 4
Mills, C. W. 94
Minnesota 61, 62, 117, 121
Miron, G. 118, 144
Montaño, E. ix

NAPCS *see* National Alliance for Public Charter Schools
National Alliance for Public Charter Schools (NAPCS) 10, 117, 118, 132
National Assessment of Education Progress 118
National Center for Education Statistics (NCES) 118, 122; Common Core of Data for 2000–01 119; Schools and Staffing Survey 119, 145
National Commission on Excellence in Education 62
National Council for Accreditation of Teacher Education 139–40
National Education Association 144
National Heritage Academies 48
Nation at Risk, A 62, 84
Nelson, C. 118
neoliberalism vii, ix, x, 1, 2, 6, 7, 9, 10, 14, 19, 20, 21, 22, 24, 25, 28, 29, 33, 35, 48, 57, 77; New Orleans 84, 87, 89, 90, 93, 94, 95; capitalism 47
New Orleans public schools 99–116; French Quarter 104; parent and family engagement and the relationship between schools and families 100–2; *see also* black educators in post-Katrina New Orleans; Bywater; Hurricane Katrina; Marigny; Orleans Parish; Plessy School; St. Claude; St. Roch
New Schools for New Orleans 90
NewSchools Venture Fund 64
New Teacher Project 50
New York State Board of Regents 141
Noack, D. 24–5
Noble Charter Schools 54, 55
No Child Left Behind 42, 84, 144

Oliver v. Orleans Parish School Board et al. 87
Ollman, B. 44
Orfield, G. 135
Orleans Parish 86, 88; Black staff 89; School Board (OPSB) 103, 106, 107, 108, 109, 113n1; *see also Oliver v. Orleans Parish School Board et al.*
Orwell, G.: *Animal Farm* 91, 92; *Lord of the Flies* 91, 92

parent engagement 99, 100, 102, 109, 110–1, 112, 113
parent trigger 2, 3, 8
Partnership for Learning 3, 5
philosophical foundations 42–7
Plessy School 99, 100, 103, 105–13
Posey-Maddox, L. 102, 110, 111

Race to the Top viii, 42
racism 87, 89, 92
Rapp, K. E. 118, 131, 133, 134, 135
Ravenswood School District 141
Ravitch, D. 7, 55, 144
Reagan, Ronald 62
Reay, D. 101
Recovery School District (RSD) 80, 85–6, 103, 106
Relay Graduate School of Education 54, 141
research 142–5; charter school efficacy 142–3; charter school innovation 143–5
Rhee, M. 41, 50; "MAP Boycott Is About Keeping Test Scores Out of Teacher Evaluations" 43, 44
Roberti, B. 88
Rochester, New York School District 26
Rochester Teachers Association 26
Roda, A. 101, 102
Rosetta Stone 27, 29
Royal Bank of Canada 24
RSD *see* Recovery School District
Rubin, C. L. 100

Schirmer, E. vii
school closures 10, 11, 14, 55
Schouten, G. 21
Scott, J. ix, 49
segregation vii, 21, 27, 118, 119, 133, 134, 135–6
Shanker, A. 62, 144
Smarick, A. 117

Smith, B. ix, 140–1, 142
Solórzano, D. G. 90
Spellings, M. 85
stakeholders 73, 78, 83
Stand for Children 3, 5
Stanford University 141, 143
state-level charter school commission 3, 9
St. Claude 99, 103, 105, 106, 107, 108, 110, 114n3
Stifel, Nicolaus and Company, 25
Stitzelein, S. ix, 140–1, 142
Strizek, G. A. 120
St. Roch 99, 103, 105, 106, 109, 114n3
StudentsFirst 41
Success Academy Charter Schools 49

Taube, J. 31, 35, 36
teacher: Kenosha 26–7, 29, 31; layoffs 47, 50, 52; pipelines 51–3; training 54–7; turnovers 42, 47, 49, 50, 83
Teacher U 141
Teach for America (TFA) 41, 42, 51–3, 54, 86, 92, 94, 141
teaching mission 139–42; charter teacher preparation 141–2; clinical preparation 139–41
teachNOLA 86, 92
TFA *see* Teach for America
Tichnor-Wagner, A. 53
Tourkin, S. C. 121
trigger 2, 3, 8

Uncommon Schools 54, 141
unionization of teachers 61–79; beginning 62–3; consequences 69–77; Hope Charter School 61, 65–71, 73, 74, 75–6, 77; literature review 63–5; methodology 65–8; relationship with governing board 71–5; relationship with school leaders 69–71; repercussions for union involvement 75–6; voice and presence 76–7
United Federation of Teachers 65
United States Supreme Court 107
United Teachers Los Angeles (UTLA) 63, 65, 69
University of Arkansas: Department of Education Reform 143
University of Colorado: School of Education 143
University of Washington: Center on Reinventing Public Education 143

Urban Prep Academy 65, 134
Urschel, J. L. 144
U.S. Department of Education 136n3; Common Core of Data for 2000–01 119; National Center for Education Statistics (NCES) 118, 122; 2003–04 National Center for Education Statistics (NCES) Schools and Staffing Survey 119, 145
U.S. Securities and Exchange Commission 25
UTLA *see* United Teachers Los Angeles
Uy, P. S. 100

Vulcan Inc. 3, 4

Wade, D. 35, 36
Walker, S. 26, 30, 31, 32, 33, 34
Walton, A. 3, 4
Walton Family Foundation 4, 5
Warren, M. R. 100
Washington Charter Law 6–9
Washington charter schools 1–18; common schools, closing, and risk of free market 9–11; First Place Scholars and after-the-fact accountability of markets 11–13; Initiative 1240 2–7, 8, 9, 10, 14; philanthropic contributions to 1240 campaign 4–6; reform 2; school governance and free market ideology 6–9
Washington Coalition for Public Charter Schools 3, 4
Washington Policy Center 10
Washington State Auditor's Office 12
Washington State Charter School Commission 6
Washington Supreme State Court 10, 14
Welch, M. J. 143–4
Wells, A. S. 49, 101, 102, 134
white abjectorship 87–90, 93
White Hat Management 48
WILL *see* Wisconsin Institute for Law and Liberty
William Frantz Elementary 107
Wirch, B. 31–2
Wisconsin Institute for Law and Liberty (WILL) 34, 35, 36
Wisconsin Supreme Court 34, 35
Wolf, M. 5

Yosso, T. 90

Zeichner, K. 55–6